IMAGES
of America

BIENVILLE PARISH

I0808780

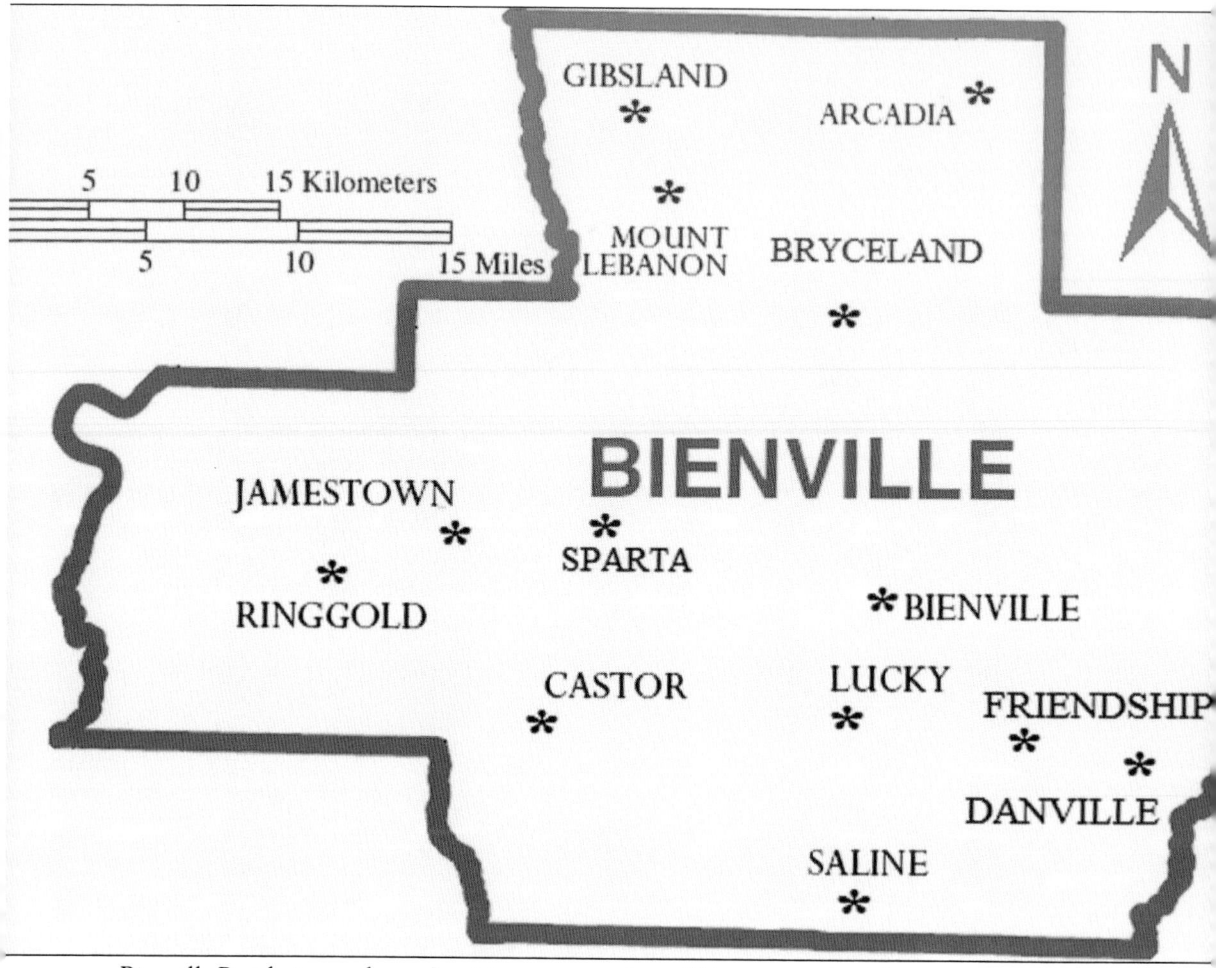

Bienville Parish, in northwest Louisiana, covers about 822 square miles. This map of the parish will be a useful reference throughout the book. Chapter 1 focuses on the Bienville Parish Courthouse, from the 1890s until the era of the recently completed courthouse. Chapter 2 highlights the northern portion of the parish, including the parish seat of Arcadia. Chapter 3 deals with the central portion of the parish, including the original parish seat of Sparta. Chapter 4 focuses on the southern portion of the parish. (Courtesy of the author.)

On the Cover: Bienville Parish can link its initial growth and prosperity to the timber industry. At the turn of the 20th century, the parish experienced an economic boom. Logging crews, such as the one in the photograph, moved into the area with their families to harvest the virgin pine forests and transport the trees to one of many local sawmills. The timber industry continues to be an important part of the local economy. (Courtesy of Mary Hamner.)

IMAGES
of America

BIENVILLE PARISH

Benjamin Brad Dison

ARCADIA
PUBLISHING

ISBN 978-1-4671-1191-1

Published by Arcadia Publishing
Charleston, South Carolina

Printed in the United States of America

Library of Congress Control Number: 2013954630

For all general information, please contact Arcadia Publishing:
Telephone 843-853-2070
Fax 843-853-0044
E-mail sales@arcadiapublishing.com
For customer service and orders:
Toll-Free 1-888-313-2665

Visit us on the Internet at www.arcadiapublishing.com

I dedicate this book to my brother Jereme Dison.
Without his help, this book would not have been possible.

Contents

ACKNOWLEDGMENTS

I would like to express my sincere gratitude to the following for allowing me to reproduce their photographs in this history of Bienville Parish: Bert Davis, Bruce Evans, Cheryl Babers, Donna Sutton, Keith Vincent, Lavon Sullivan, Mary Crochet, Mary Hamner, Muriel Sullivan, Nanette Choate, Pat Mathews, Wanda Culpepper, Galen White of the Louisiana & North West Railroad, the wonderful volunteers at the Stage Coach Trail Museum, Saline High School librarian Rebekah Barnett, the *Bienville Democrat*, and the agents of the Federal Bureau of Investigation. I would also like to thank my aunt Lavon Sullivan for helping me contact contributors; my brother Jereme for the countless hours he spent helping me edit photographs; and Victoria Sheppard for helping me scan all of the photographs in this book.

Introduction

On March 14, 1848, the Louisiana State Legislature divided Claiborne Parish in half and named the lower portion Bienville Parish, in honor of French Canadian explorer Jean-Baptiste Le Moyne, Sieur de Bienville. He had served as the governor of French Louisiana for four separate terms, a total of 30 years, and is credited as the founder of New Orleans. Although the parish bears his name, Bienville explored the Gulf of Mexico coastline and the mouth of the Mississippi River, and never traversed what is now Bienville Parish.

In the 1830s, Reuben Drake left his home in South Carolina and scouted for land in Louisiana to which to move his family. They established the first permanent settlement in what became Bienville Parish and named it Mount Lebanon. As they were devout Baptists, the early pioneers quickly built a church and school, which became the focus of the community. By 1853, the school had grown into Mount Lebanon University. At first, the university was a men's college, but it soon converted to a coed college. During the Civil War, classes were suspended as the Confederacy commandeered the college and used the campus as a hospital for sick and wounded soldiers. After the war, Mount Lebanon University resumed its classes. In 1906, following years of financial troubles, the school was consolidated into Louisiana College in Pineville, Louisiana.

Over time, small communities developed throughout the region, but Bienville Parish was sparsely populated during the 19th century. Until the last decade of the century, the small town of Sparta was the cultural and political center of the parish. Sparta had no immediate access to a navigable waterway, and all goods and supplies were transported overland by horse-drawn wagons. Visitors to the region wrote to their families about the vast acreage of virgin pine timber. Entrepreneurs quickly realized the potential profits that pine lumber could bring, but they lacked the infrastructure to move the harvested lumber to market.

In the late 1880s, workers completed the Vicksburg, Shreveport & Texas Railroad, an east-west railway that passed through the northern portion of Bienville Parish and bypassed Sparta. The community of Arcadia was originally located about a mile south of the railroad, and its citizens moved the town to its present location to be along the rail line. Towns along the railroad, such as Arcadia and Gibsland, became boomtowns, and communities that were bypassed, such as Sparta and Sailes, began to decline. Citizens of Arcadia, Bienville, and Gibsland rallied for a more suitable parish seat and held an election to decide the matter. Shortly after the election results were in, several wagons pulled up beside the courthouse in Sparta, and the wagon drivers haphazardly loaded the parish records destined for Arcadia. Controversy still surrounds the "midnight raid," as many citizens of Bienville continue to argue that "the parish seat was stolen."

In the latter part of the 19th century, the population in Bienville Parish grew rapidly due to the booming timber industry. Railroad companies built more miles of track throughout the parish to reach the remote pine trees. Teams of woodcutters built temporary wooden-railed railroads, called trams, to transport the fresh-cut timber to the main railroad line. Once loggers exhausted the timber supply along the tram, they moved to another location. Mill companies built sawmills along the route of the railroad to process the rough timber into finished lumber. The timber industry required a large number of workers, and multitudes of people arrived with their families seeking new opportunities. Many sawmills in the parish paid their employees with tokens or company notes that could only be spent at the sawmill's company stores, called commissaries.

Towns grew around the sawmills. As the infrastructure grew, other support businesses came in and provided opportunities besides those immediately involved with the timber industry. Each town had different enterprises that supported the workers in the region, providing a number of goods and services, including general stores, millineries, hotels, restaurants, and cotton gins. These businesses also played an important role in the developing communities. They served as gathering places for people to form community bonds and aided in the creation of settlements that would outlast the timber industry.

Farmers in the region were putting the newly cleared land to good use. They planted a variety of crops, including corn, beans, and tomatoes, but perhaps the most well-known was watermelons. The sandy soil around villages like Saline provided the ideal conditions for a bumper crop. Workers at the packing mill in Saline loaded crops onto train cars destined for distant locations. Saline became synonymous with watermelons, and Saline Watermelons were shipped worldwide.

Churches and schools were the foundations of the early communities. Most towns had a single one-room building that functioned as a school during the week and as a church on weekends. For many farmers in the parish, churches provided the only source of activity away from their farms. In the 1920s, motorized buses transported students over longer distances in a shorter period of time, and the several small schools consolidated into newly built multiroom schools. Although churches and schools no longer used the same building, they continued to bind many residents to the region.

During the Great Depression, Bienville Parish made national and worldwide headlines as the location where the Bonnie and Clyde gang came to a gruesome end. Bonnie Parker and Clyde Barrow robbed banks, stores, and gas stations, stole numerous cars, and murdered several police officers and citizens in the Midwest and the South. Law enforcement officers learned that Bonnie and Clyde were in the area and were planning to rendezvous with another gang member in Bienville Parish. Knowing the danger they faced, the officers decided their only option was an ambush. Arthur Penn's 1967 film *Bonnie and Clyde* romanticized the duo's exploits and transformed them into pop-culture icons. Most contributors to this book, however, had a less-than-romantic view of Bonnie and Clyde and considered their link with the parish to be a negative one.

This book covers the time period from the mid-1800s until the early 1960s, and it is presented in chronological order by community. For the purposes of this book, the parish is divided into three sections—north, central, and south. I collected the photographs from family, friends, neighbors, and friends that I made during the research process. I reached out to the communities through the parish's local newspaper, the *Bienville Democrat*, as well as provided flyers to local churches. In addition, social media websites such as Facebook proved to be invaluable to this project. I have enjoyed working on this book, and I hope that former and present citizens of Bienville Parish and of neighboring parishes will be proud to have this renewed connection to past communities that still have roots a century later.

One

Bienville Parish Courthouse

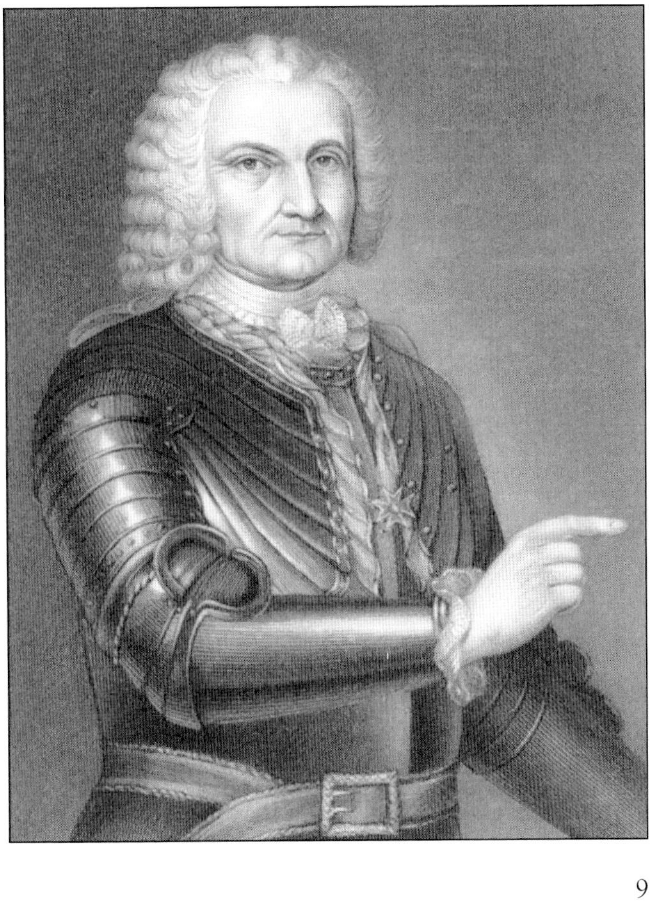

Bienville Parish was named after the French Canadian explorer Jean-Baptiste Le Moyne, Sieur de Bienville. Although the parish was named in his honor, it is unlikely that he explored the area that now comprises Bienville Parish. Between 1701 and 1743, Bienville was appointed governor of Louisiana four separate times. In 1743, he resigned as governor and retired to France. (Courtesy of J.C. Buttre.)

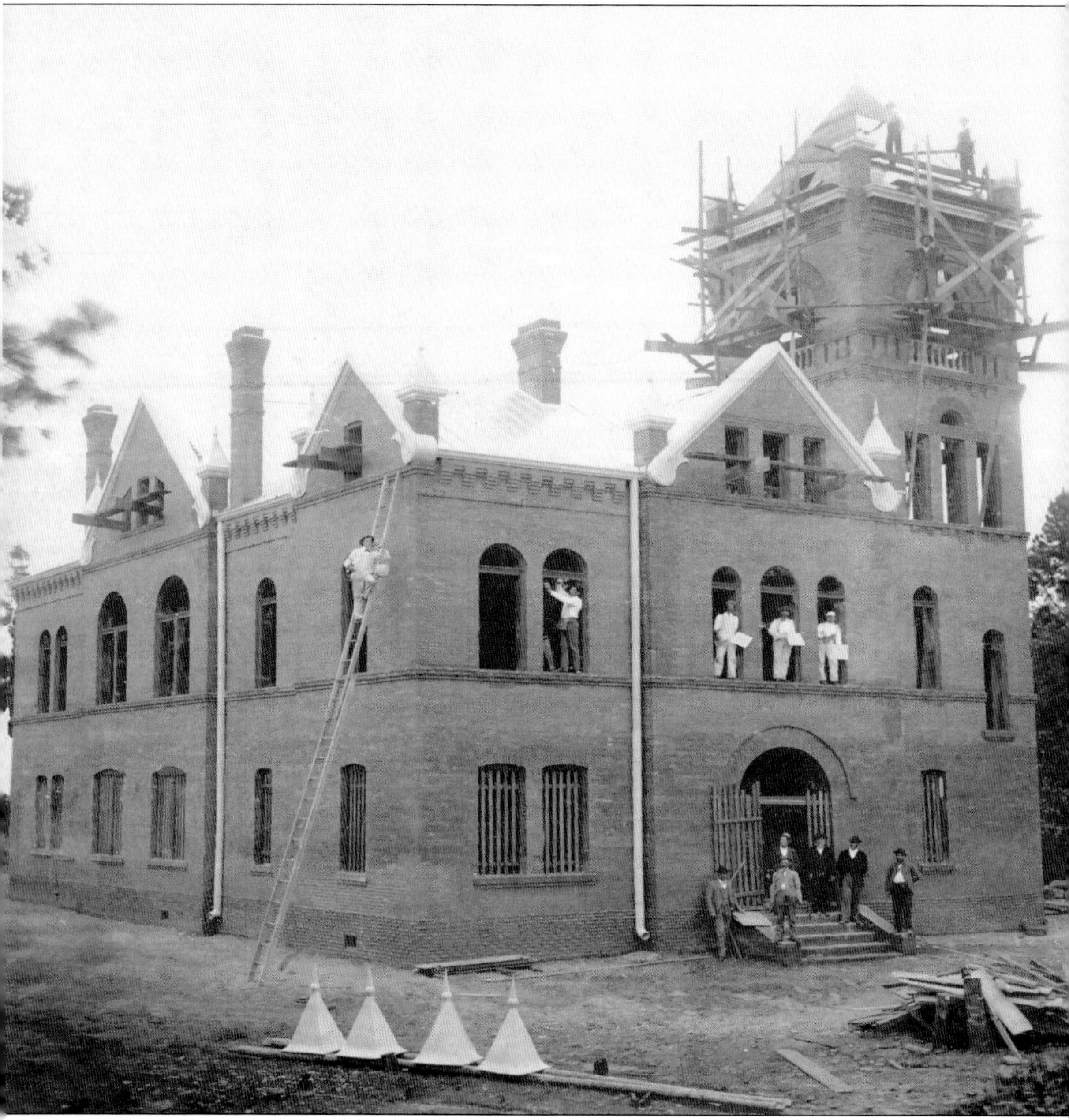

On September 30, 1895, workers pose for a photograph while constructing the Bienville Parish Courthouse. The police jury awarded the contract to F.B. & W.S. Hull of Jackson, Mississippi. Francis Blair Hull owned a lumberyard in Jackson and formed a construction company in the early 1870s. In 1876, Francis's brother William joined his construction business. (Courtesy of Stage Coach Trail Museum.)

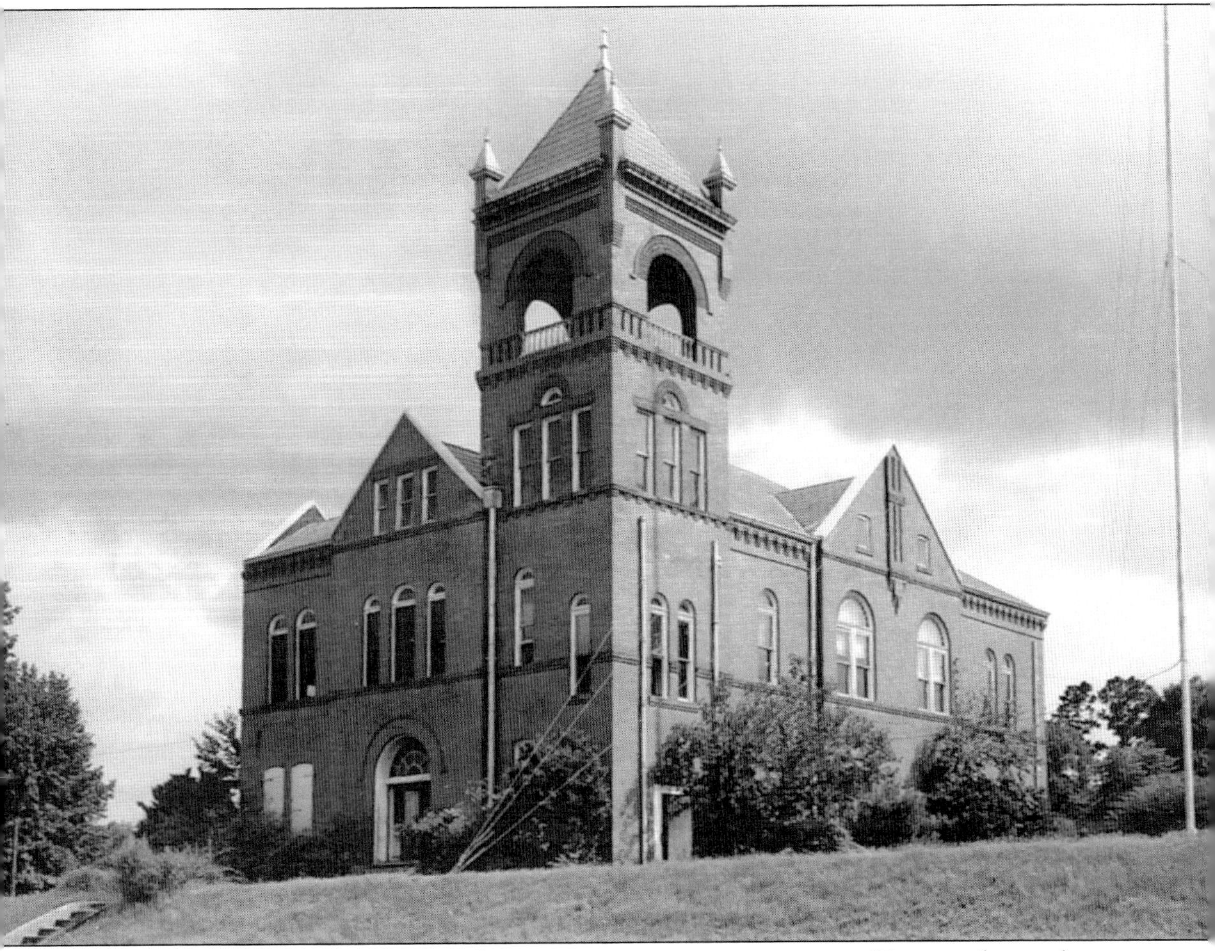

On April 6, 1926, the courthouse still maintains its majestic appearance 30 years after workers completed it. Like many architects of the time, William Hull received no formal training, learning on the job and by reading books and journals. This courthouse served the citizens of the parish until the early 1950s. (Courtesy of Keith Vincent.)

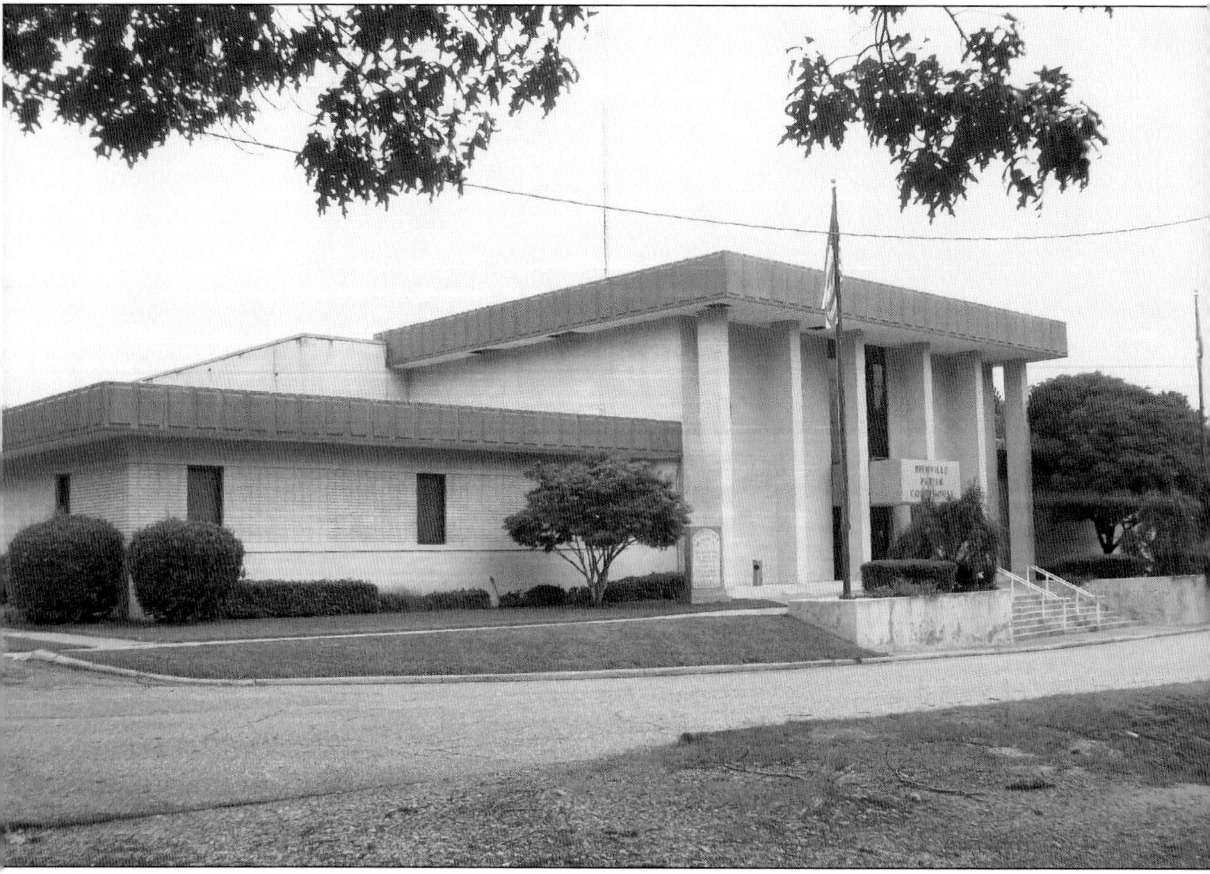

By 1950, the courthouse, which was built in 1895, was outdated, unsafe, and was said to be "approaching the status of an antique." The police jury was planning to build for 75 or 100 years into the future and wanted to double the floor space of the original courthouse. In the early 1950s, architect C. Scott Yeager designed and Allen Construction Company built a 24,422-square-foot courthouse. (Courtesy of the author.)

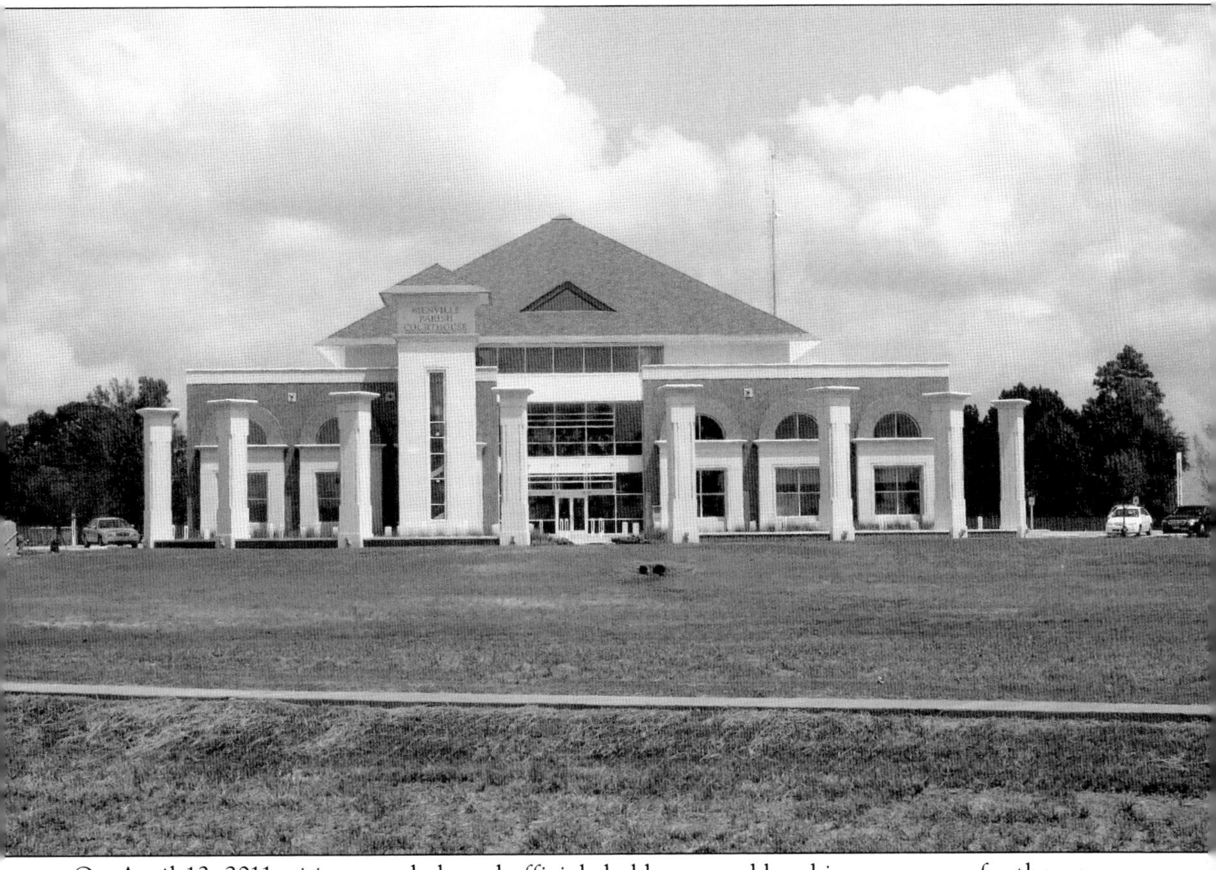

On April 13, 2011, citizens and elected officials held a ground-breaking ceremony for the new Bienville Parish Courthouse. On March 9, 2011, the police jury accepted Lincoln Builders' bid of $10,063,000 to construct the 50,723-square-foot building off Interstate 20. This structure replaced the courthouse built in 1953. The new courthouse more than doubled the size of the previous courthouse. (Courtesy of the author.)

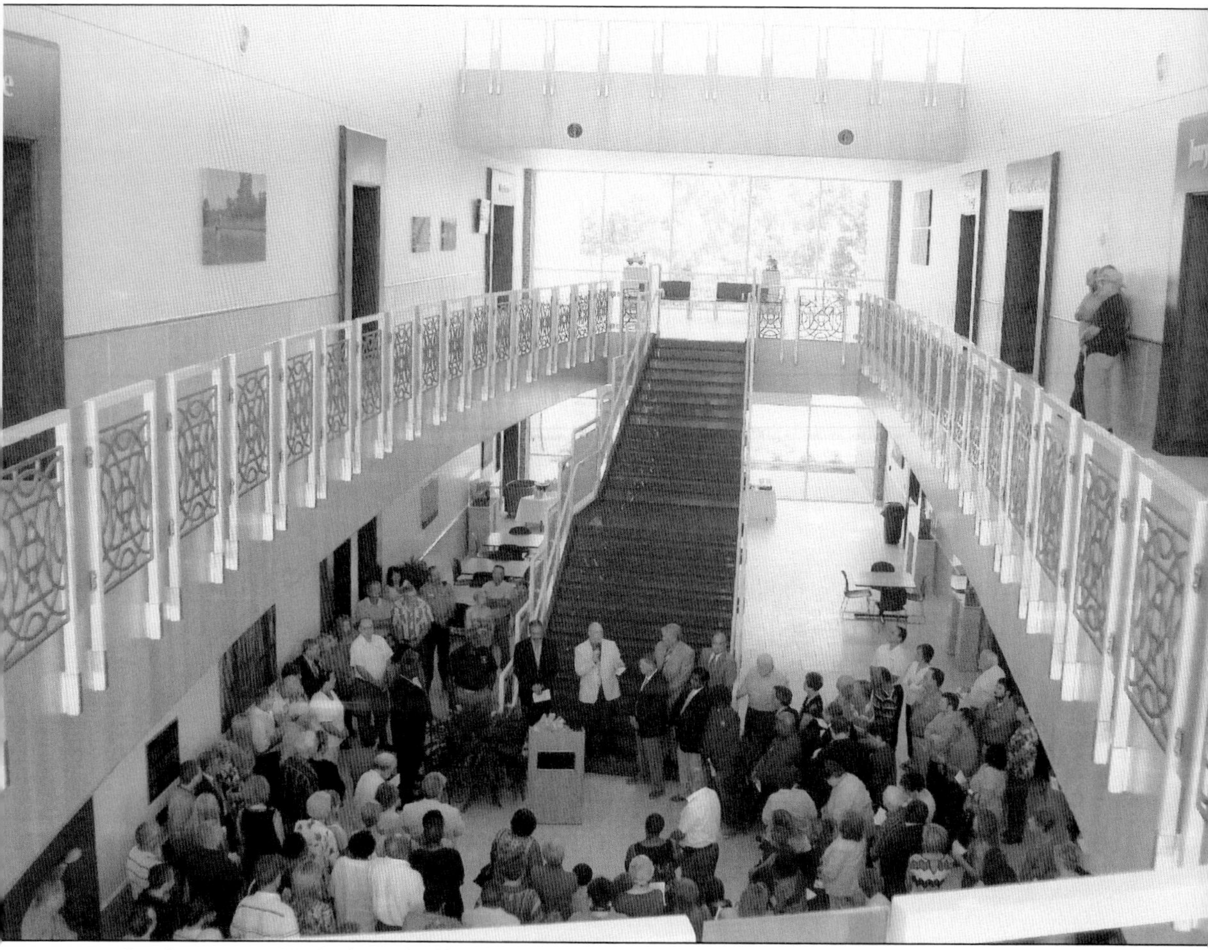

On August 10, 2013, elected officials of Bienville Parish held a ribbon-cutting and grand-opening ceremony at the new courthouse. Speakers included Rodney Warren, Jim Martin, John Balance, Jonathon Stewart, Rev. Jeff Hoffman, Bill Sims, Greg Wilson, and Rep. Patrick Jefferson. Citizens of the parish created the artwork displayed in the courthouse, all of which represents different aspects of the parish. (Courtesy of the author.)

Two

North Bienville Parish

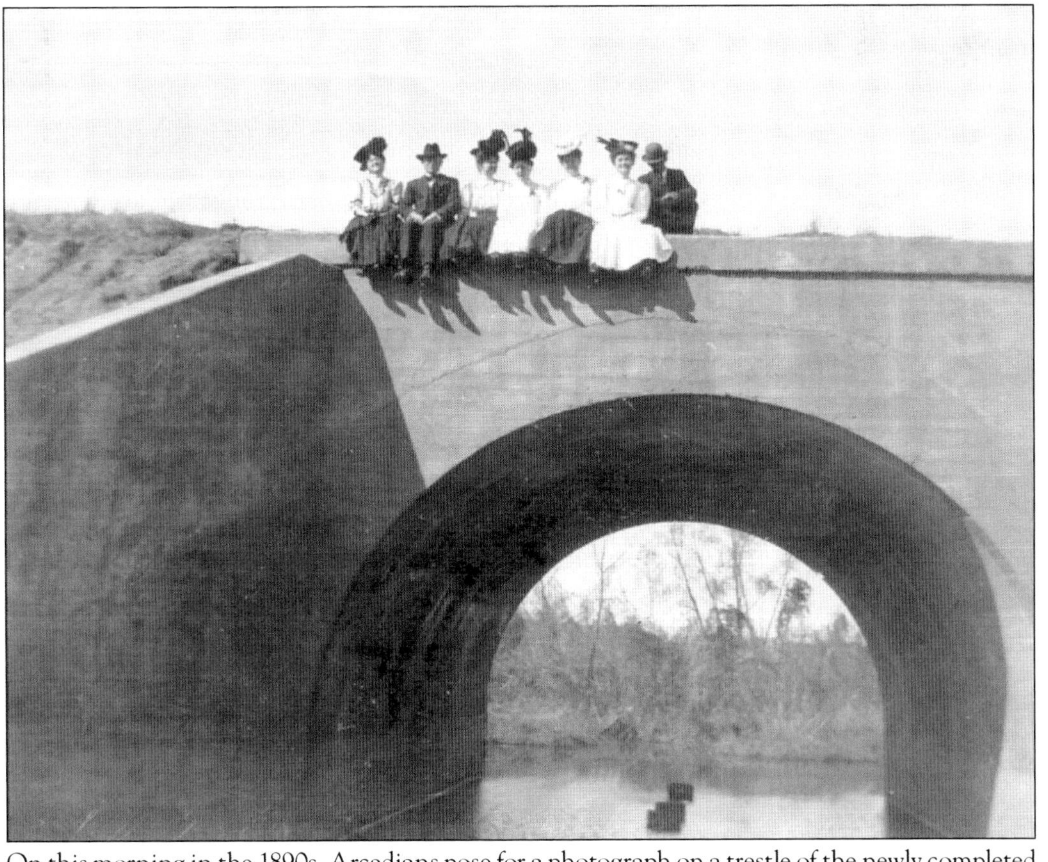

On this morning in the 1890s, Arcadians pose for a photograph on a trestle of the newly completed Vicksburg, Shreveport & Pacific Railroad (VS&P). Built in the early 1880s, this concrete trestle survives, though it is now overgrown with vegetation. It is located two miles west of Highway 9 on Highway 80. (Courtesy of Bert Davis.)

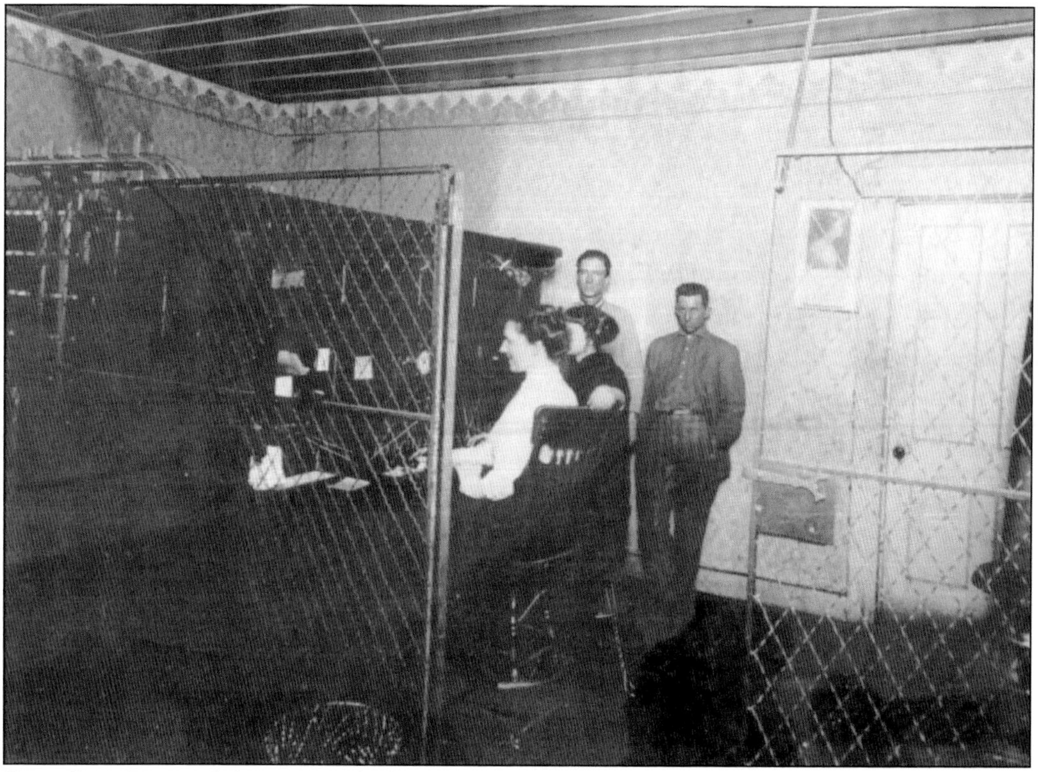

From the 1870s until the 1960s, telephone companies used manual switchboards and switchboard operators to connect callers. The operator manually connected a cord to the proper circuit in order to complete the call. On January 24, 1912, local switchboard operator Eula Grifin connects a call at Arcadia's early telephone office as manager W.R. Moore (left) and lineman R.W. Ozley look on. (Courtesy of Stage Coach Trail Museum.)

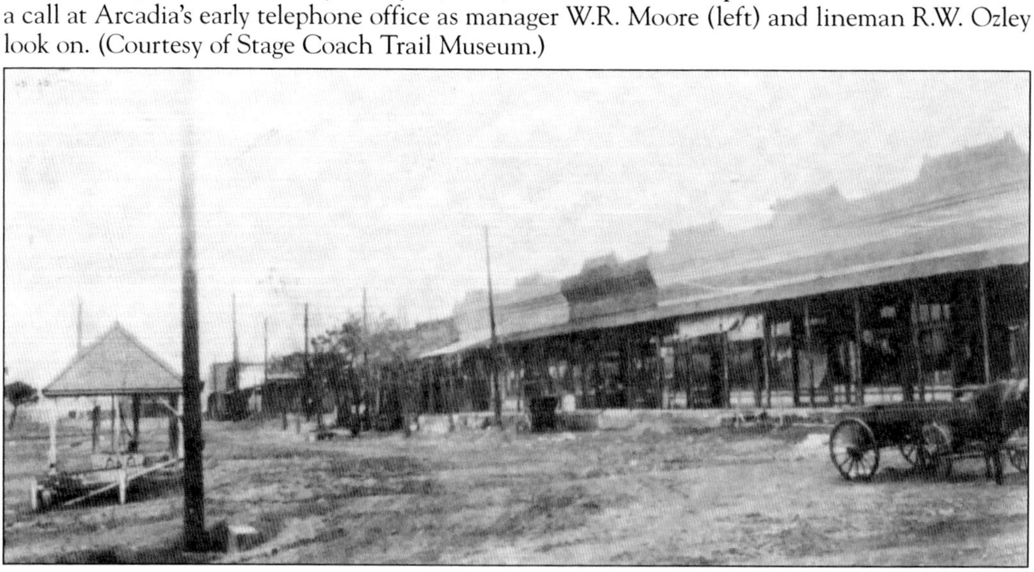

Postmarked December 17, 1913, this real-photo postcard shows Arcadia as a rural town before the era of the automobile. Arcadia's Main Street shops faced the Vicksburg, Shreveport & Pacific Railroad tracks, which brought locals and visitors to the town. The well in the left foreground provided water for the townspeople and their horses. (Courtesy of Nanette Choate.)

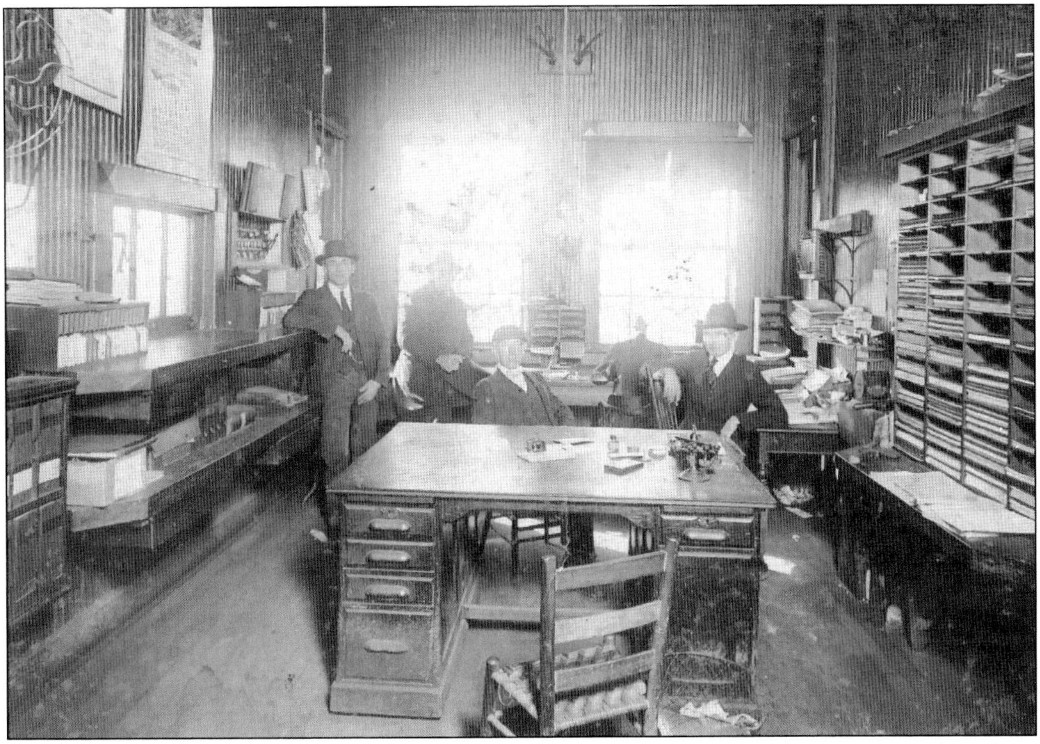

On April 3, 1919, S.A. Cook owned and edited a weekly newspaper that came out on Thursdays, the *Bienville Democrat*. A yearly subscription cost $1.50. In the mid-1920s, the staff of the *Bienville Democrat* poses for this photograph. The shelves on the right contain the hardbound copies of the newspaper. The original building is located at 2326 Maple Street. (Courtesy of Bert Davis.)

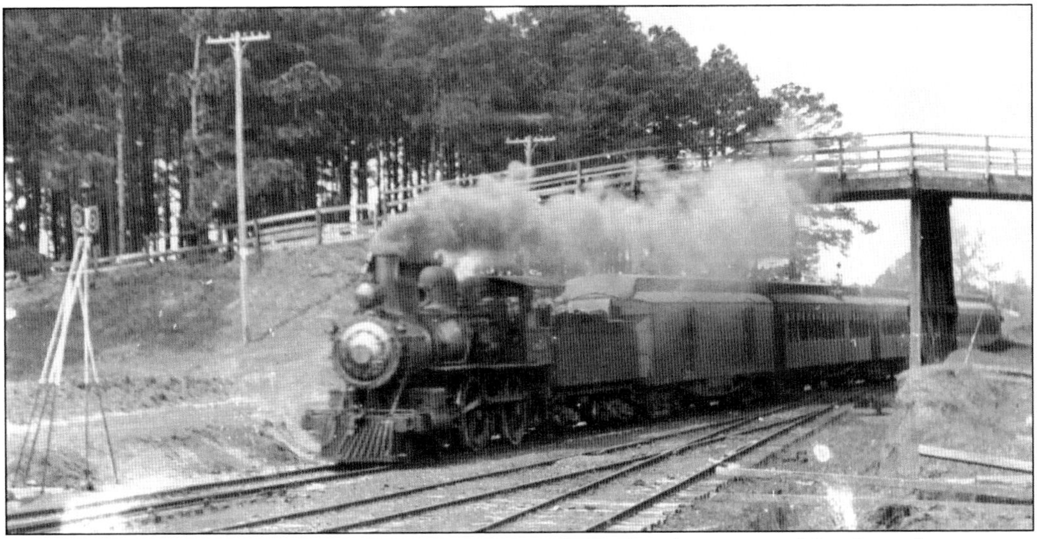

Completed in 1884, the Vicksburg, Shreveport & Pacific Railroad transported freight and passengers between Shreveport and Vicksburg, Mississippi, and included stops at Arcadia and Gibsland. New Arcadia, established half a mile north of old Arcadia to reap the benefits of the railroad, grew quickly with the new connection. Here, a VS&P passenger train arrives in Gibsland in May 1921. (Courtesy of Louisiana & North West Railroad.)

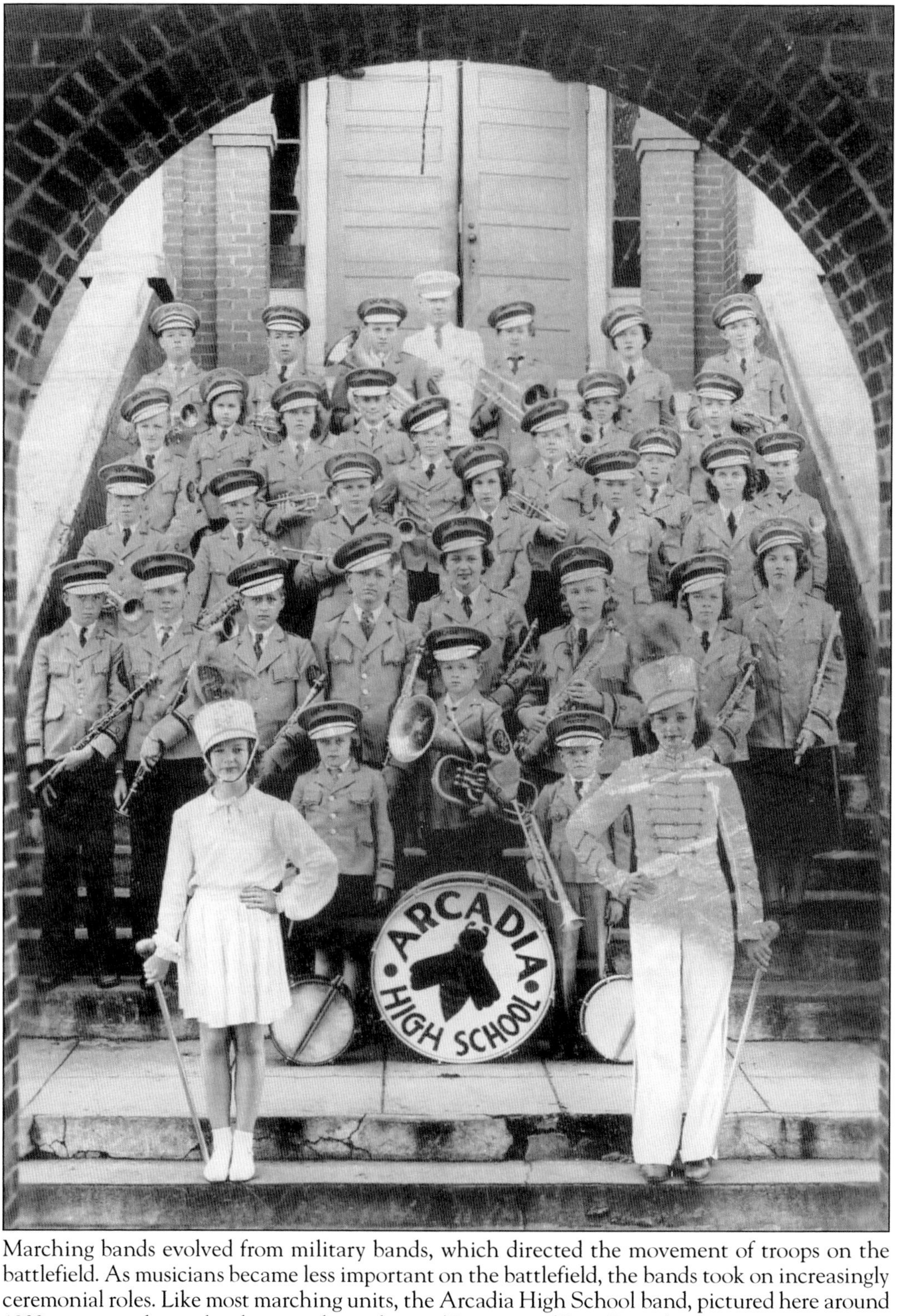

Marching bands evolved from military bands, which directed the movement of troops on the battlefield. As musicians became less important on the battlefield, the bands took on increasingly ceremonial roles. Like most marching units, the Arcadia High School band, pictured here around 1933, wears traditional military-style uniforms. (Courtesy of Bert Davis.)

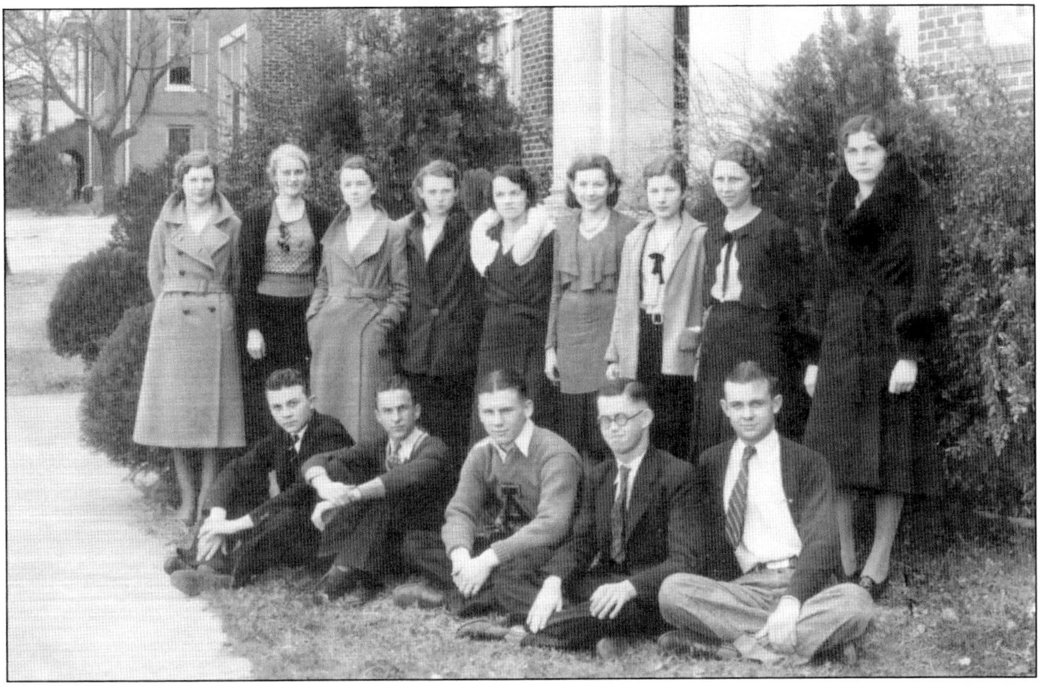

On the evening of March 25, 1932, Arcadia High School seniors acted in Carl Pierce's comedic play *Love Trouble* at Arcadia's city hall. The tagline for the play was "'Love Trouble' is a disease from which only a few are immune." The play was said to be a sure cure for the "contagious malady." The cost of admission was 30¢ for adults and 15¢ for kids. (Courtesy of Bert Davis.)

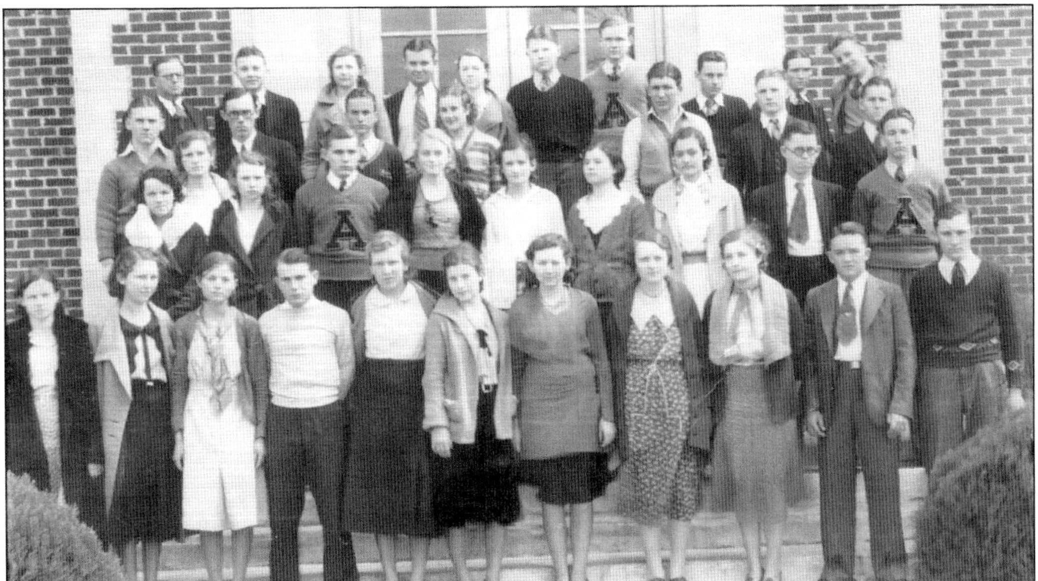

On May 24, 1932, Mr. and Mrs. Julius Williams held an evening of entertainment honoring the 1932 graduating class of Arcadia High School, which included their daughter Mildred Williams. The rooms were decorated with the class flowers, rose and sweat pea. The senior class divided into teams and played the popular dice game progressive bunco before enjoying a buffet supper. (Courtesy of Bert Davis.)

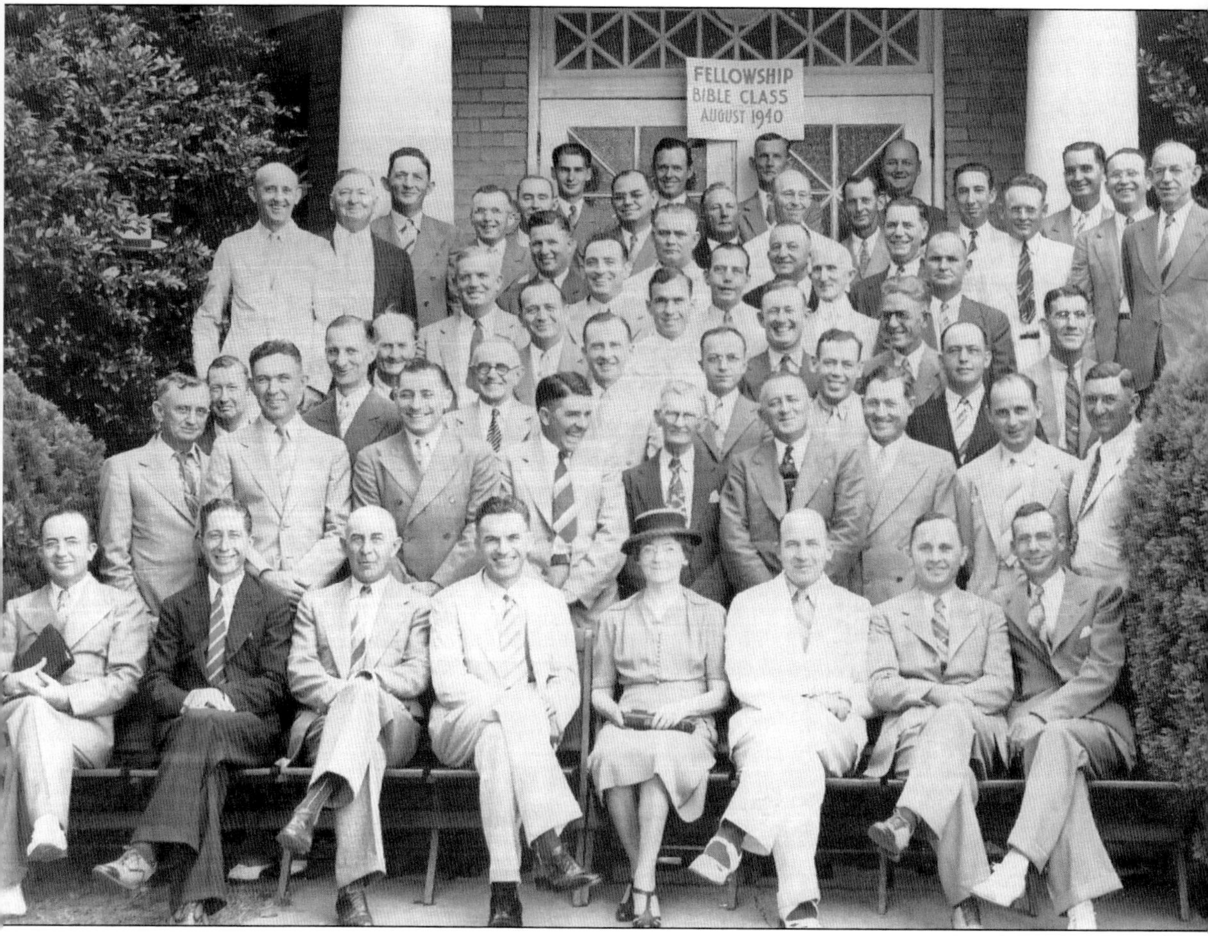

In 1931, Mrs. Bert Davis (first row, center) became the second teacher in the Fellowship Bible Class at Arcadia Baptist Church. With just 16 members in its first year, the church's membership had grown substantially by 1940 (the year this photograph was taken) through Davis's efforts. In addition to its local religious work, the class cared for an orphan in the Louisiana Baptist Orphans Home in Monroe. Pastor C.L. Caldwell is located in the first row, at far left. (Courtesy of Bert Davis.)

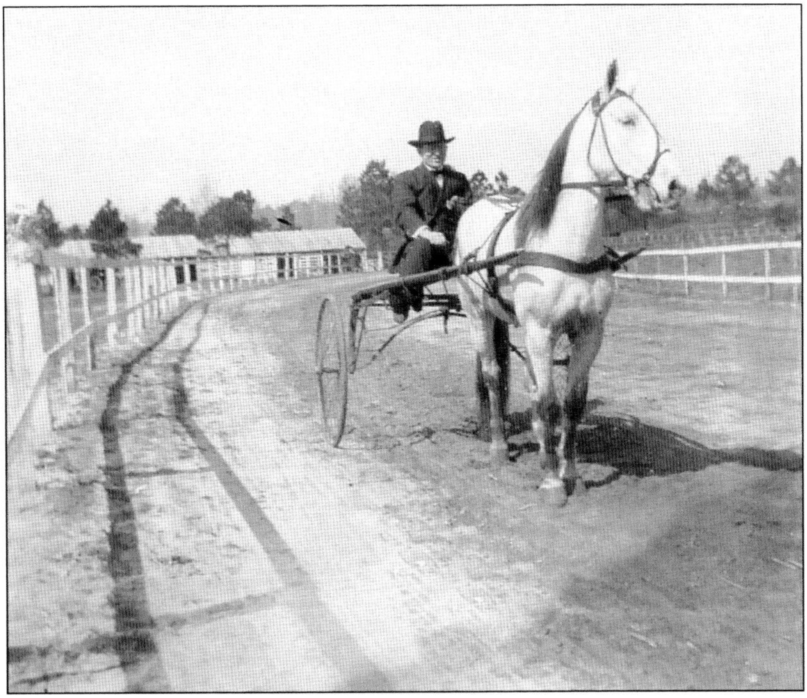

In 1907, Bert Davis and his racehorse, Lillian B, pose for a photograph on an oval racetrack. Horse racing in the United States dates to 1665, with the creation of the Newmarket course in Salisbury, New York. Horse racing was an expensive and prestigious hobby that Bert Davis enjoyed. (Courtesy of Bert Davis.)

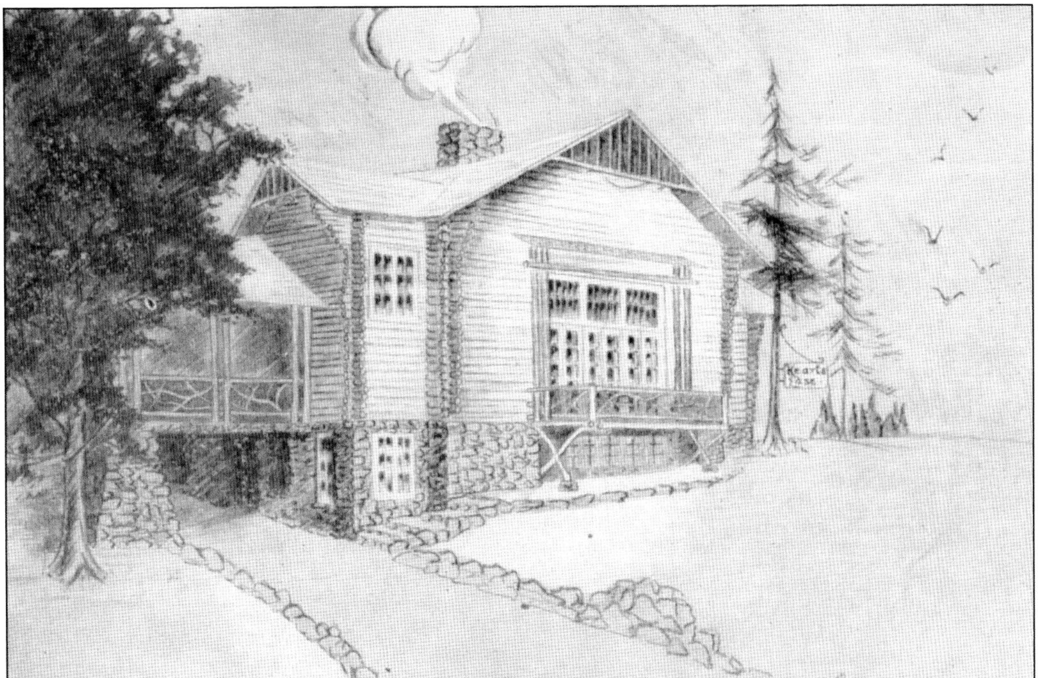

This hand-drawn image of Hearts Ease, the home of V.C. and Nena Pipes, was used on greeting cards. For over 30 years, V.C. was a jeweler and expert watch repairer in Arcadia until his death in 1948. Mr. and Mrs. Pipes entertained a variety of guests at Hearts Ease, including the poet Emma Wilson Emory. Hearts Ease is located at the corner of Third and Elm Streets. (Courtesy of Bert Davis.)

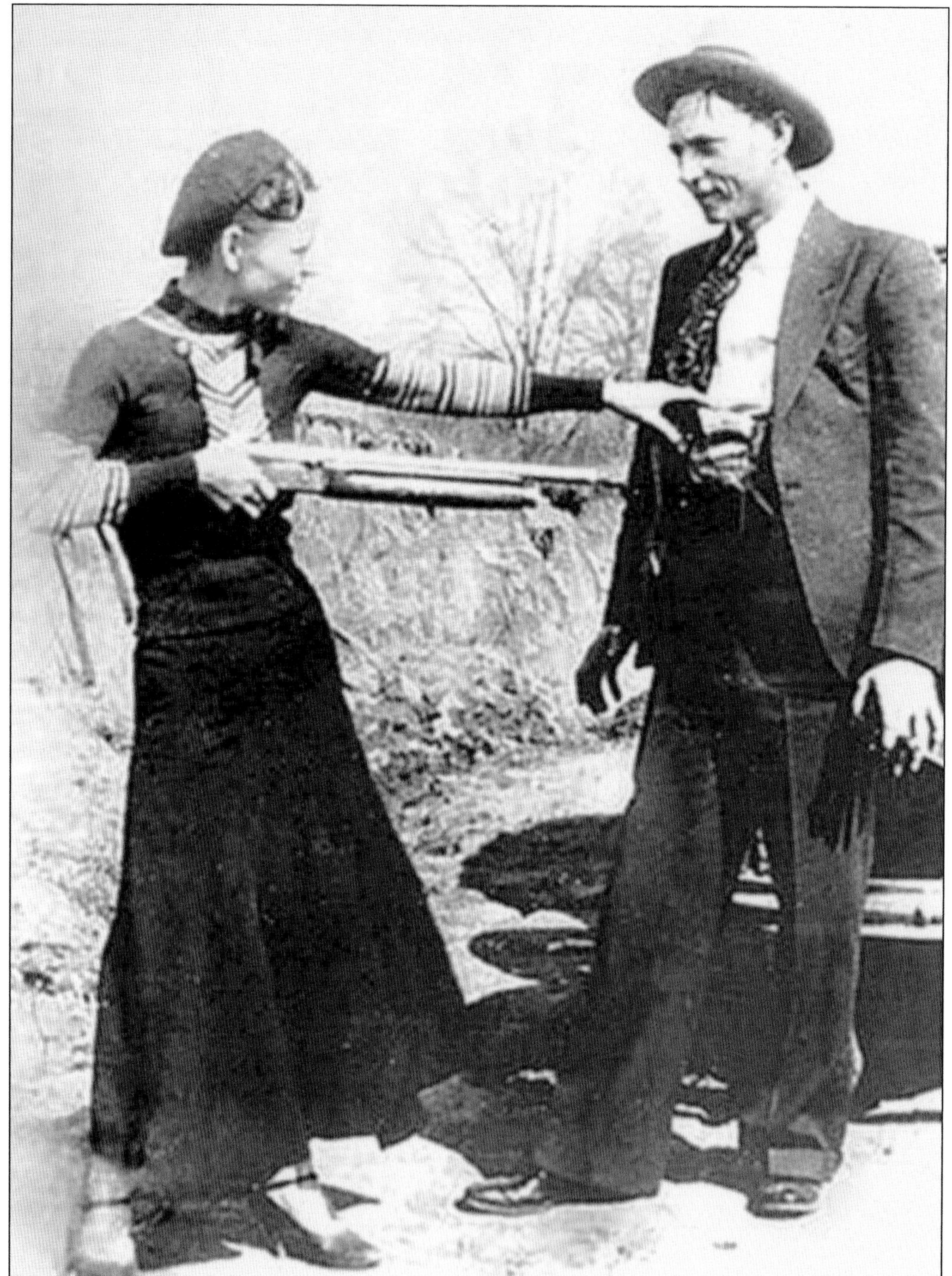

Bonnie Parker and Clyde Barrow were members of the Barrow Gang, which committed crimes including theft, armed robbery, and murder in the central United States. In March 1933, Bonnie holds Clyde at gunpoint in this playfully staged photograph that was taken by another member of the gang. Police found film containing this image in the Barrow Gang's Joplin, Missouri, hideout. (Courtesy of the Federal Bureau of Investigation.)

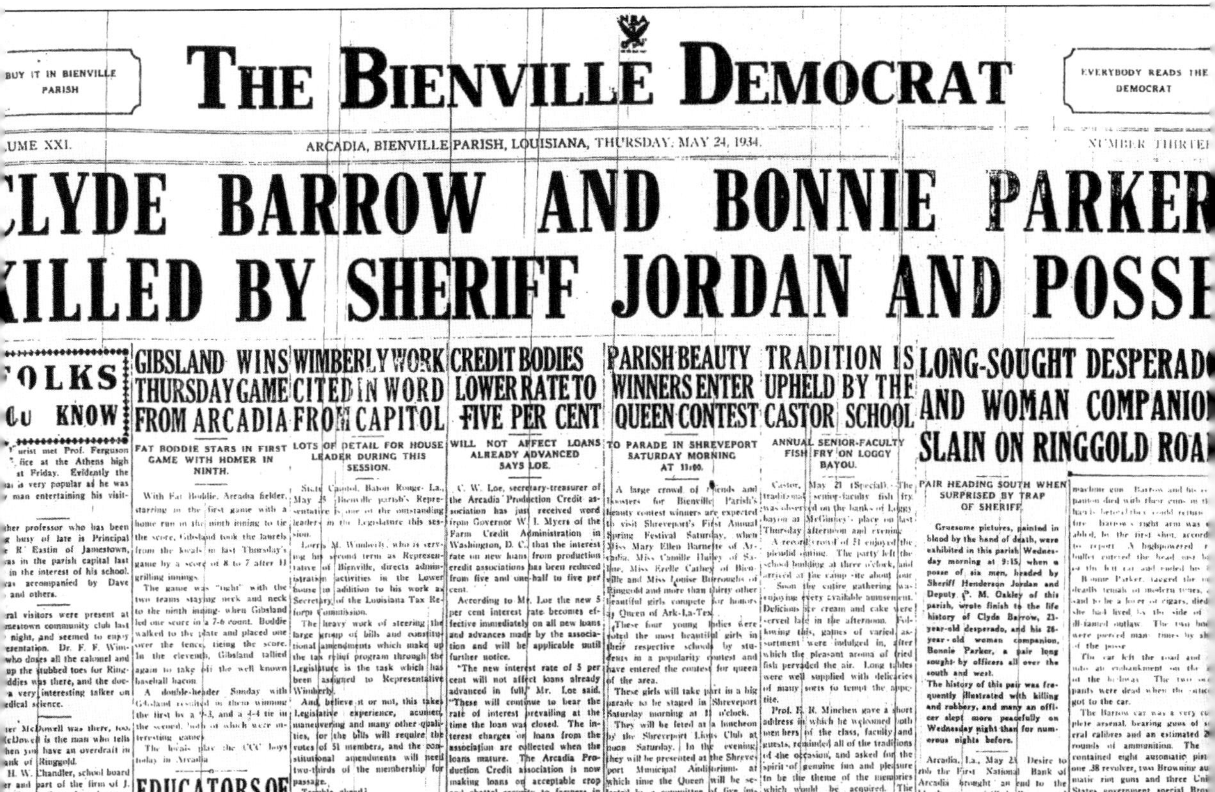

BUY IT IN BIENVILLE PARISH

THE BIENVILLE DEMOCRAT

EVERYBODY READS THE DEMOCRAT

UME XXI. ARCADIA, BIENVILLE PARISH, LOUISIANA, THURSDAY, MAY 24, 1934. NUMBER THIRTE

CLYDE BARROW AND BONNIE PARKER KILLED BY SHERIFF JORDAN AND POSSE

FOLKS YOU KNOW

GIBSLAND WINS THURSDAY GAME FROM ARCADIA

FAT BODDIE STARS IN FIRST GAME WITH HOMER IN NINTH.

WIMBERLY WORK CITED IN WORD FROM CAPITOL

LOTS OF DETAIL FOR HOUSE LEADER DURING THIS SESSION.

CREDIT BODIES LOWER RATE TO FIVE PER CENT

WILL NOT AFFECT LOANS ALREADY ADVANCED SAYS LOE.

C. W. Loe, secretary-treasurer of the Arcadia Production Credit association has just received word from Governor W. I. Myers of the Farm Credit Administration in Washington, D. C., that the interest rate on new loans from production credit associations has been reduced from five and one-half to five per cent.

PARISH BEAUTY WINNERS ENTER QUEEN CONTEST

TO PARADE IN SHREVEPORT SATURDAY MORNING AT 11:00.

TRADITION IS UPHELD BY THE CASTOR SCHOOL

ANNUAL SENIOR-FACULTY FISH FRY ON LOGGY BAYOU.

LONG-SOUGHT DESPERADO AND WOMAN COMPANION SLAIN ON RINGGOLD ROAD

PAIR HEADING SOUTH WHEN SURPRISED BY TRAP OF SHERIFF

Gruesome pictures, painted in blood by the hand of death, were exhibited in this parish Wednesday morning at 9:15, when a posse of six men, headed by Sheriff Henderson Jordan and Deputy P. M. Oakley of this parish, wrote finish to the life history of Clyde Barrow, 23-year-old desperado, and his 26-year-old woman companion, Bonnie Parker, a pair long sought by officers all over the south and west.

The history of this pair was frequently illustrated with killing and robbery, and many an officer slept more peacefully on Wednesday night than for numerous nights before.

EDUCATORS OF STATE EXPRESS APPRECIATION

GO ON RECORD AS APPROV-

CLUB PROGRAM

On May 24, 1934, the *Bienville Democrat* relayed the news that the nationwide hunt for the wanted criminals Bonnie and Clyde had ended the previous day. Law enforcement officers ambushed and killed the duo just a few miles southwest of Gibsland. Masses of people arrived to view the bodies of Bonnie and Clyde at Conger's Funeral Home in Arcadia. (Courtesy of the *Bienville Democrat*.)

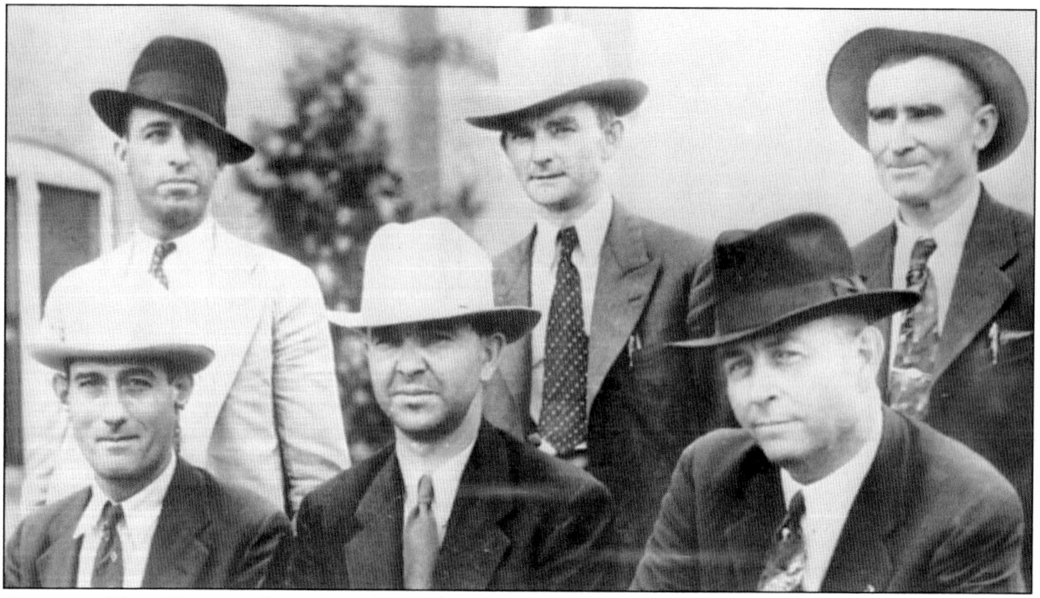

A posse of four Texas and two Louisiana deputies ambushed and killed Bonnie and Clyde. Shown here are, from left to right, (first row) Bob Alcorn (Texas), Bienville Parish sheriff Henderson Jordan, and Frank Hamer (Texas); (second row) Ted Hinton (Texas), Bienville Parish sheriff's deputy Prentiss Morel Oakley, and B.M. "Manny" Gault (Texas). (Courtesy of the Federal Bureau of Investigation.)

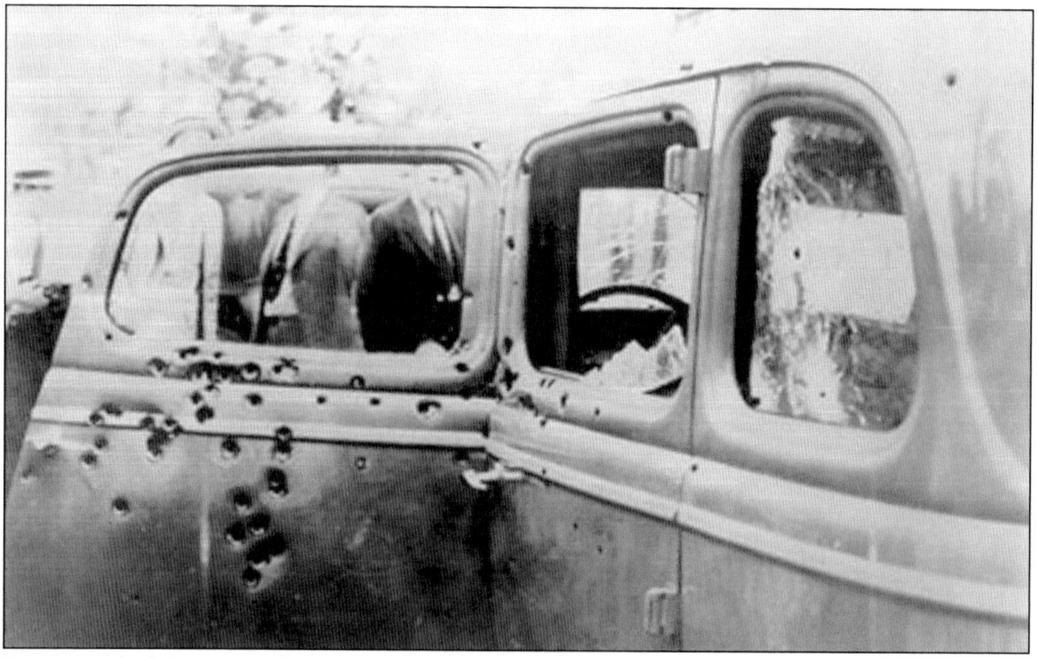

Bonnie and Clyde repeatedly escaped capture, but not on the morning of May 23. At approximately 9:15 a.m. on that day, a posse hid in the bushes until the men heard Barrow's stolen Ford V8 arriving at a high rate of speed. Once the couple was identified, the posse fired approximately 130 rounds of ammunition into the car, killing Bonnie and Clyde. (Courtesy of the Federal Bureau of Investigation.)

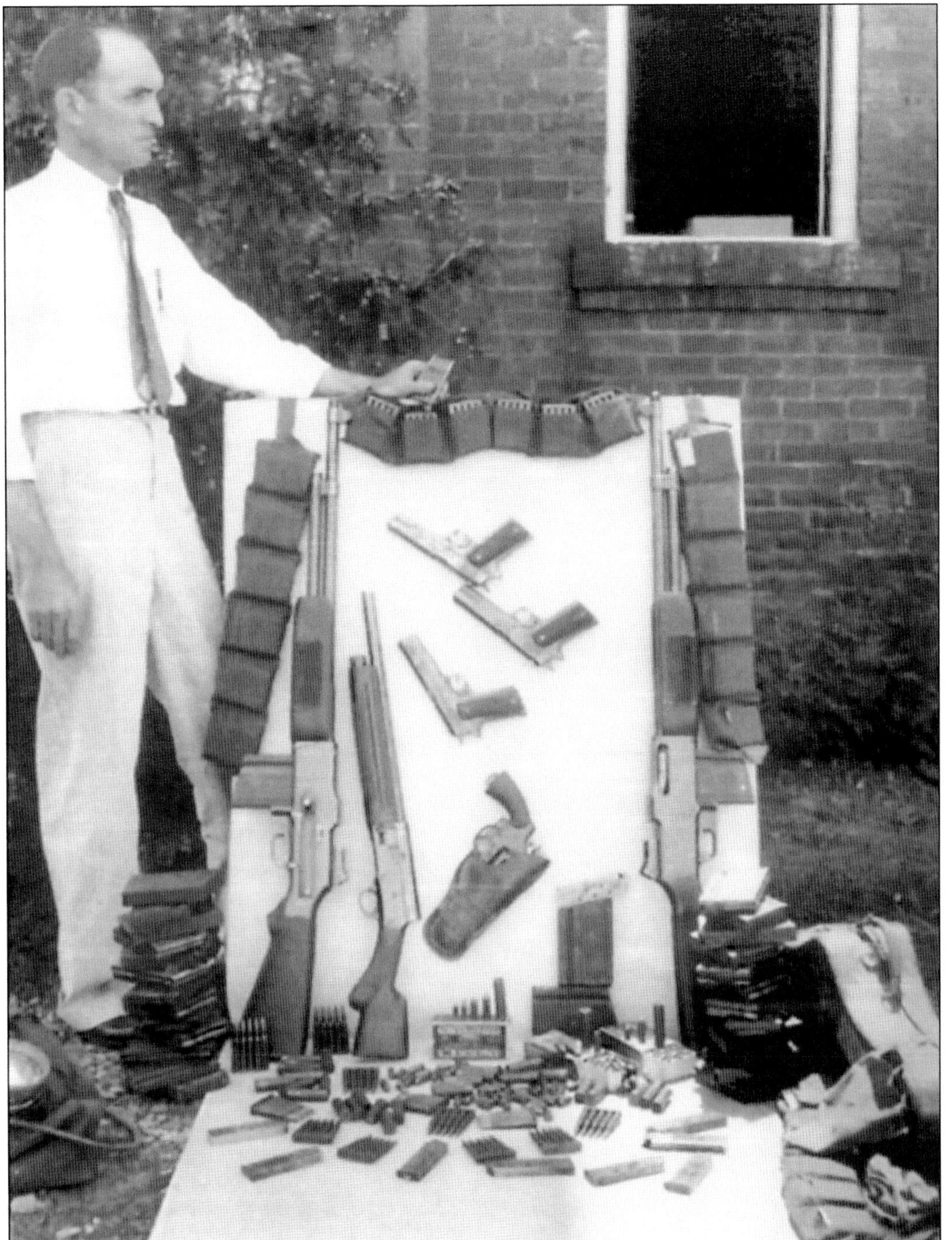

In contrast to the playfulness shown in the photographs taken by the Barrow Gang, Bonnie and Clyde were armed and dangerous criminals. When police officers searched the Ford V8, they found an arsenal of weapons, including handguns, sawed-off semiautomatic shotguns, automatic rifles, several thousand rounds of ammunition, and 15 license plates from various states. (Courtesy of the Federal Bureau of Investigation.)

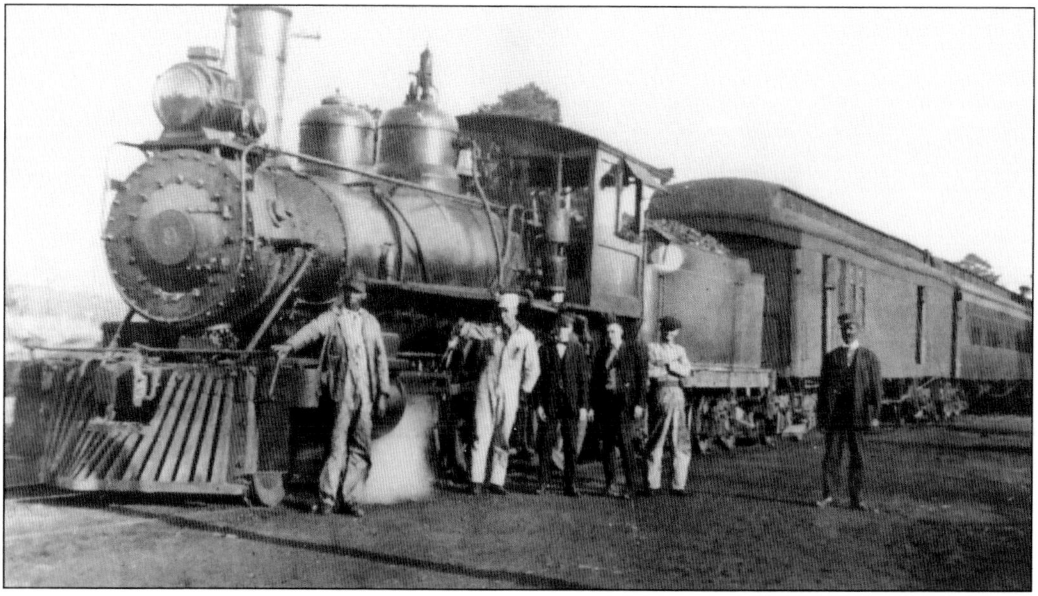

In 1920, the crew of Louisiana & North West's daily passenger train No. 9 pauses for a photograph at the union station in Gibsland. When the train arrived at the station, a mass of passengers hurried to board or disembark the train. Several businesses thrived along the rail line. Near this station were hotels, stores, and a blacksmith shop. (Courtesy of Louisiana & North West Railroad.)

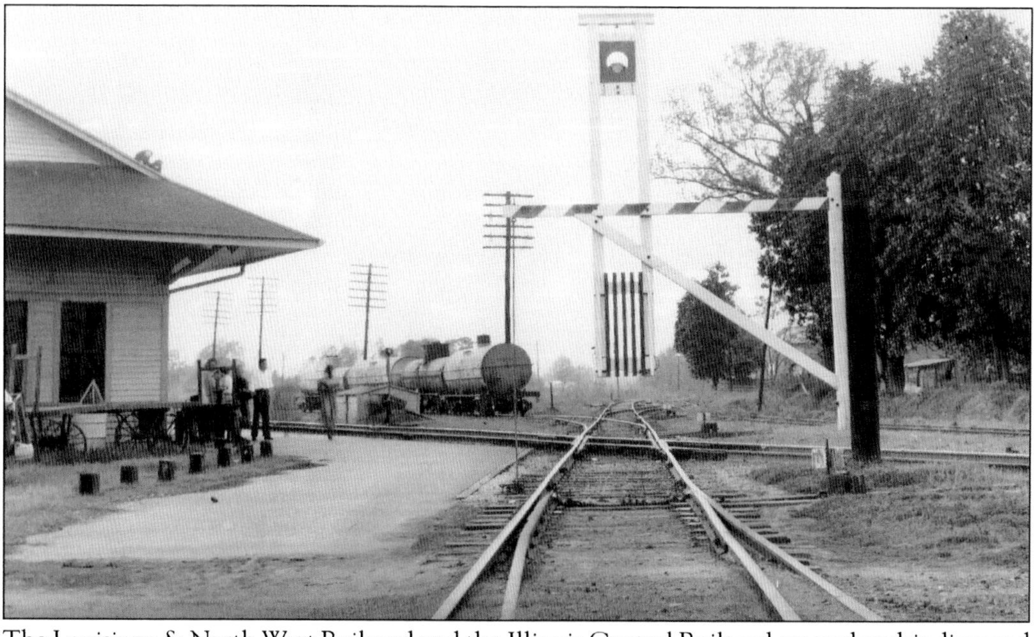

The Louisiana & North West Railroad and the Illinois Central Railroad crossed at this diamond at Gibsland, seen here in September 1949. At its height, the tracks at Gibsland were busy with up to eight daily passenger trains, most of which were overloaded. At one time, Gibsland had four platforms for the loading and unloading of passengers and freight. (Courtesy of Louisiana & North West Railroad.)

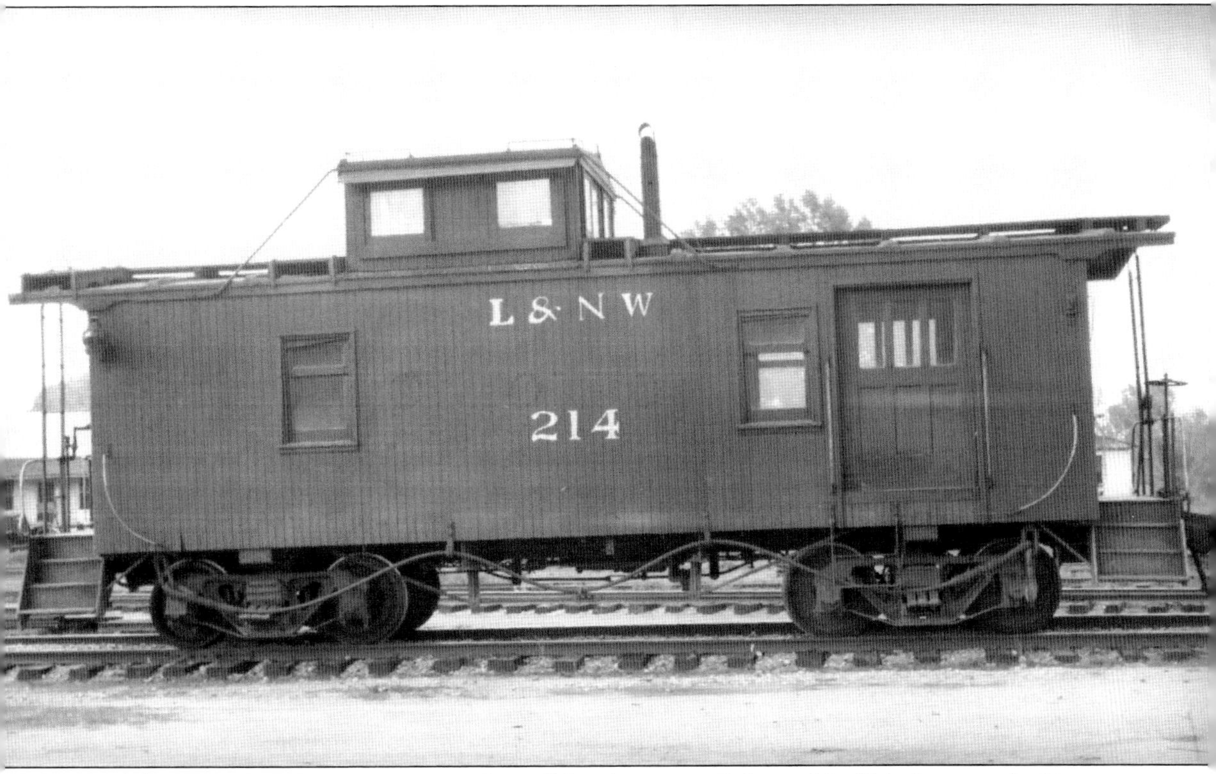

Until the 1980s, cabooses were required on all freight trains. Caboose No. 214, photographed here in 1950, provided the train crew with shelter and temporary living quarters for longer trips. The conductor had a table in the caboose for keeping records. Crews often decorated the caboose for a homier feel. Advancements in modern technology, such as electronic sensors, have rendered cabooses obsolete. (Courtesy of Louisiana & North West Railroad.)

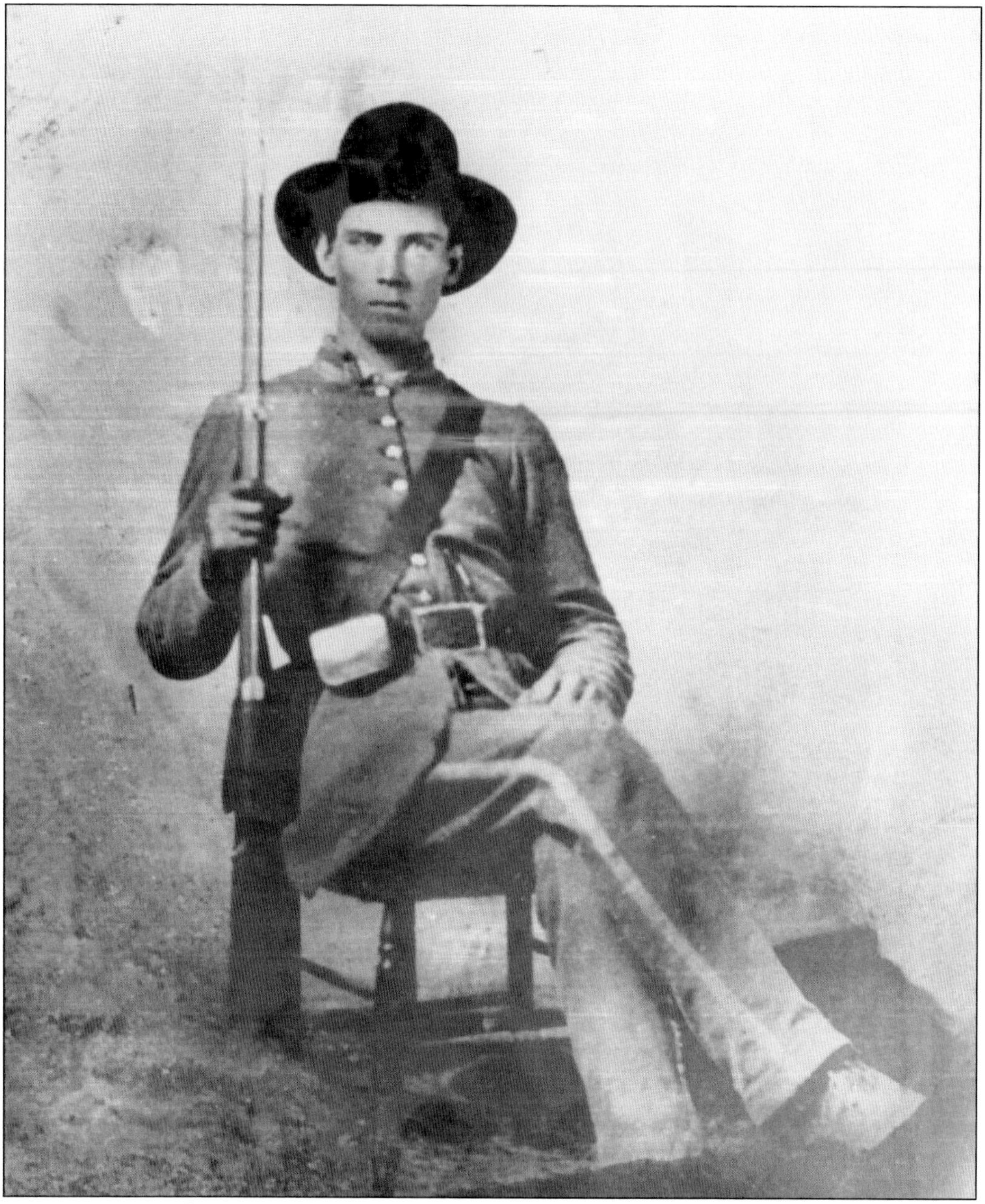

Many young men from Bienville Parish fought for the Confederacy, but few photographs of them survive. During the Civil War, William T. Burnett was a private in the 8th Louisiana Infantry Company G and trained at Camp Moore, Louisiana. Company G originated in Minden, and the company was nicknamed "The Minden Blues." Burnett survived the war and returned to Mount Lebanon. (Courtesy of Stage Coach Trail Museum.)

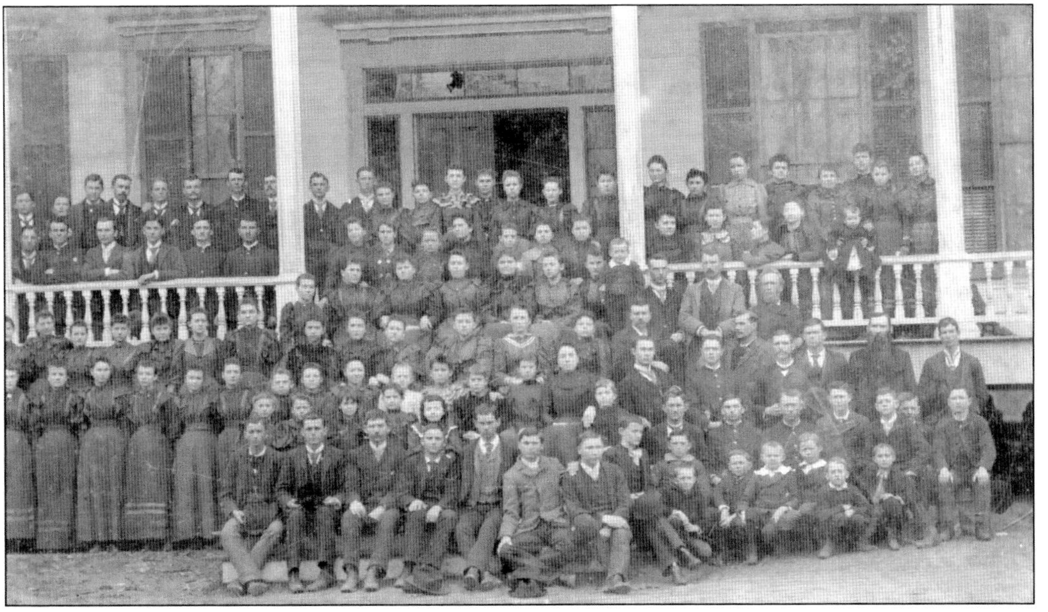

Founded in 1853, Mount Lebanon University became the leading educational center of North Louisiana. At its height, it claimed 127 students. In September 1863, the Confederate army commandeered the buildings and used them as a hospital. Classes resumed after the Civil War. In the 1893–1894 school year, when this photograph was taken, the Mount Lebanon University student body was large. (Courtesy of Stage Coach Trail Museum.)

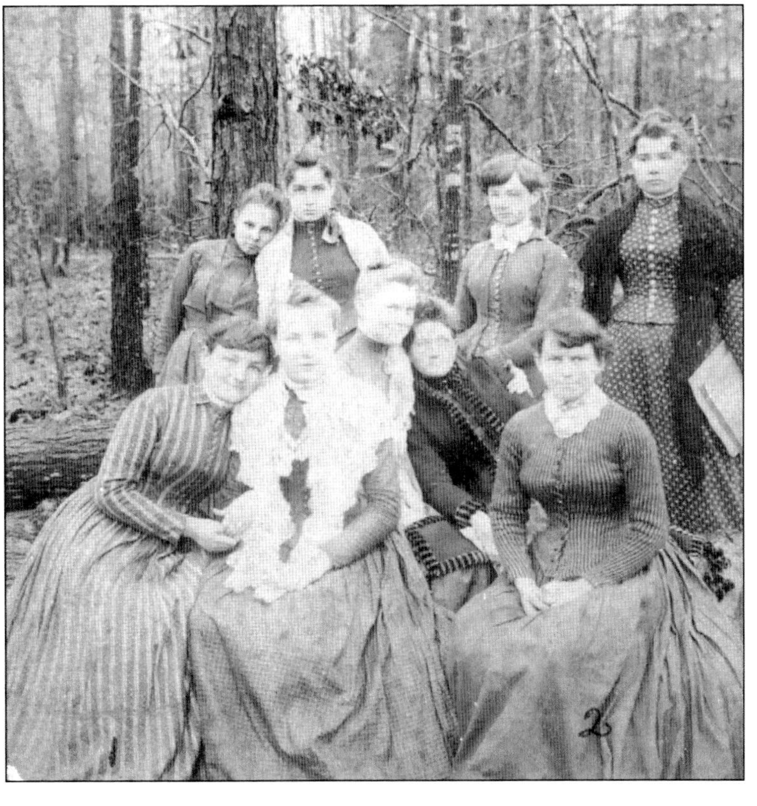

Soon after the founding of Mount Lebanon University, which was built as a men's college, a female college was also formed at Mount Lebanon to meet the needs of the young ladies of North Louisiana. Enrollment was limited by the ability of the young lady's family to pay tuition. The college prepared women to become teachers, "their only socially acceptable occupation." (Courtesy of Stage Coach Trail Museum.)

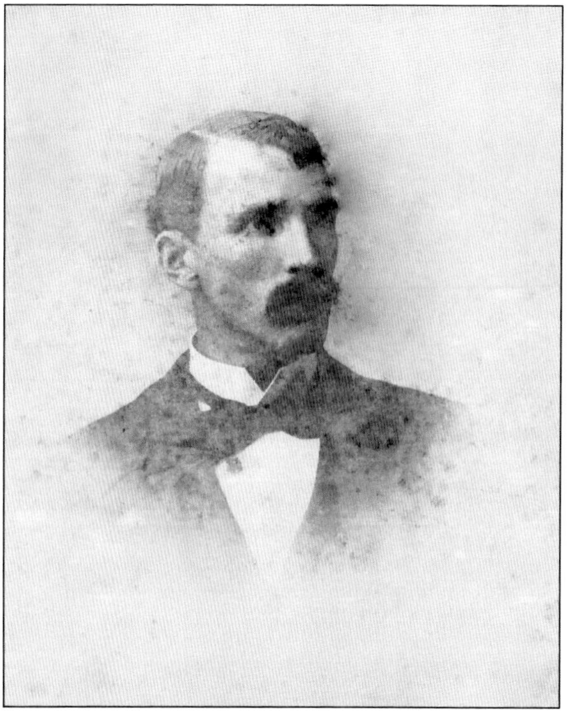

In the late 1800s, William Claiborne Robinson was a professor of mathematics and also served as president of Mount Lebanon University. He also taught mathematics at Louisiana Polytechnic Institute, now Louisiana Tech University. From 1899 to 1900, Robinson served as the second president of what is now Louisiana Tech. Robinson Hall at Louisiana Tech was named in his honor. (Courtesy of Stage Coach Trail Museum.)

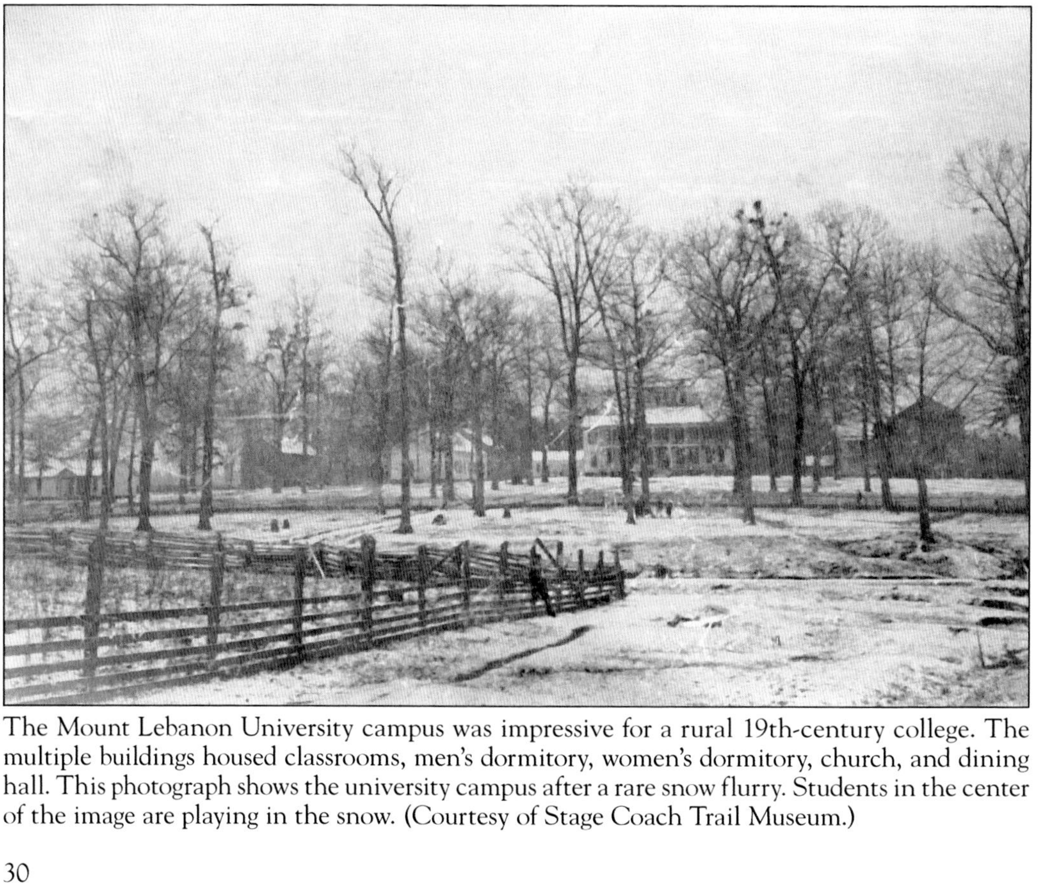

The Mount Lebanon University campus was impressive for a rural 19th-century college. The multiple buildings housed classrooms, men's dormitory, women's dormitory, church, and dining hall. This photograph shows the university campus after a rare snow flurry. Students in the center of the image are playing in the snow. (Courtesy of Stage Coach Trail Museum.)

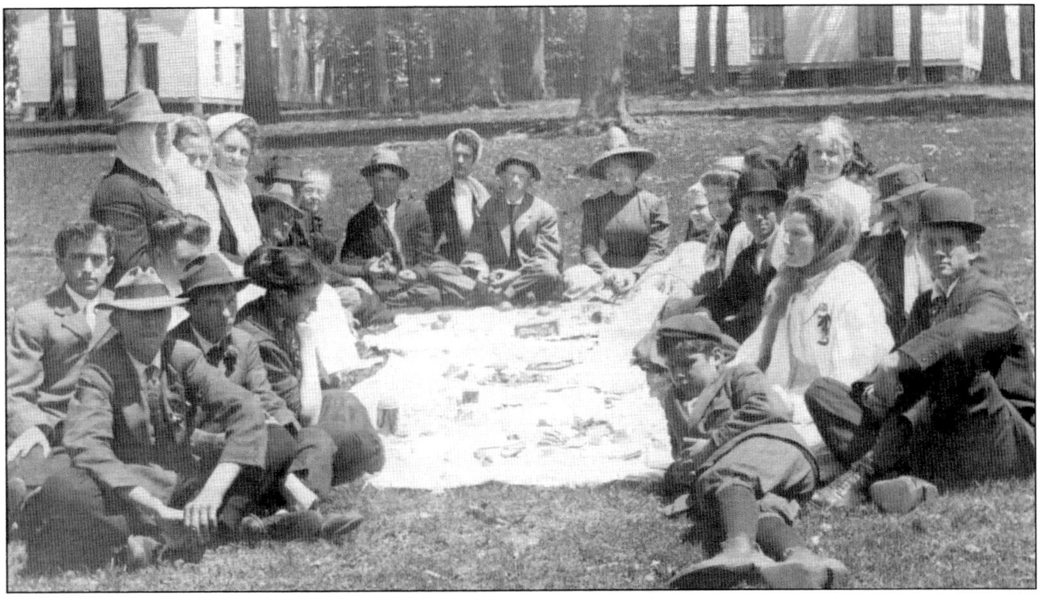

In the late 1800s, students and teachers took a break from schoolwork and held a picnic on the Mount Lebanon University campus. At this outing, they ate apples, plums, and other fruits, along with biscuits and bread. The female student in the foreground at left is taking this time to catch up on her reading. (Courtesy of Stage Coach Trail Museum.)

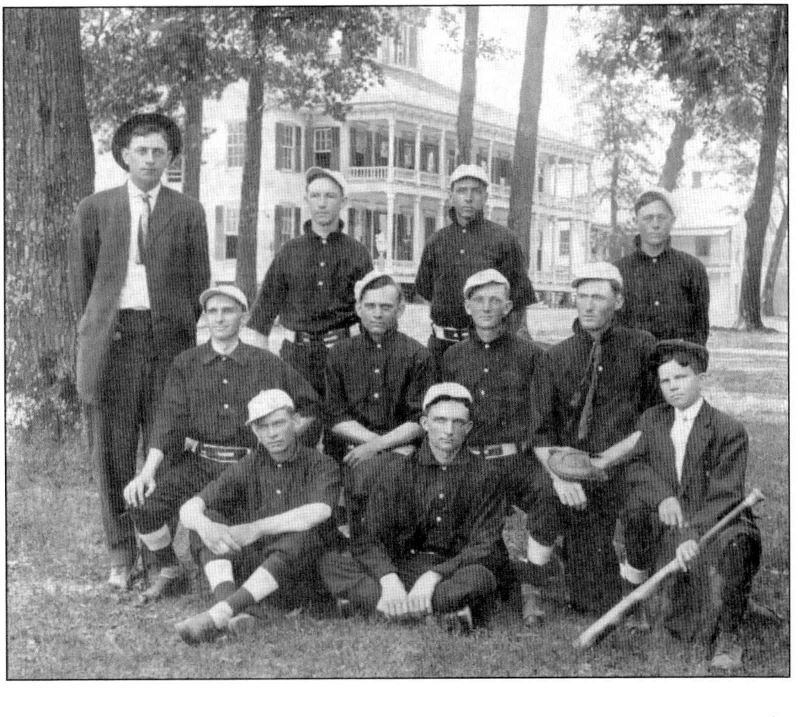

In the 1850s, bat-and-ball games had become popular, and colleges formed baseball teams and leagues. In the late 1800s, Mount Lebanon University formed its own baseball team. College athletes had a rigorous schedule of attending classes, studying, practicing sports, and competing against other universities. (Courtesy of Stage Coach Trail Museum.)

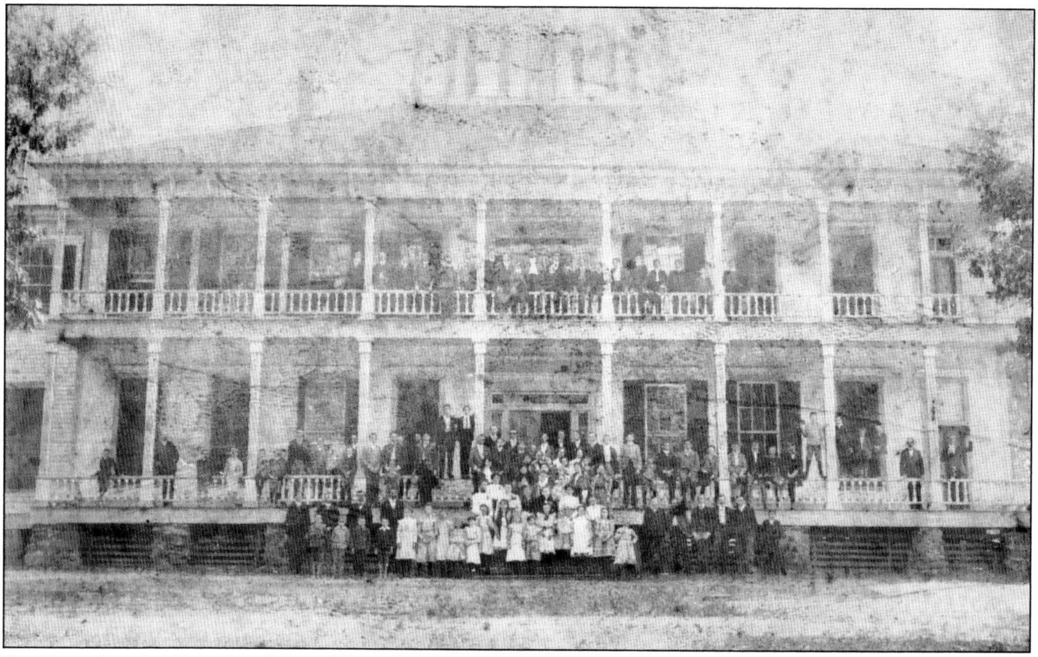

On October 4, 1902, the date of this photograph, the college had fewer students and was struggling financially. In 1899, Mount Lebanon University had come under the control of the Louisiana Baptist Convention. In 1906, following years of financial troubles, Mount Lebanon University was consolidated into Louisiana College in Pineville. (Courtesy of Stage Coach Trail Museum.)

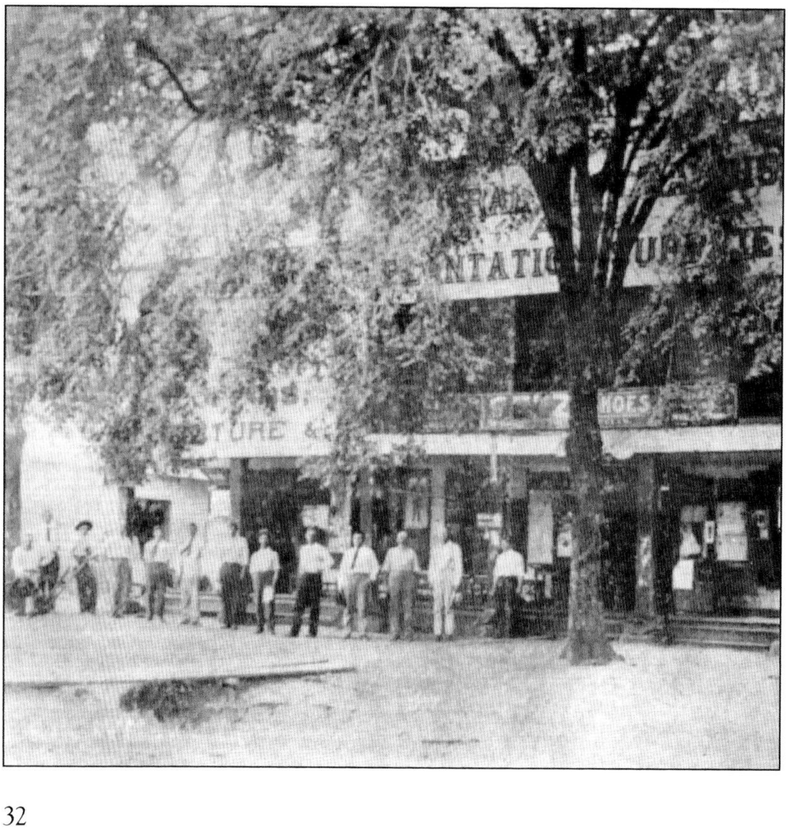

In the late 1800s, citizens of Mount Lebanon have gathered in front of Baker & Co. General Merchandise and Plantation Supplies for this photograph. Rural towns usually had at least one small general store to provide the necessities of life. Mount Lebanon's general store was larger than most in the rural towns in Bienville Parish. (Courtesy of Stage Coach Trail Museum.)

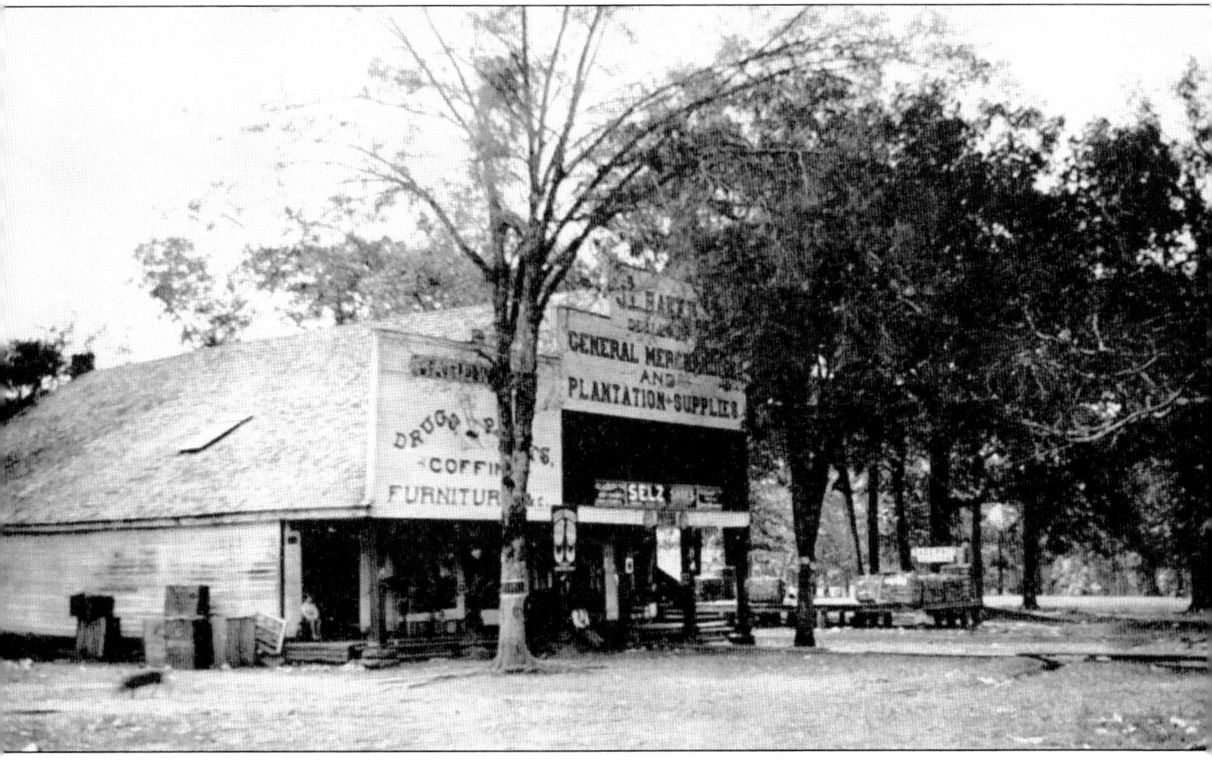

Baker & Co. sold a variety of items, including plantation supplies, shoes, clothing, drugs, furniture, cotton, and coffins. During rainy weather, the dirt streets turned into mud. A wooden sidewalk provided a clean crossing from the general store to the businesses on the other side of the street. (Courtesy of Stage Coach Trail Museum.)

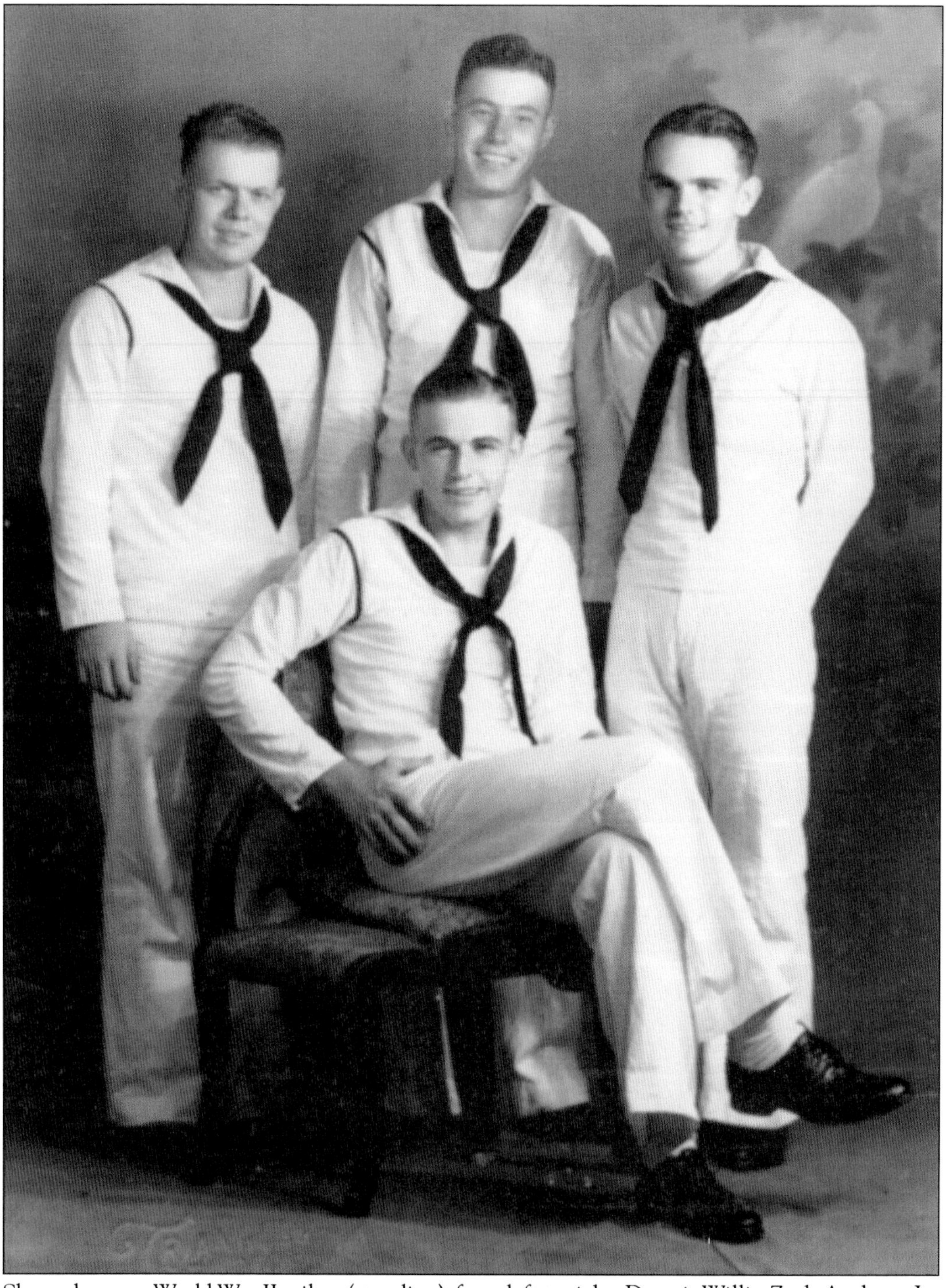

Shown here are World War II sailors (standing), from left to right, Donnis Willis, Zach Andrews Jr., Edwin Hoofer, and (seated) Milton Russel. They served aboard the USS *Houston* during the Battle of Sunda Strait off the coast of Java. Andrews was the first soldier from Bienville Parish listed as missing in action. On May 1, 1942, a Japanese torpedo sank the *Houston*, and Andrews and Hoofer were killed in action. (Courtesy of Stage Coach Trail Museum.)

Three

Central Bienville Parish

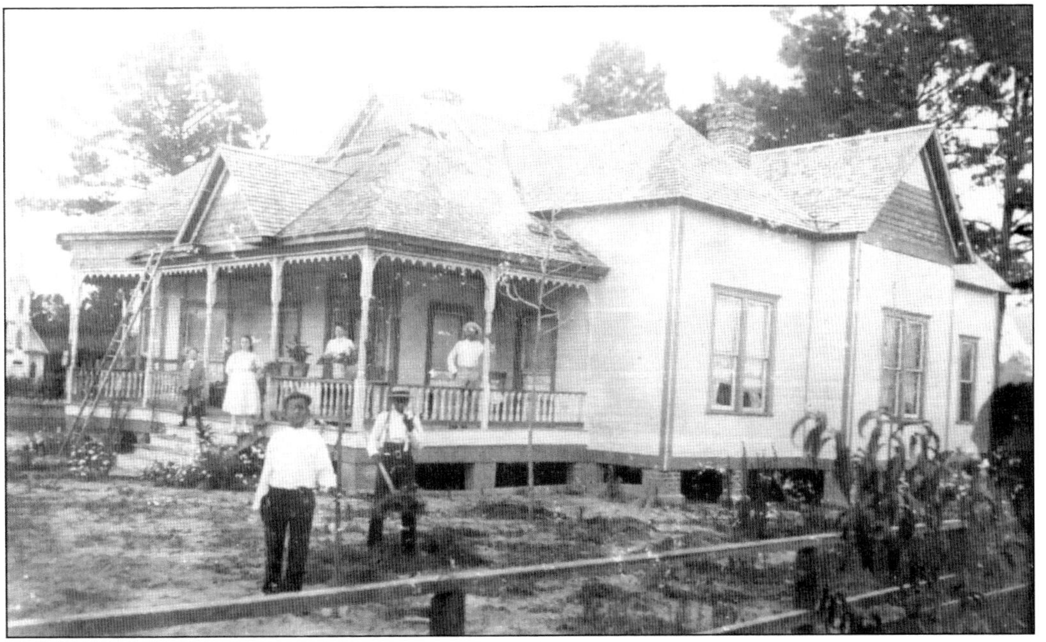

The George Washington Sutton house was originally built in Sparta in the 1800s. Sutton purchased the house, had it cut into sections, moved it to Bienville on wagons, and had it reassembled near the Methodist church. Shown here posing on the front porch about 1900 are, from left to right, George Cecil Sutton, Dixie Sutton, Willie Palmer Sutton, and George Washington Sutton. The boys in the yard are unidentified. (Courtesy of Donna Sutton.)

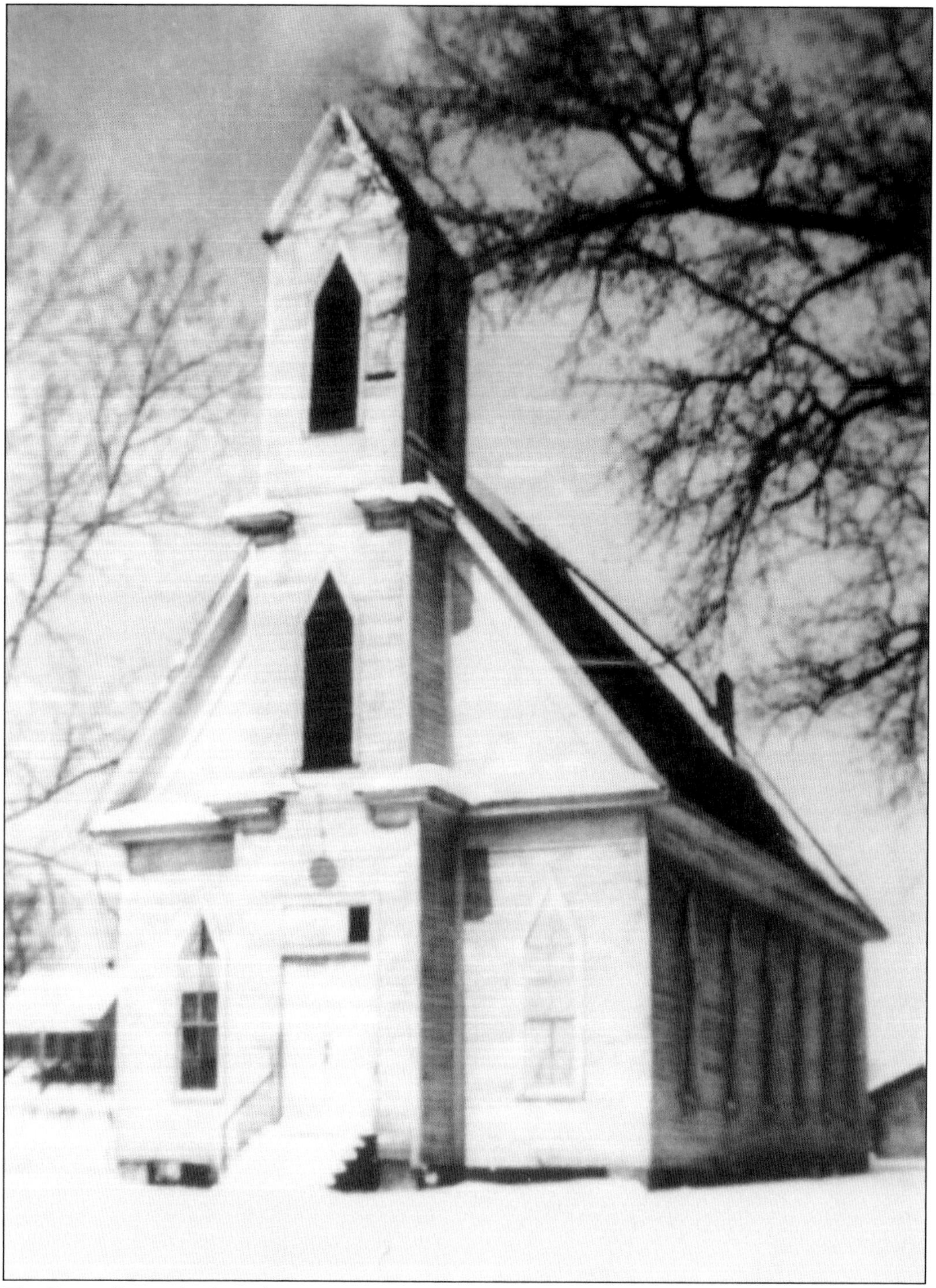

The Bienville Methodist Church is seen here after a rare winter's snow. The church was located on Spruce Street, at the site of the current Bienville United Methodist Church. Through the years, the church has had a large succession of preachers, including Rev. J.G. Sloane in the 1920s and Rev. W.P. Shows in the 1940s. (Courtesy of Donna Sutton.)

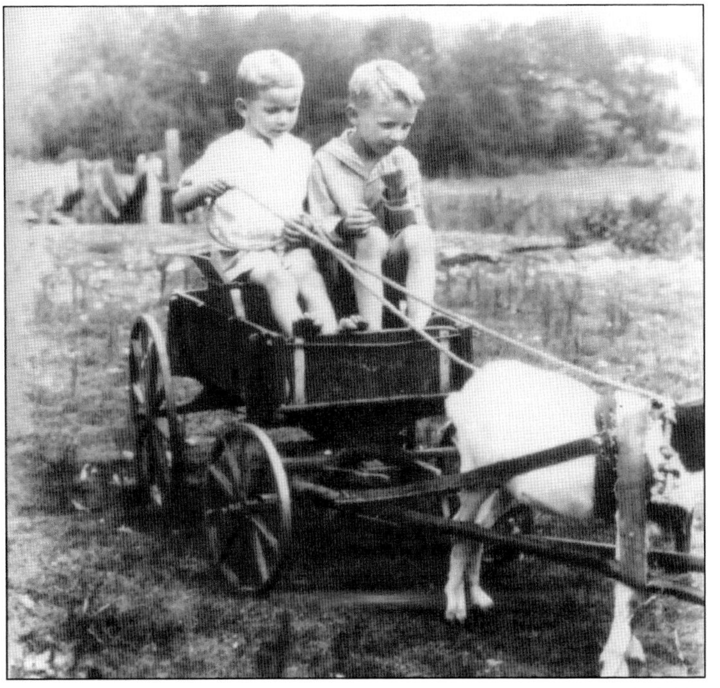

In the mid-1920s, Harold E. (left) and George Cecil Sutton Jr. enjoy a ride in their goat-drawn farm wagon. Sears, Roebuck and Company began selling this model of "Boys' Farm Wagons" in the 1890s for under $7, with the option to purchase a goat or dog harness. Goat-drawn carts were a popular toy at the turn of the 20th century. (Courtesy of Donna Sutton.)

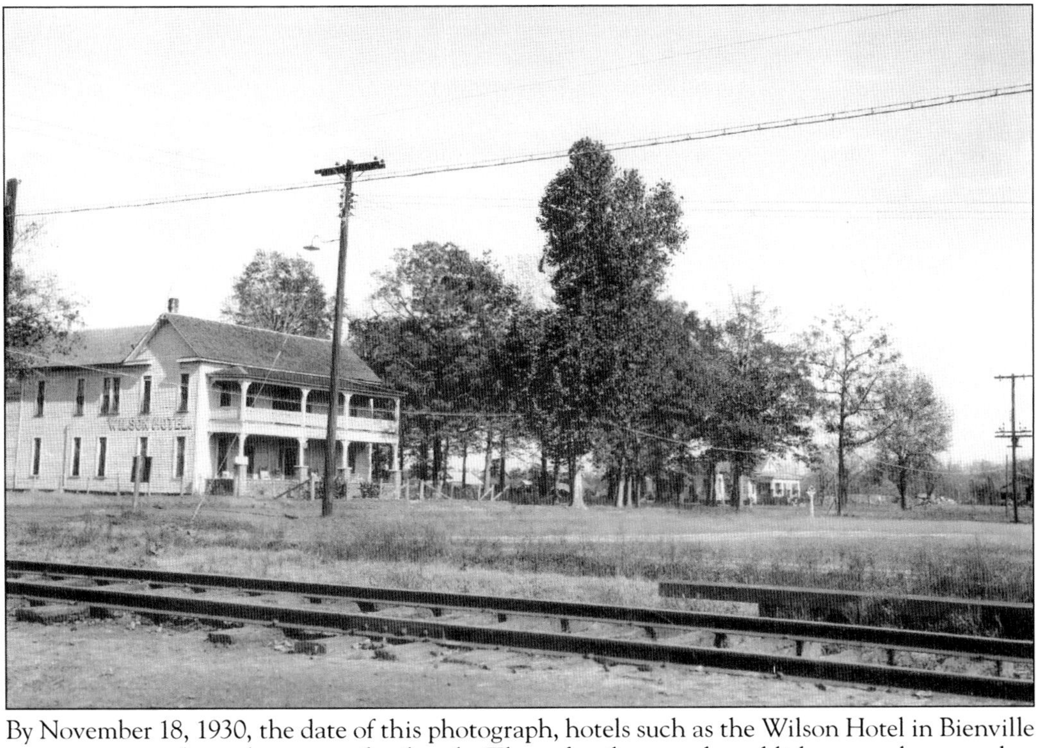

By November 18, 1930, the date of this photograph, hotels such as the Wilson Hotel in Bienville were common along the route of railroads. These family-owned establishments also served as residences for the owner's family. Hungry travelers ate at the family's dinner table. W.M. Wilson owned and operated the Wilson Hotel until his death in May 1933. (Courtesy of Louisiana & North West Railroad.)

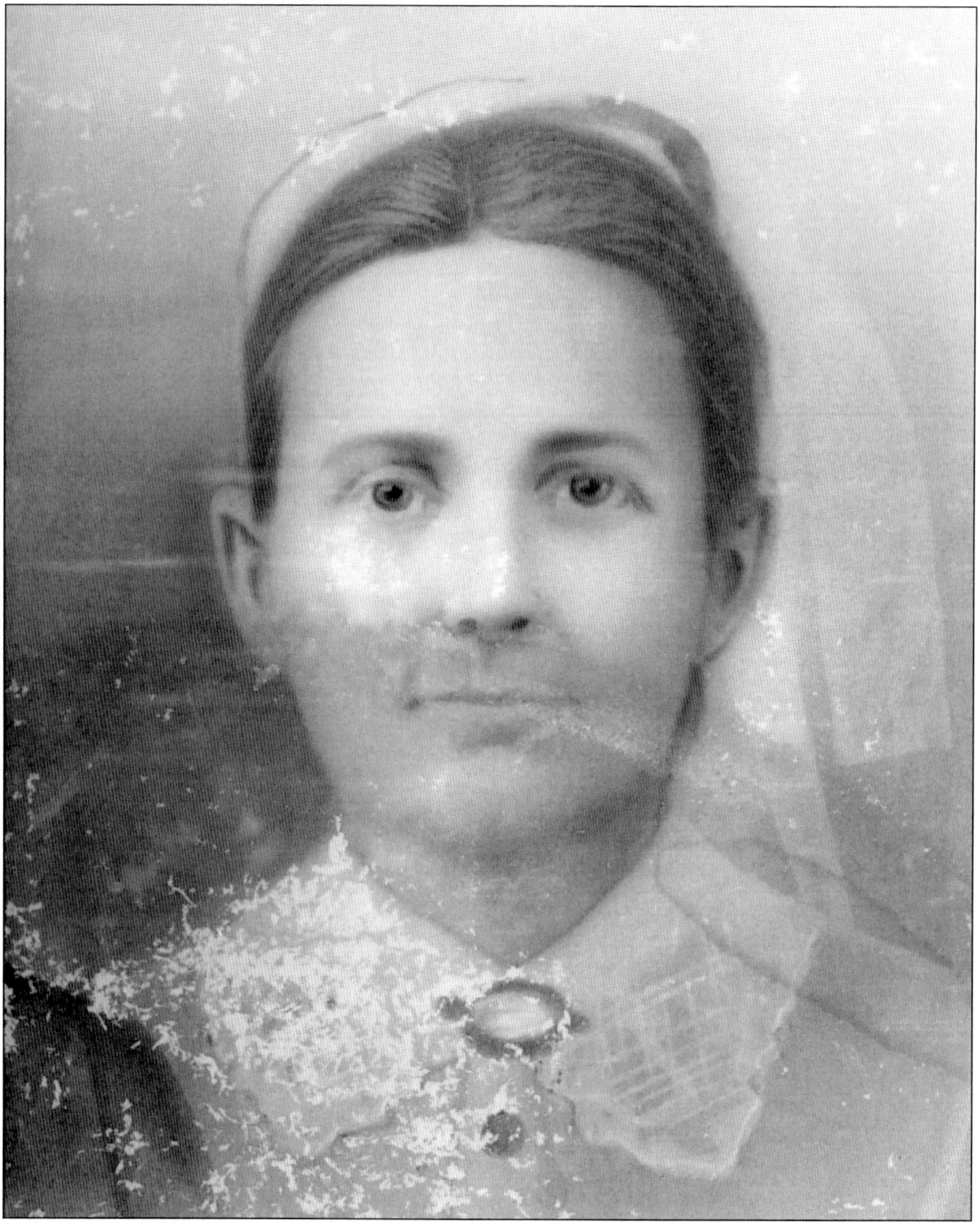

Originally called Salt Springs, Castor had approximately 2,640 acres of underlying deposits of salt. In the 1840s, Alfred P. King began salt operations and founded King Salt Works. The finished product varied in price from $3 to $10 for a 60-pound bushel. King's daughter (her first name is not known), shown here, undoubtedly helped in the boiling down of the salt. (Courtesy of Mary Hamner.)

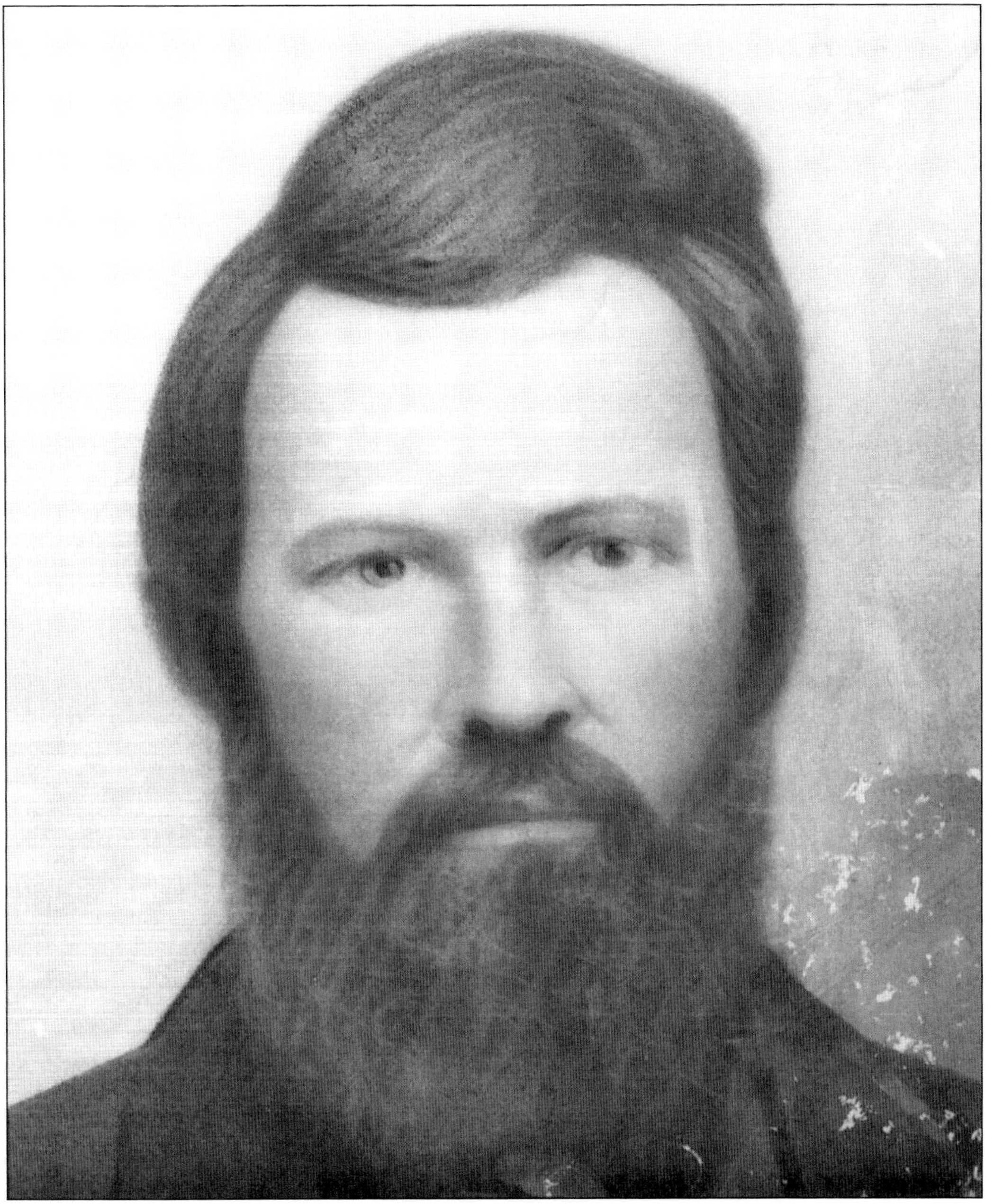

Alfred Pickney King's son-in-law (pictured) also helped in the salt operations at King Salt Works. Before the Civil War, King Salt Works shipped salt to other states in the union. During the war, a Federal blockade interfered with salt shipments, and the commodity became scarce. People came to King Salt Works from Alabama, Arkansas, and Mississippi to acquire salt. (Courtesy of Mary Hamner.)

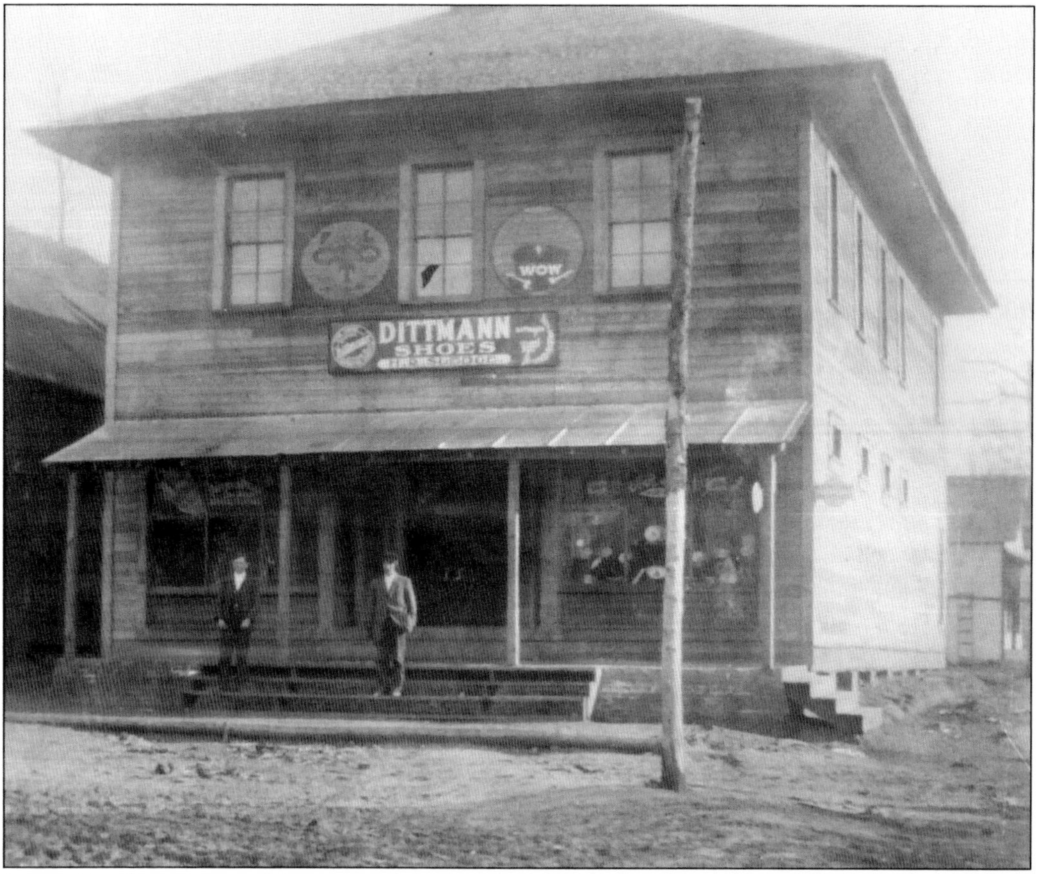

Henry R. Sledge operated a general store in Castor, seen here around 1922. His son Rupert worked in the store while his father went "politicking." "Happy" Henry was the clerk of court of Bienville Parish from 1923 until his death in 1939. The Independent Order of Odd Fellows and the Woodmen of the World life insurance fraternal societies were located on the top floor. (Courtesy of Mary Hamner.)

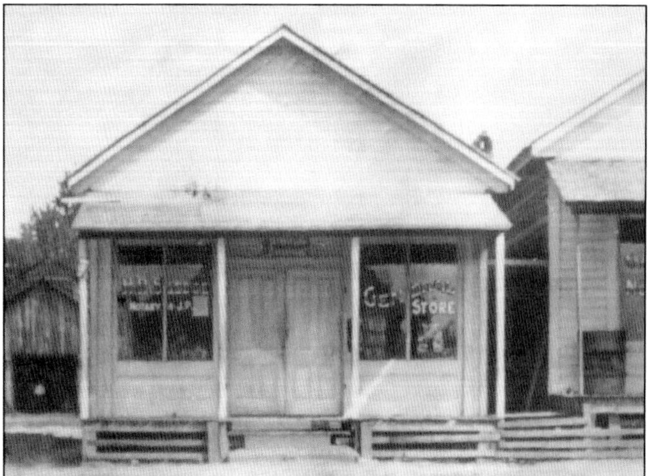

As well as serving as clerk of court for Bienville Parish, "Happy" Henry was justice of the peace and provided notary services for the citizens of Castor. Sledge's justice of the peace and notary office was located in this extension of his general store on Highway 4. (Courtesy of Mary Hamner.)

Dr. Chester Harper Sledge, brother of Henry Sledge, graduated from the University of Tennessee in 1909 and practiced dentistry in Castor from 1910 until his death in 1946. He operated a dentist office in the back of Sledge's store. Rather than disposing of teeth hygienically, Dr. Sledge simply tossed them out of the back window. (Courtesy of Mary Hamner.)

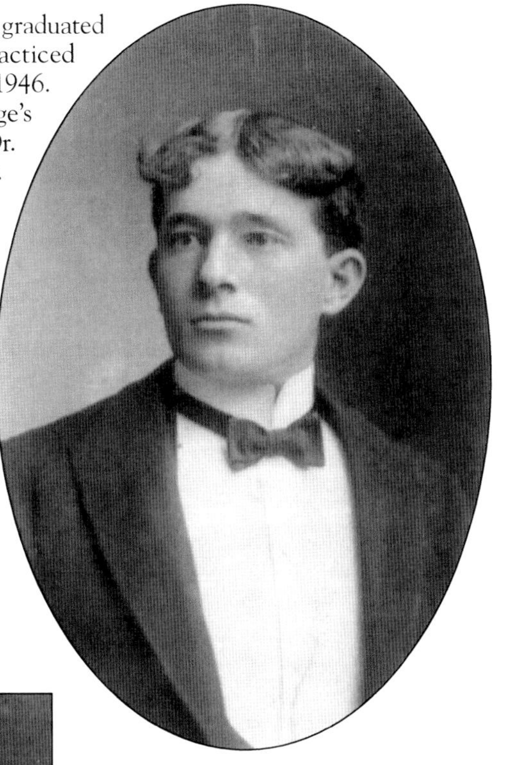

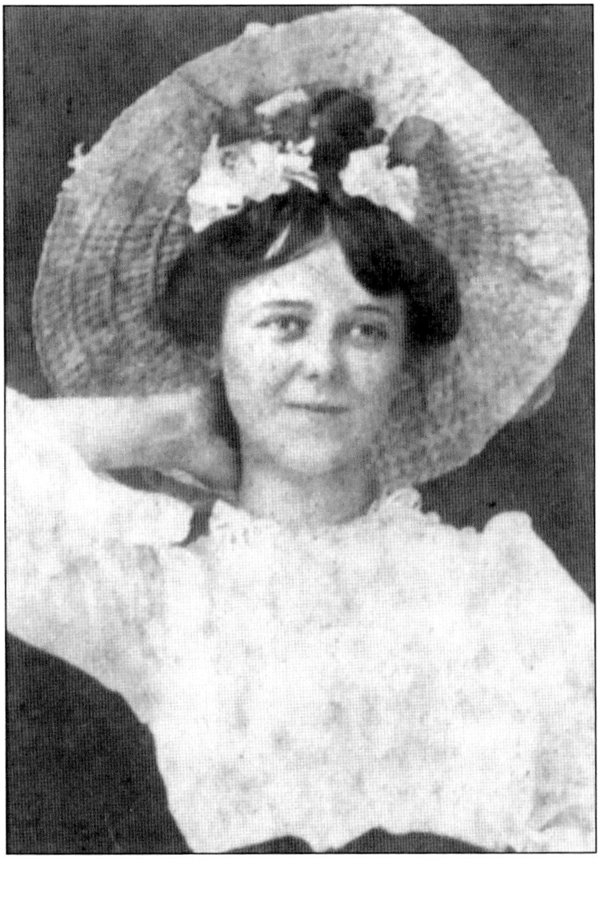

Mrs. J.C. Nix remembered Dr. Sledge's wife, Kittie Vincent Sledge (pictured), as friendly, helpful, encouraging, and one of the most devout Christians she had ever met. Sledge served in every capacity at the Castor Methodist Church at one time or another. She was a Sunday school superintendent for several years, president of the Women's Society of Christian Service, and chairman of the women's group Spiritual Growth. (Courtesy of Mary Hamner.)

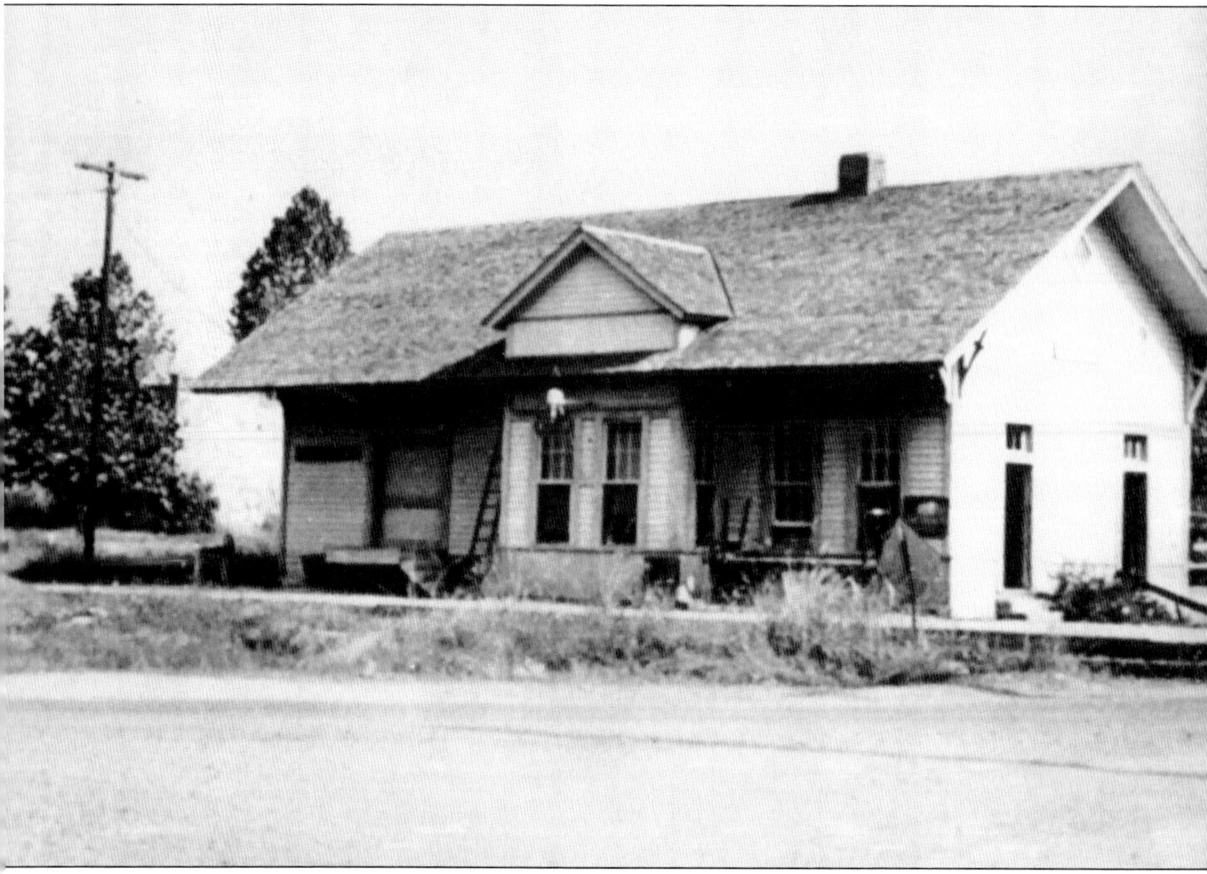

In 1896, William Buchanan built the Louisiana & Arkansas Railway (L&A) through Bienville Parish. In the mid-1940s, trains regularly stopped at the L&A depot at Castor to load or unload passengers and freight. In 1945, the Louisiana & Arkansas merged with the Kansas City Southern. When passenger service was discontinued in Castor, B.H. Davis bought and moved the depot building to his farm. (Courtesy of Mary Hamner.)

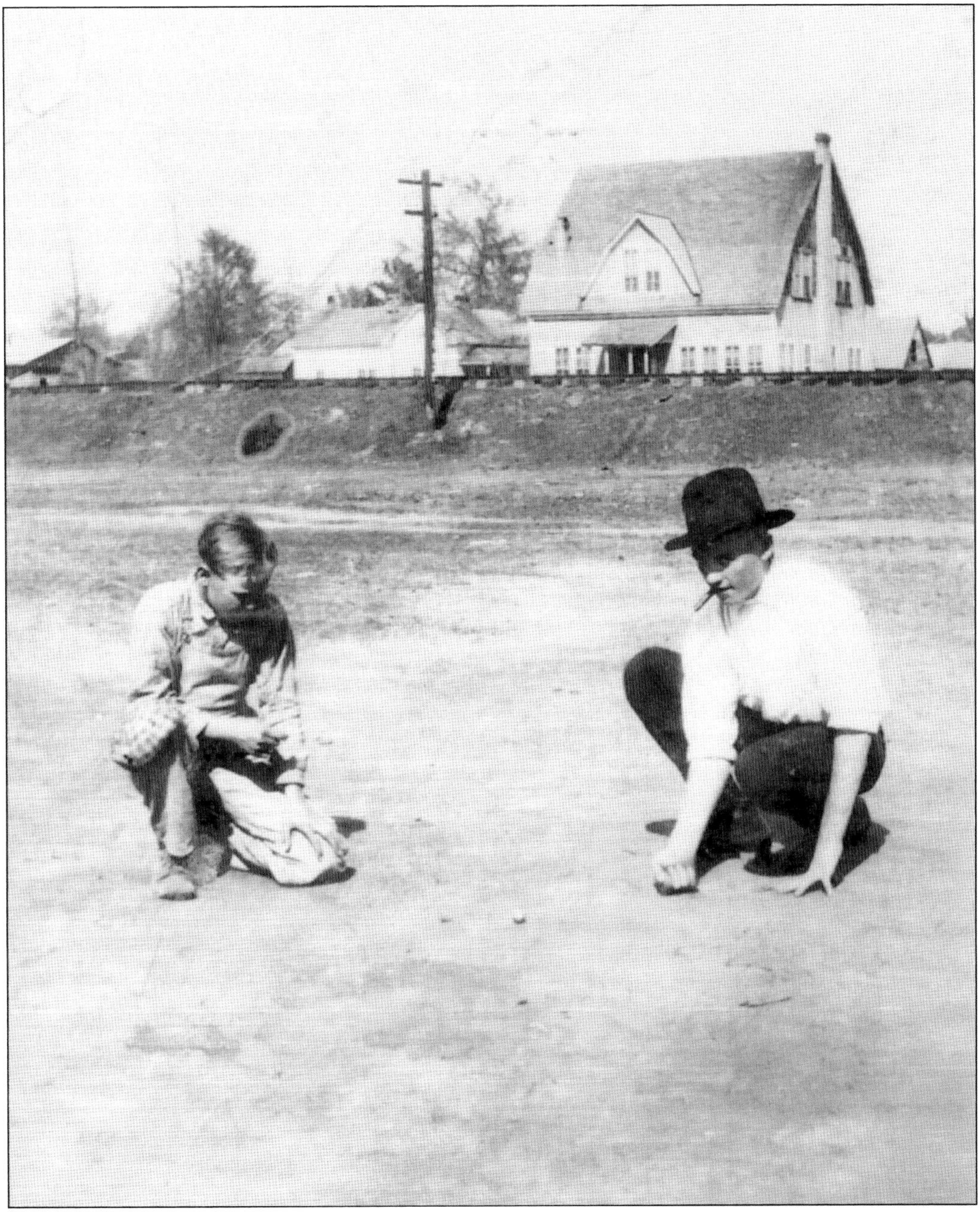

L.T. Foster (left) and Clint Simpson play marbles on the Castor High School grounds in the 1920s. Marble collectors refer to the 1920s and 1930s as the golden age of marbles because of the game's popularity during that time. The multistory building in the background is the Dorgan Hotel, owned by John Dorgan. To the left is the Wimberly house. (Courtesy of Mary Hamner.)

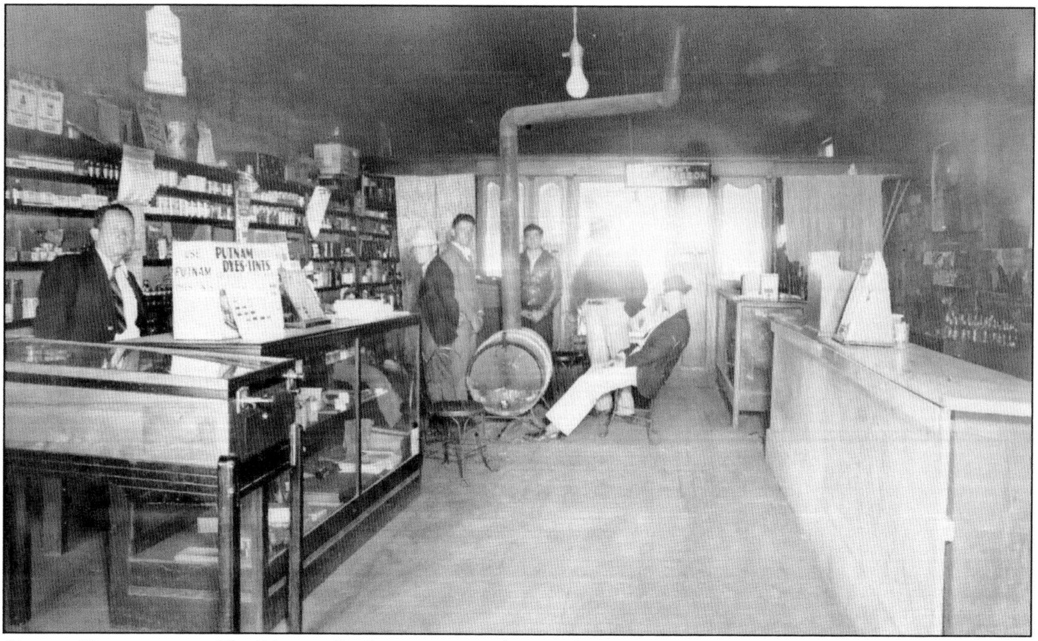

Castor Drugs, owned by Ventie B. Stewart, was located next to Castor State Bank and across from the old barbershop on Highway 4. Stewart also operated a dance hall in the back of the store. Passed in 1933, Ordinance No. 18 made the sale of alcoholic beverages legal in Castor. (Courtesy of Stage Coach Trail Museum.)

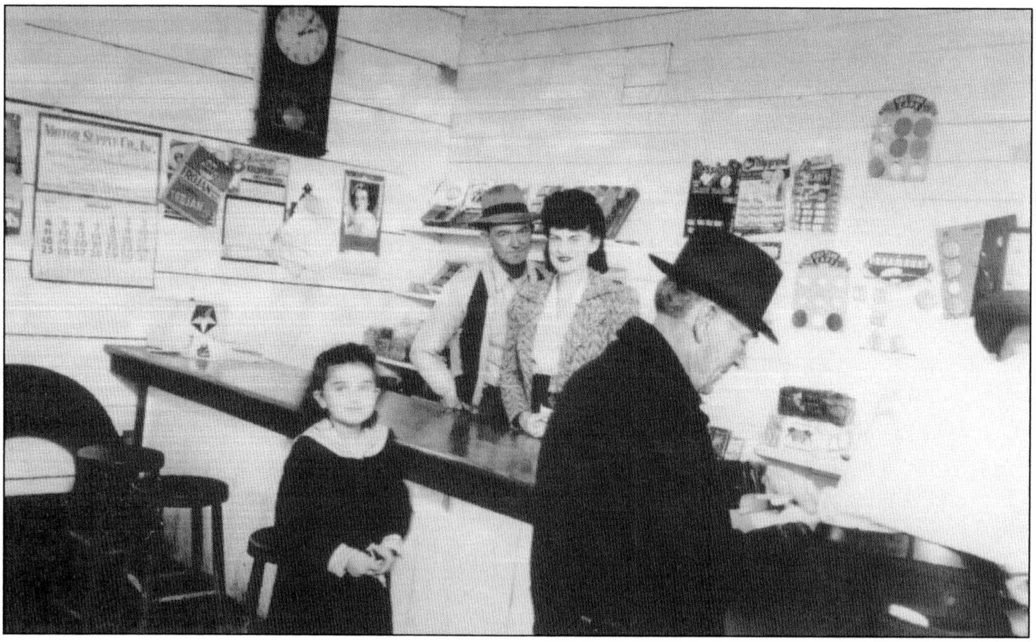

The Bogans pose for a photograph inside Bogan's Citgo service station in January 1942. In addition to gasoline, Bogan sold a variety of radiator caps, razor blades, cigars, and snacks. Shown here are, from left to right, second grader Floye Bogan, Floyd Allen Bogan, Mary Nell Bogan, Castor barber Leland Cloud, and Edward Bogan (partially visible at far right). (Courtesy of Sally Bissionnette and Floye Bogan Rains.)

Charles Barnett was a longtime pastor of the First Baptist Church of Castor. Most churches in Bienville Parish are of the Baptist denomination, and most of those are members of the Southern Baptist Convention (SBC), which is the world's largest Baptist organization. The SBC is the second-largest Christian body in the United States; the Catholic Church is the largest. (Courtesy of Mary Hamner.)

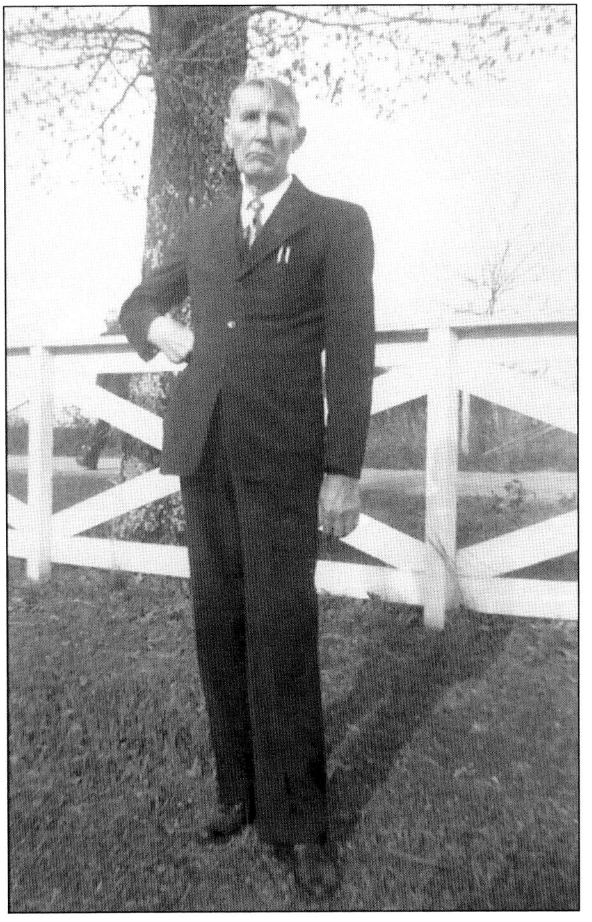

The Louisiana & Arkansas Railway built south from Sibley, and an extension through Castor to Ashland was completed on September 23, 1900. In the early 1900s, citizens at the Castor depot pose for a photograph with the southbound train. Each day, two passenger trains passed through Castor, one going north and one traveling south. (Courtesy of Wayne Sullivan and Sally Bissionnette.)

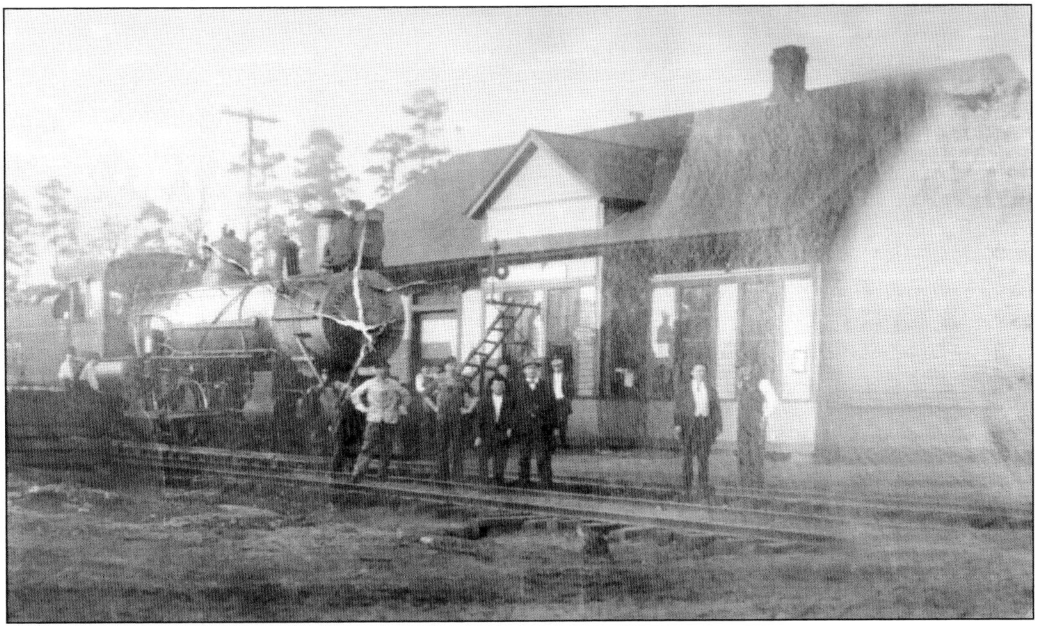

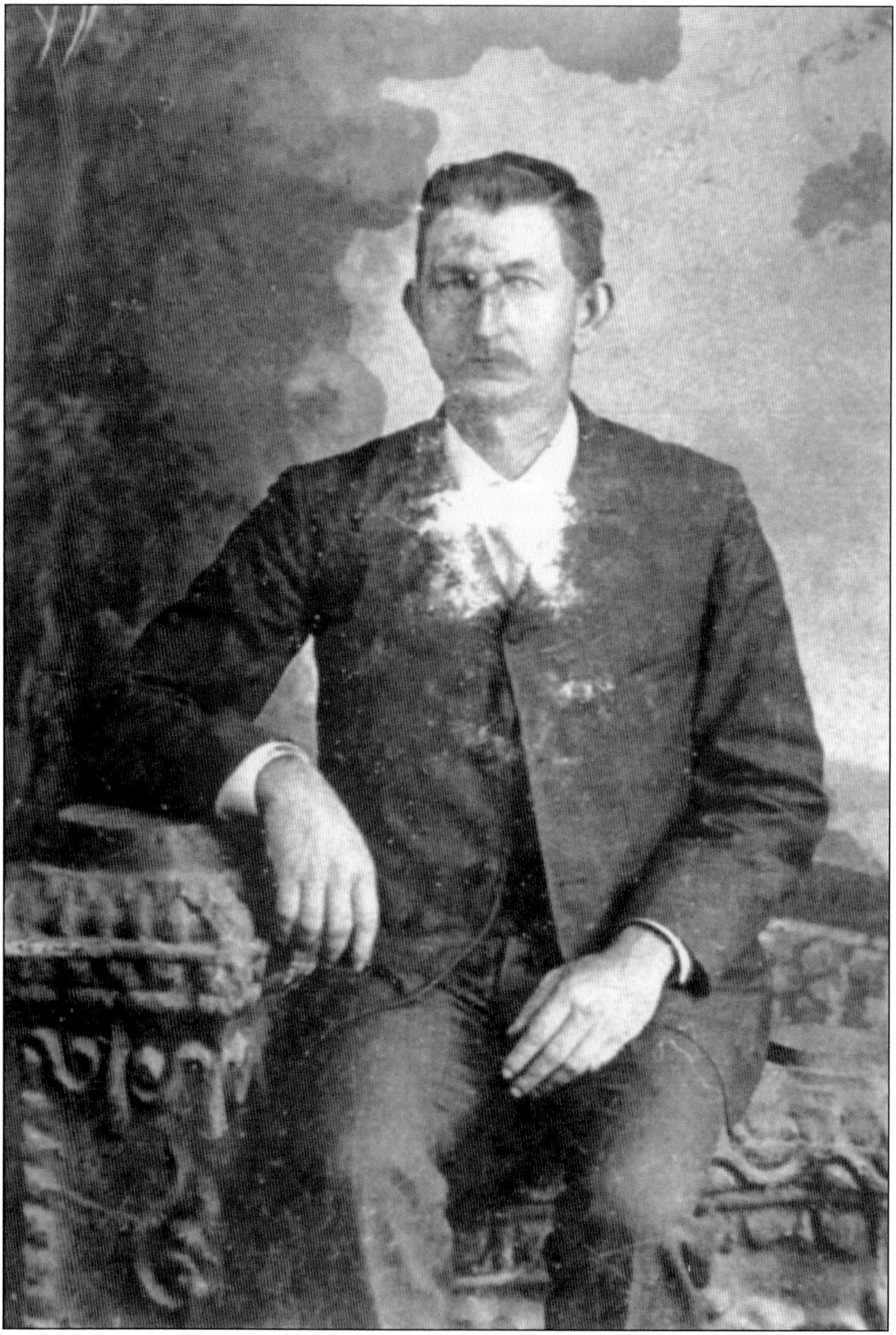

Jesse McInnis, Castor's first postmaster, served from 1901 until 1923. McInnis was also a schoolteacher and owner of a general store. The local population considered him a dreamer. He believed that there was life on the moon and predicted that man would go there someday. He was at least half right. (Courtesy of Mary Hamner.)

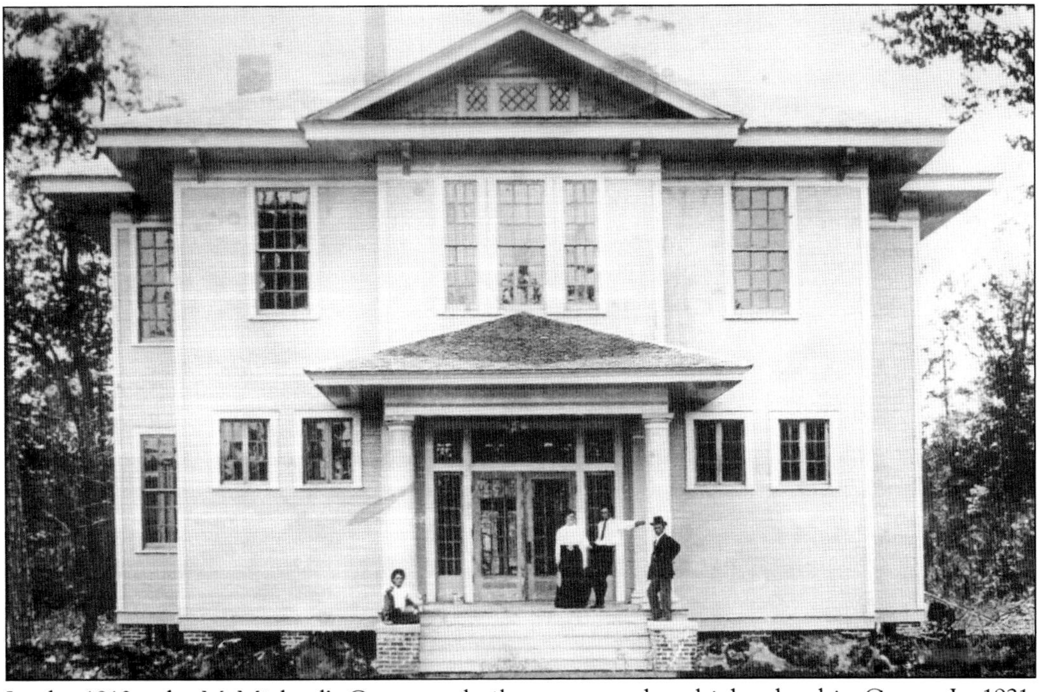

In the 1910s, the McMichael's Company built a new, modern high school in Castor. In 1921, the student body had grown to 283 students, of which 85 were high school students. Under the guidance of principal W.M. Caskey, the number of students grew each year. The senior class of 1921 was the largest in the school's history to that point. (Courtesy of Mary Hamner.)

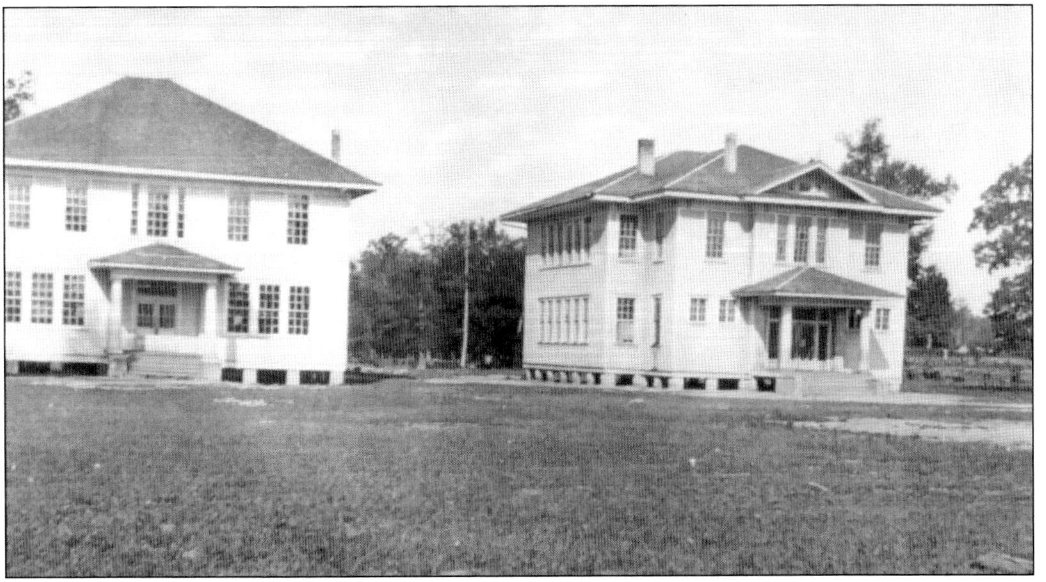

On January 3, 1923, at 11:00 p.m., a defective flue in the older of the two buildings caused a fire, which destroyed both Castor High School buildings. The same building caught on fire several weeks before the fire of January 3, but it was quickly extinguished. In July 1923, the school board contracted J.C. Corbin to erect a new brick Castor High School building. (Courtesy of Mary Hamner.)

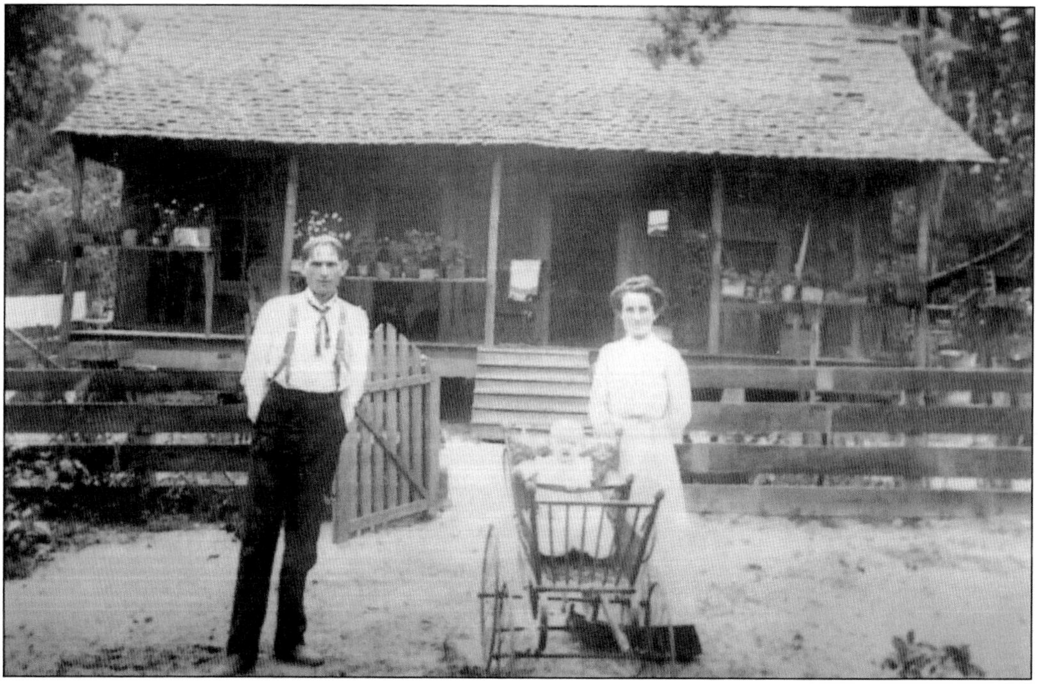

In 1898, Thomas Wardlaw Neal built the first store in Castor and sold tickets for the Louisiana & Arkansas Railway. On December 23, 1900, he married Belle Cook, and they moved into the house currently known as the Person House. There, three of their four children were born. The family moved back to the farm in 1910. (Courtesy of Mary Hamner.)

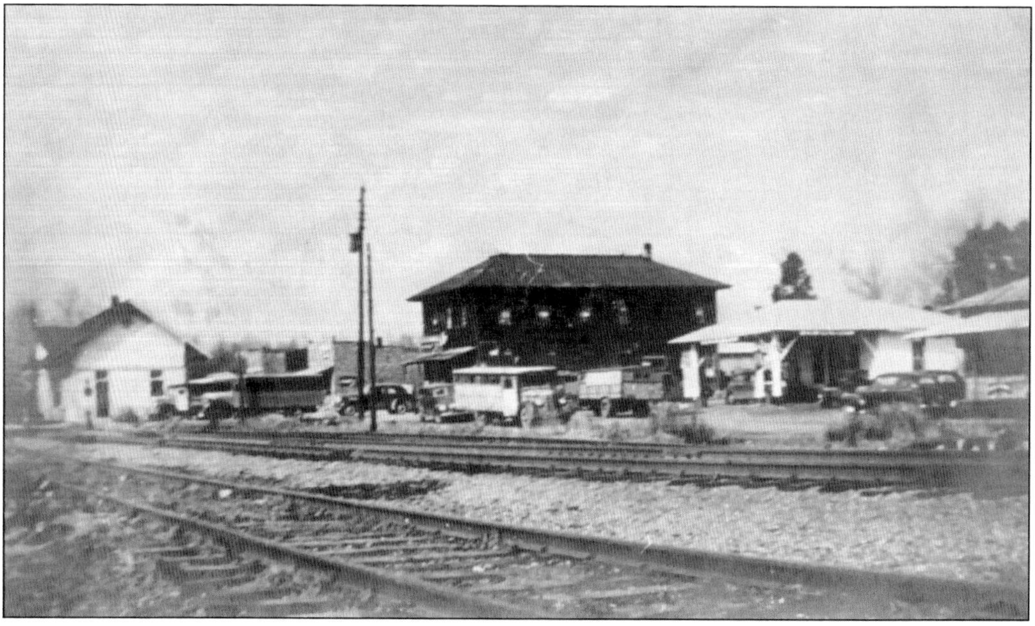

This northeast view of Castor in the mid-1940s shows the Louisiana & Arkansas Railway depot on the left. The large building in the center is Seldge's store. Floyd Bogan's Citgo service station is on the right. The school bus in the center of the photograph had burlap window curtains, which were rolled up on hot days. (Courtesy of Mary Hamner.)

R.B. Matthews served as Castor postmaster from 1925 until June 1941. At the time of this photograph, in the late 1920s, Matthews carried the outgoing mail to the Louisiana & Arkansas Railway depot and exchanged it for incoming mail. Items in the mail ranged from postcards and letters to parcels ordered from Sears & Roebuck. (Courtesy of Mary Hamner.)

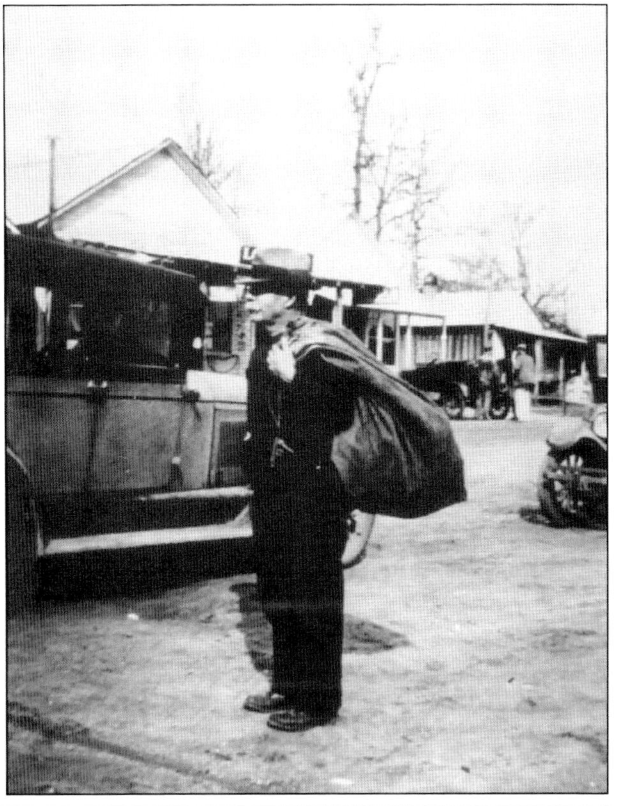

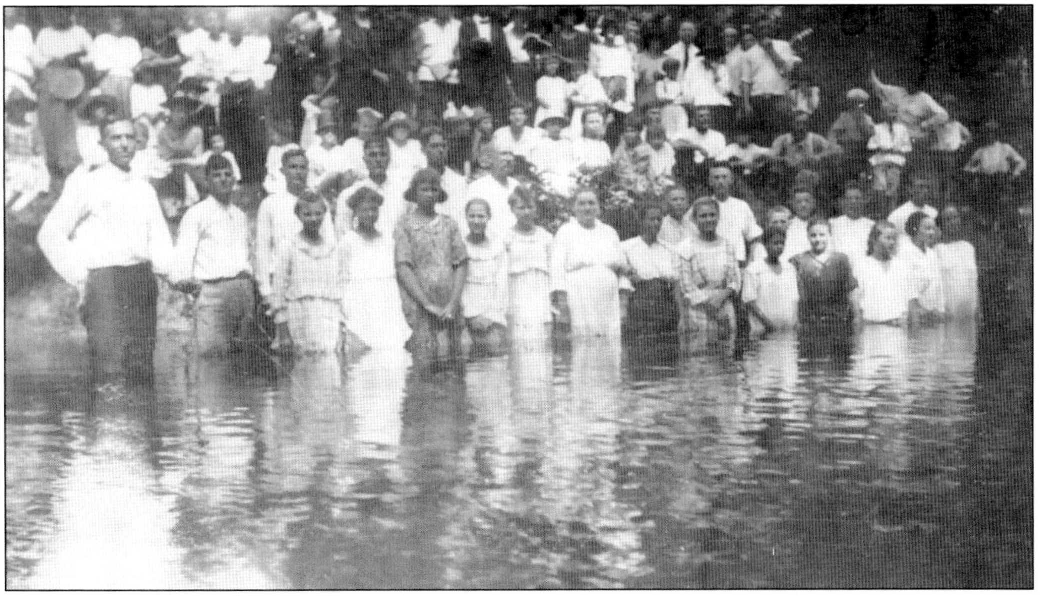

Castor Creek was used for baptismal services as late as 1945. Those making professions of faith waited until the water in the creek warmed up a little in the summer for their baptisms. The congregation stood and watched from the muddy banks of the creek. Ministers stood waist-deep, while new converts struggled to maintain their footings as they waded out to be dipped. (Courtesy of Mary Hamner.)

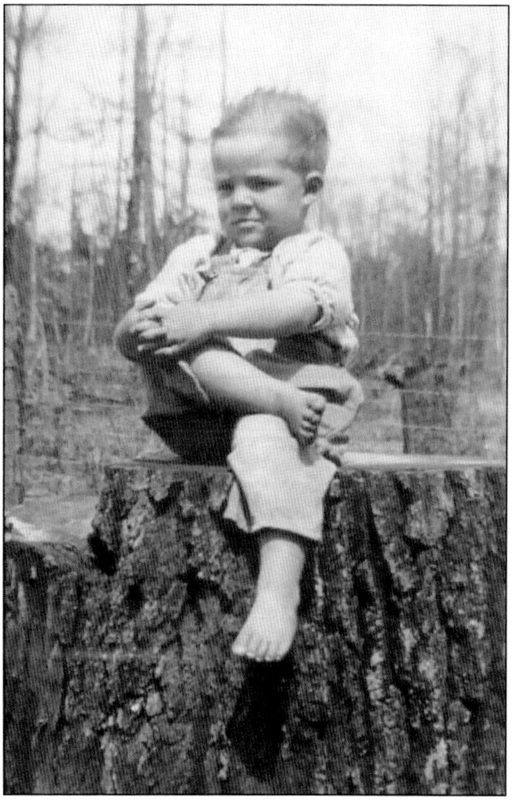

Castor's early economy was largely based on the logging industry, which became an aspect of everyday life. Loggers cut trees with hand tools, then transported logs on wagons either to the railroad or, if they were close enough, directly to the mill. In the late 1920s, young Lemey Franklin Puckett sits atop what was left from a logging operation. (Courtesy of Mary Hamner.)

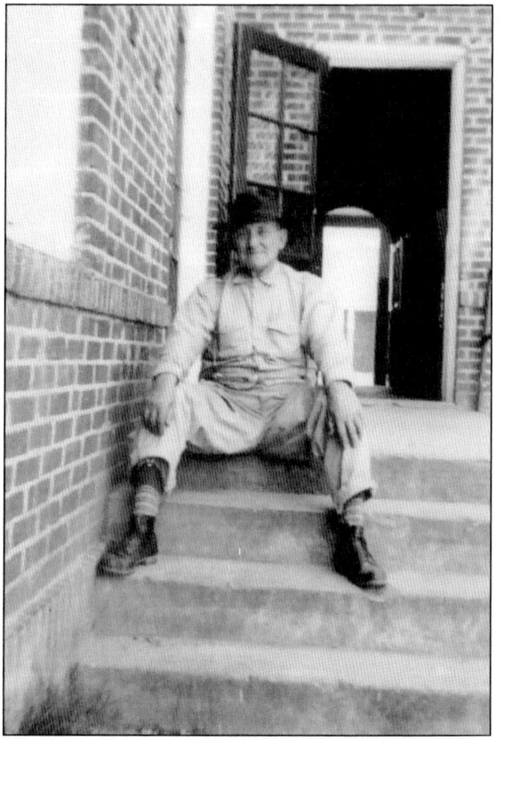

"Uncle" Charlie Bogan worked as a janitor at Castor High School. In 1955, the *Bienville Democrat* reported on Nancy Jacob, a former Castor High School student who struggled with paralysis. She remembered days at school when she would suddenly collapse, and "Uncle Charlie" would be there to help her back up. She fondly remembered that Bogan carried her on his shoulders from class to class. (Courtesy of Mary Hamner.)

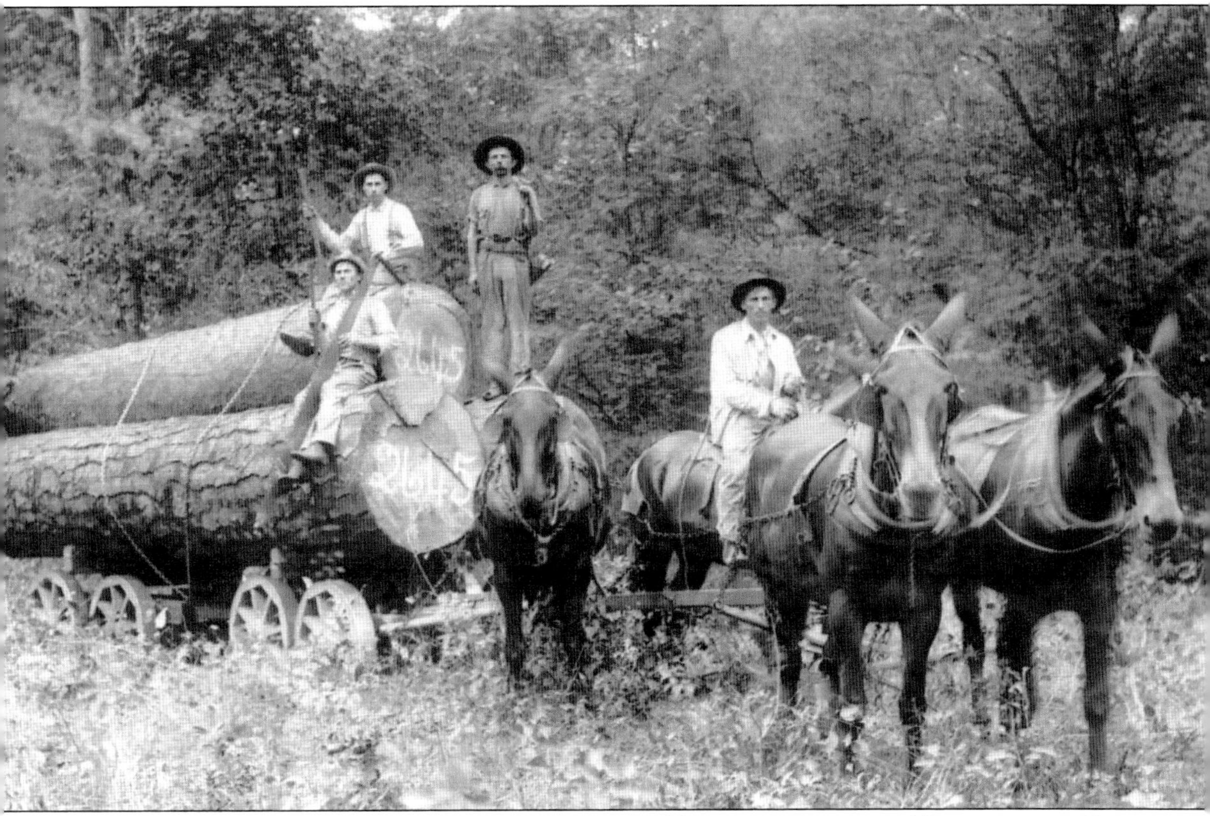

In April 1900, the Bienville Lumber Company sawmill began operations in Alberta, a sawmill town about a mile south of Castor. The Henry Pleasant Wardlaw Team was one of the many teams that hauled huge pine logs to the Bienville Lumber Company. Shown here are, from left to right, Jake Russel, Shep Givens, Russel Nelson, and John Price (driver on mule). The numbers on the logs represent board feet. (Courtesy of Mary Hamner.)

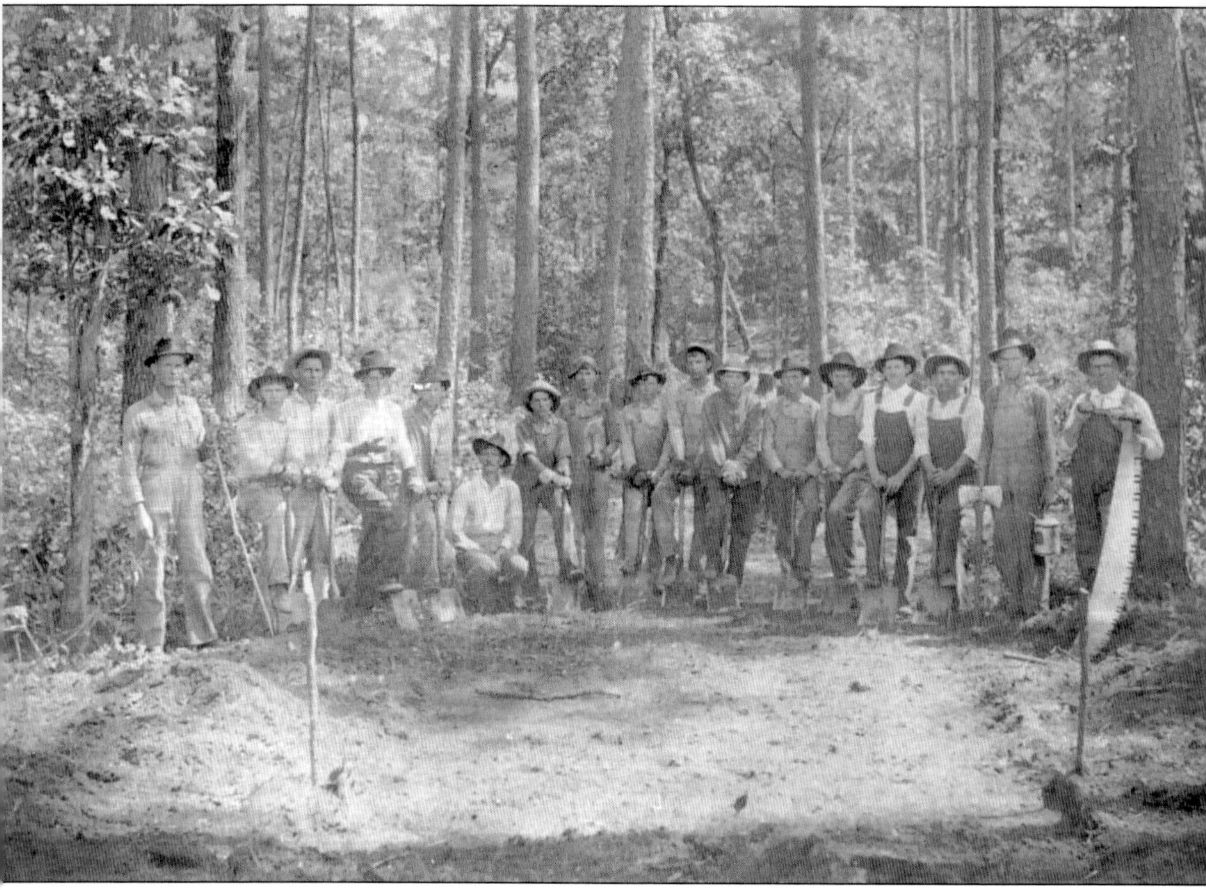

In 1902, workers in Alberta cleared a tramway. Rather than steel rails, most tramways had wooden rails, because they were inexpensive and easy to move. The two-man felling team, called "flatheads," used a double-bit axe to "bed" or notch the tree trunk, then used a two-man crosscut saw to cut down the tree. Kerosene was poured on the blade for lubrication. (Courtesy of Mary Hamner.)

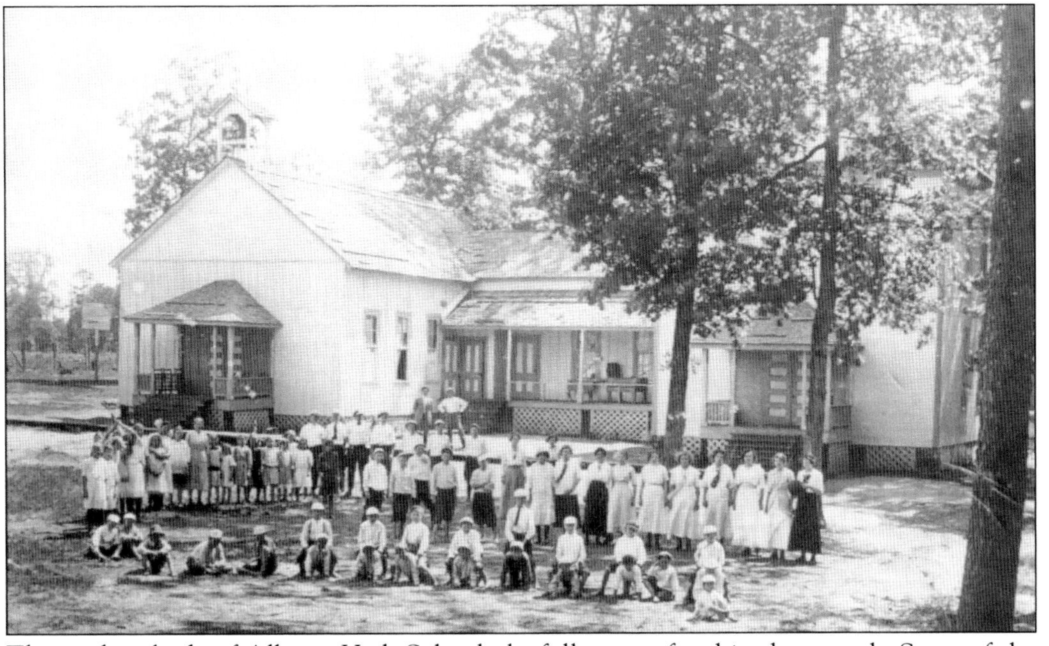

The student body of Alberta High School playfully poses for this photograph. Some of the boys in the front row sit atop other boys, as if they were cowboys. Alberta's school had a raised wooden walkway so the students could walk between rooms without going through the dirt or mud. (Courtesy of Mary Hamner.)

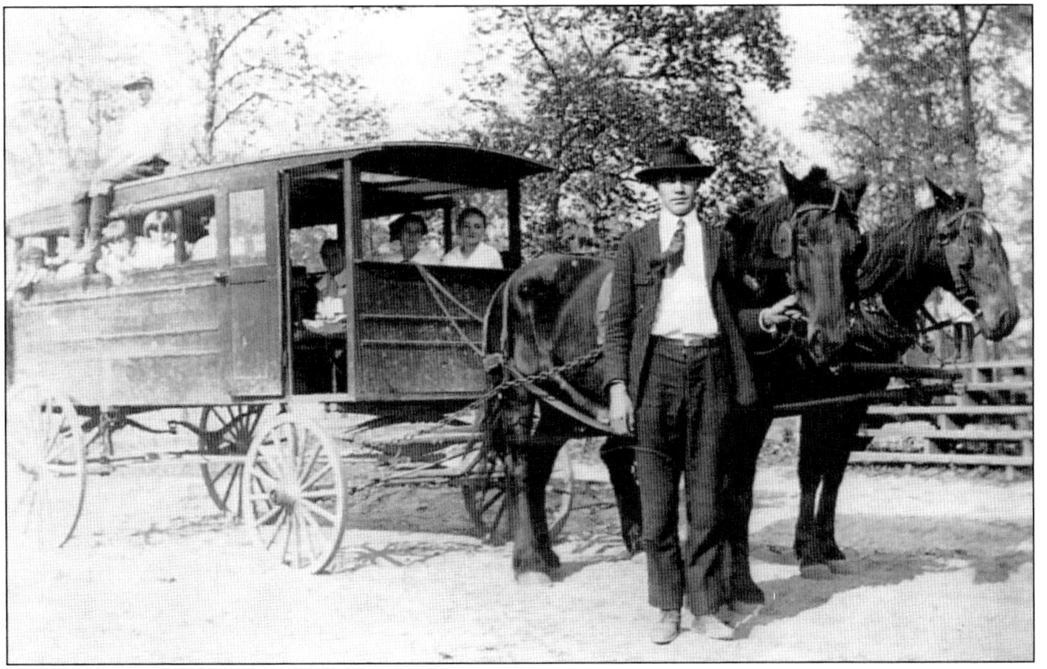

In the 19th and early 20th centuries, schools used kid hacks, horse-drawn cabs such as the one in this photograph, to transport children to and from school. A kid hack generally held under 20 children, with two bench seats that ran the length of the cab. The burlap window curtains were raised in warm weather and lowered in cold or rainy weather. (Courtesy of Mary Hamner.)

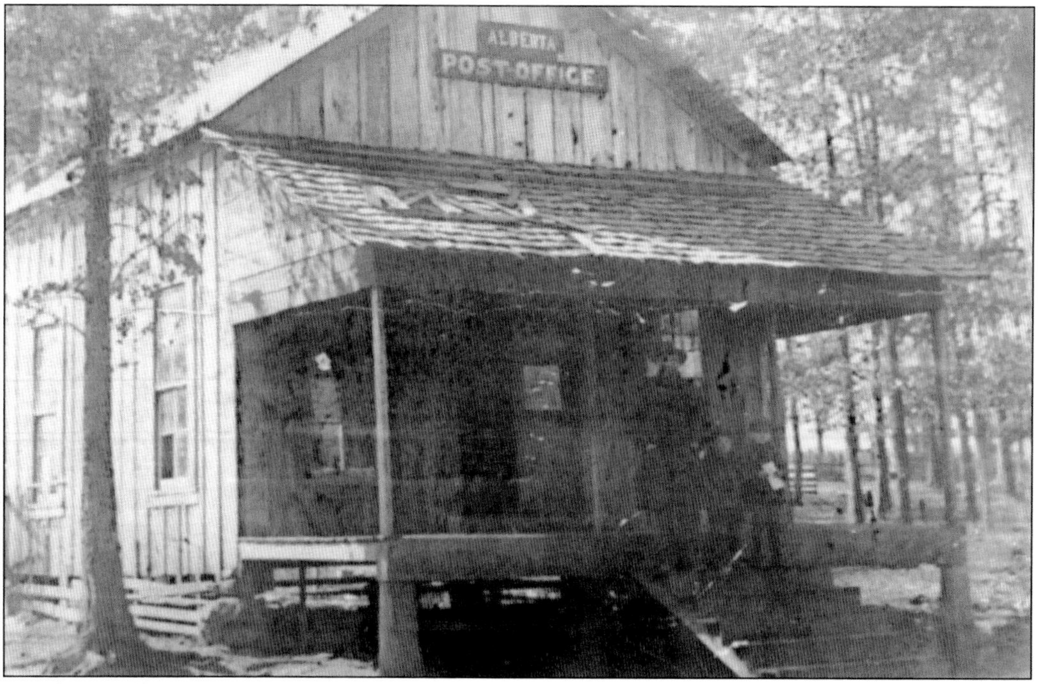

Rural post offices were farmers' main connection with the outside world. The Alberta Post Office served the community from the late 1800s until 1927, at which time Castor Post Office began handling mail for Alberta. During those years, it cost just 2¢ to send a letter. In 1896, Sears, Roebuck and Company published its first large mail-order catalog, which enabled isolated farmers to purchase almost anything through the mail. (Courtesy of Mary Hamner.)

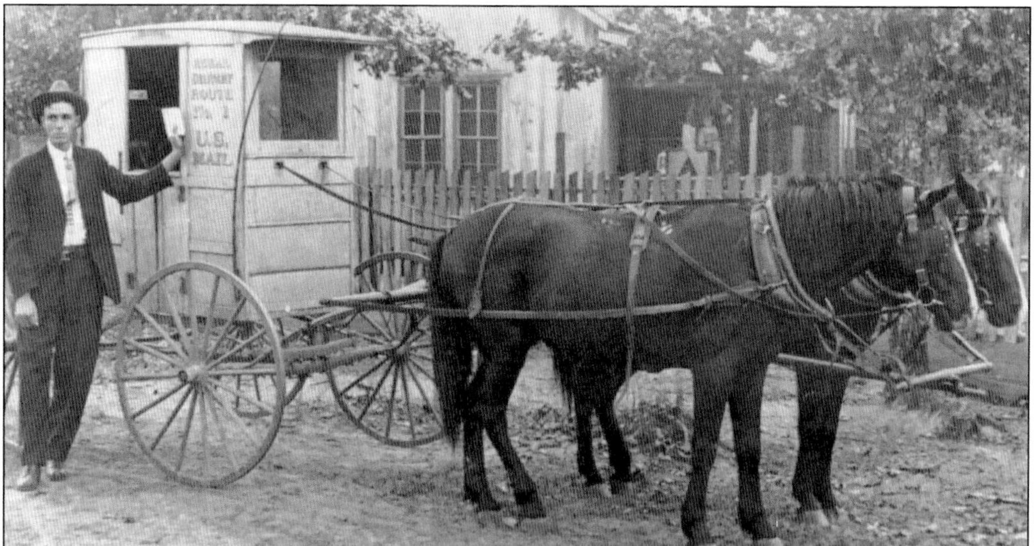

Rural Free Delivery (RFD) became a permanent postal service in 1902. Each RFD vehicle functioned as a miniature post office on wheels, with carriers able to receive and postmark mail and sell stamps, money orders, and other postal supplies. Earning $104.16 per month in 1917, H.L. Hadwin delivered mail along his 26-mile route in the Alberta area. Hadwin was responsible for the purchase and upkeep of his vehicle and horses. (Courtesy of Mary Hamner.)

Gayla (left), Ruby (center), and Guy Cooke pose for a photograph outside their home in Alberta. The dirt streets of Alberta were good enough for the horse and buggy, but made for a dusty trip on dry days. The passing of horses and buggies left endless clouds of dust along the streets. Many travelers along the dirt streets experienced a constant gritty taste in their mouths. (Courtesy of Mary Hamner.)

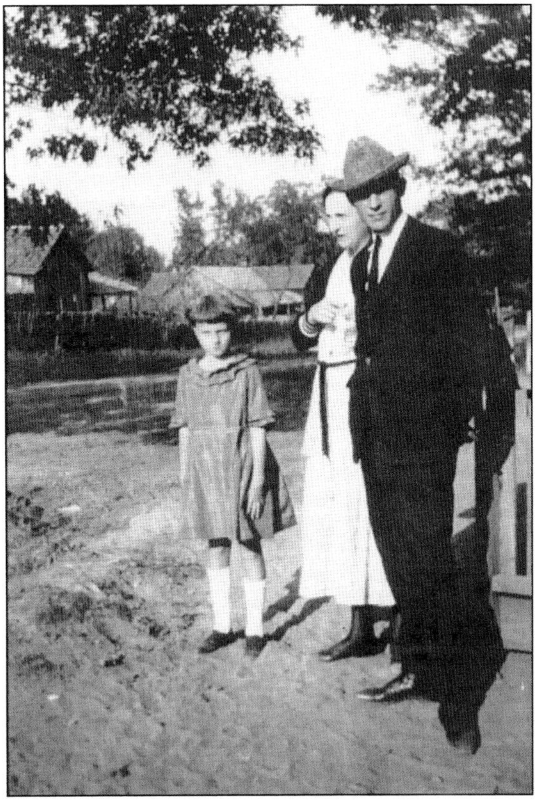

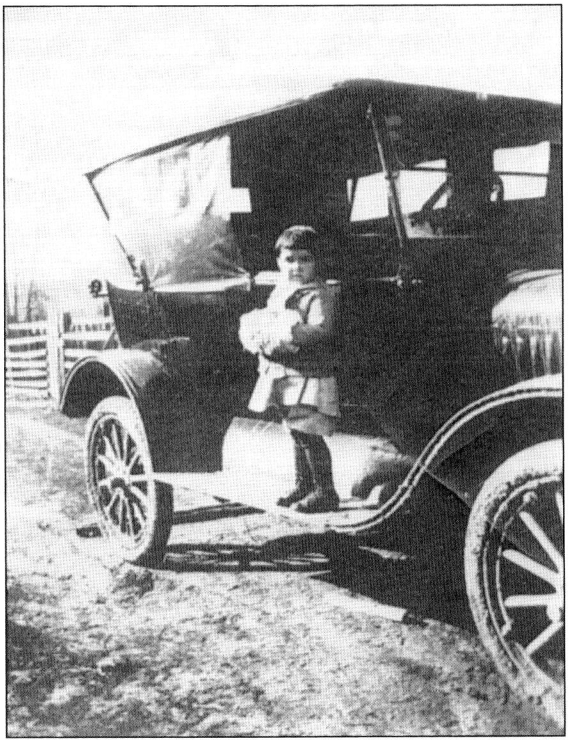

Willie Mae Bishop stands on the running board of a Ford Model T in the 1920s. The Model T was one of the first automobiles in the area. The Tin Lizzie, as it was commonly called, was the first truly affordable automobile and the first mass-produced automobile. With the introduction of the car in rural America came the need for better roads. (Courtesy of Mary Hamner.)

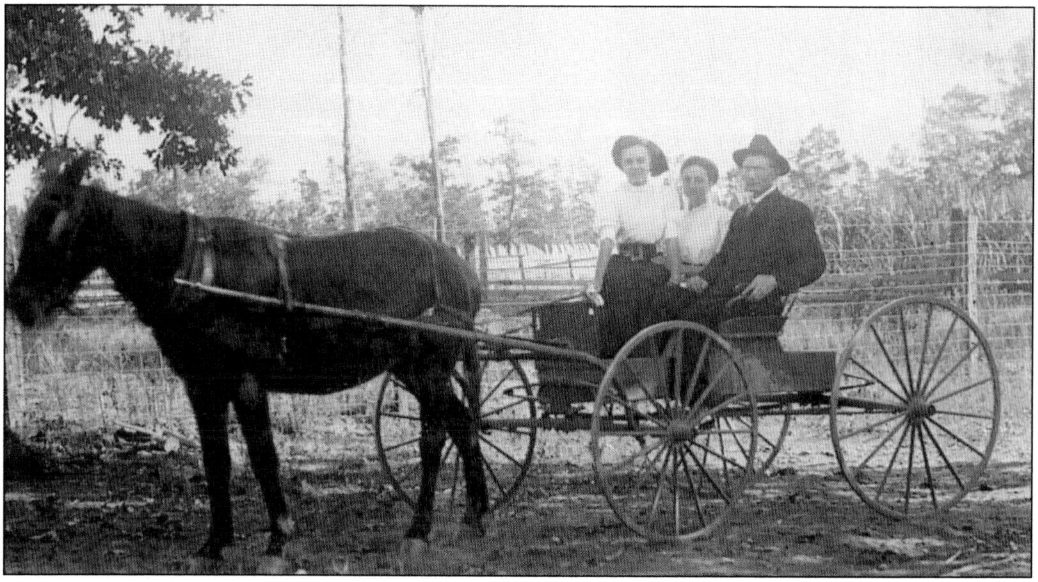

In the early 1900s, Lena Cooke (left), Ruby Wardlaw (center), and Peerless Ballard pause during their ride in a buggy in Alberta. This type of small, single buggy was used primarily for transporting up to three people, as it had just one bench seat and no bed for transporting produce or other farm supplies. (Courtesy of Mary Hamner.)

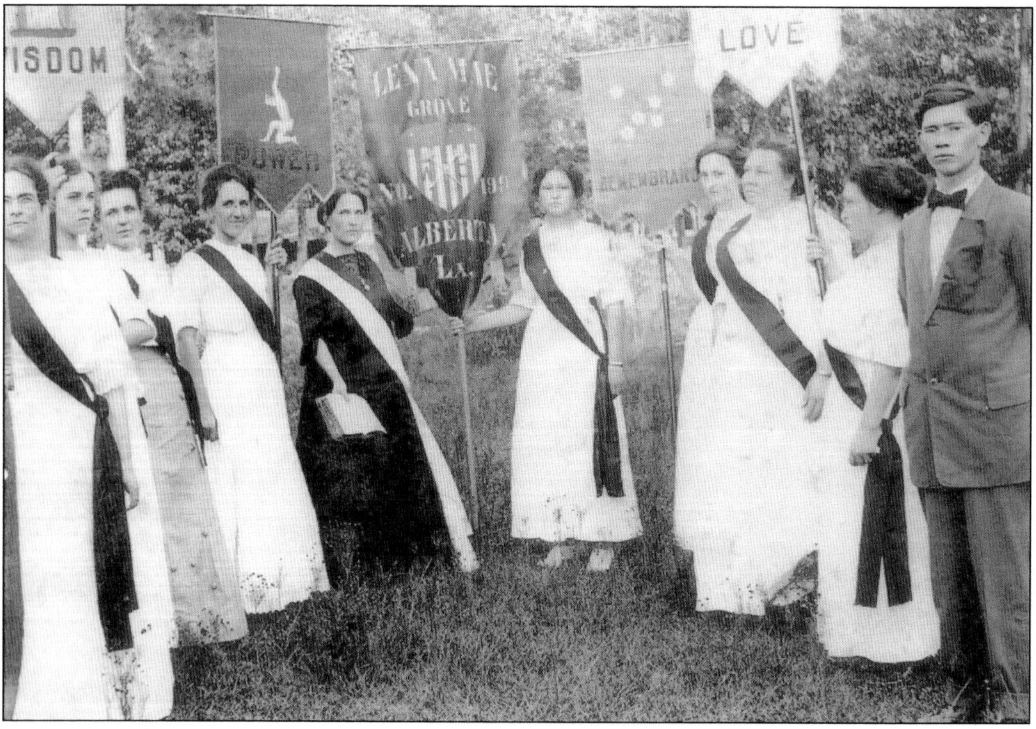

Societies, such as Alberta's Lena Mae Grove No. 199, were based on four pillars—Wisdom, Power, Remembrance, and Love. Religion was the foundation for this society, as is evident by the group leader in the black dress and white sash holding the opened Bible toward the photographer. In contrast, the other ladies wear white dresses and black sashes. (Courtesy of Mary Hamner.)

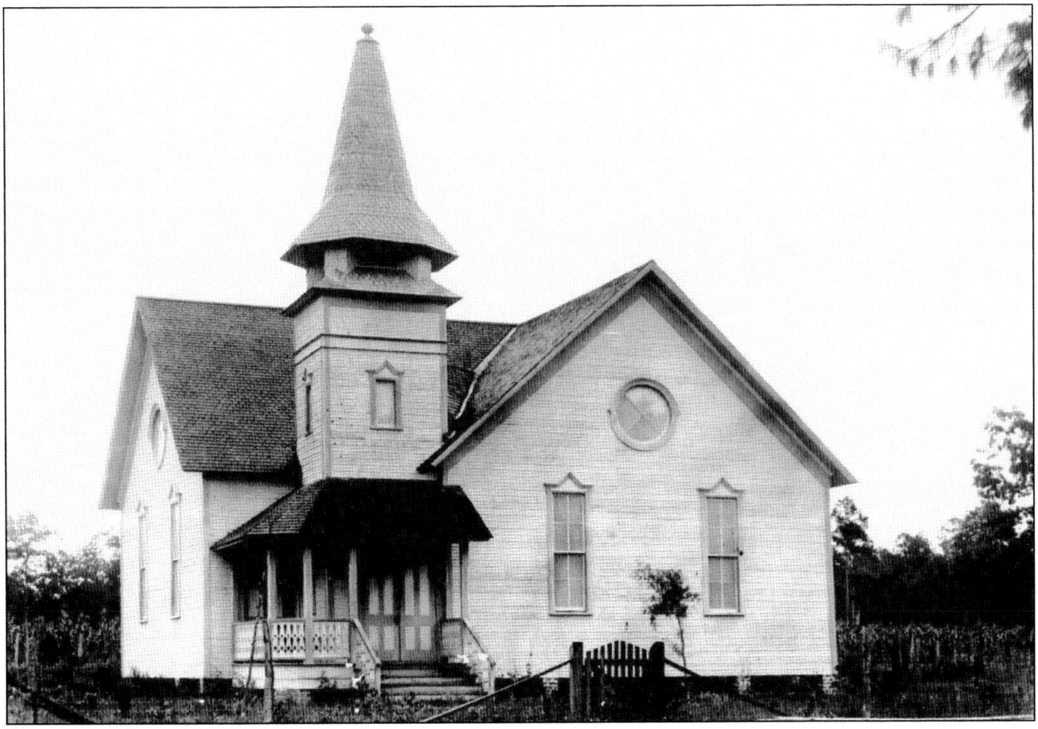

The Alberta Methodist Church, seen here around 1900, was a place of worship for most locals. The ringing of the bell in the steeple signified the beginning of church services and alerted those in the area of danger. It was also rung in celebration of weddings and holidays. Since the only mechanical sound in the area was that of a sawmill, the church bell could be heard several miles away. (Courtesy of Mary Hamner.)

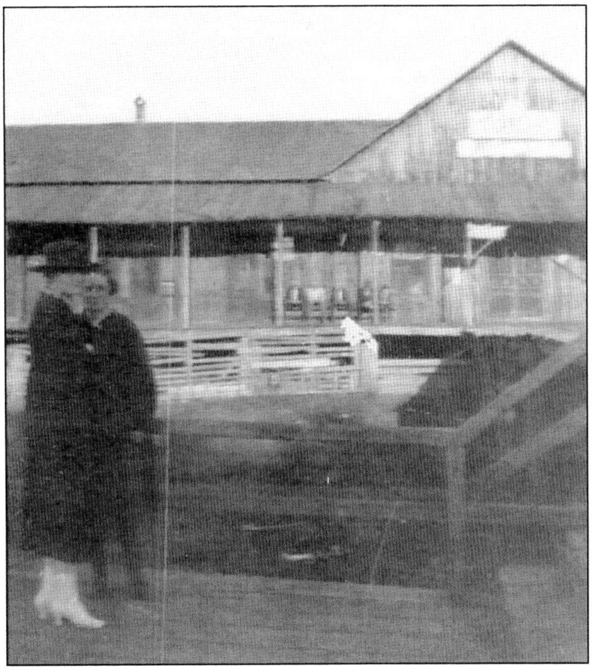

Most sawmills paid their workers in the form of mill script—paper vouchers or metal tokens—rather than a paycheck. Alberta's commissary, seen here around 1900, sold groceries, supplies, furniture, and clothing. By using this system, sawmills made money from their workers in two ways: by the products they produced, and by the items they purchased at the commissary. (Courtesy of Mary Hamner.)

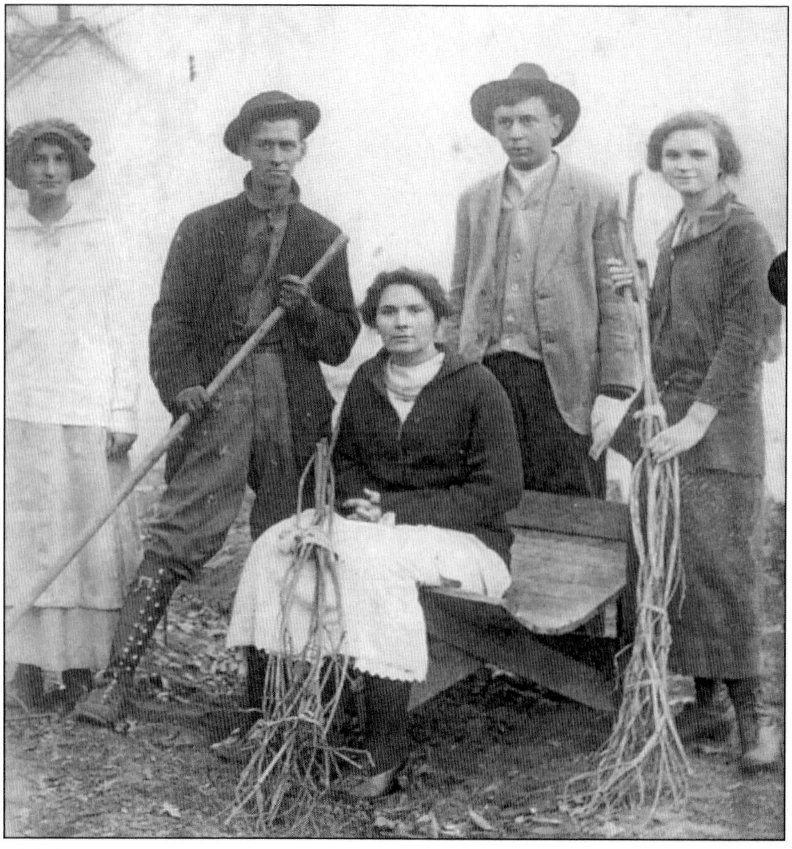

In the early 1900s, farmers made many of their tools by hand. Tools were often hard to get and expensive, so many farmers used their ingenuity to get by. Here, two women show off their handmade yard brooms. The word *broom* is derived from the name of a thorny shrub that was cut and used for sweeping. (Courtesy of Mary Hamner.)

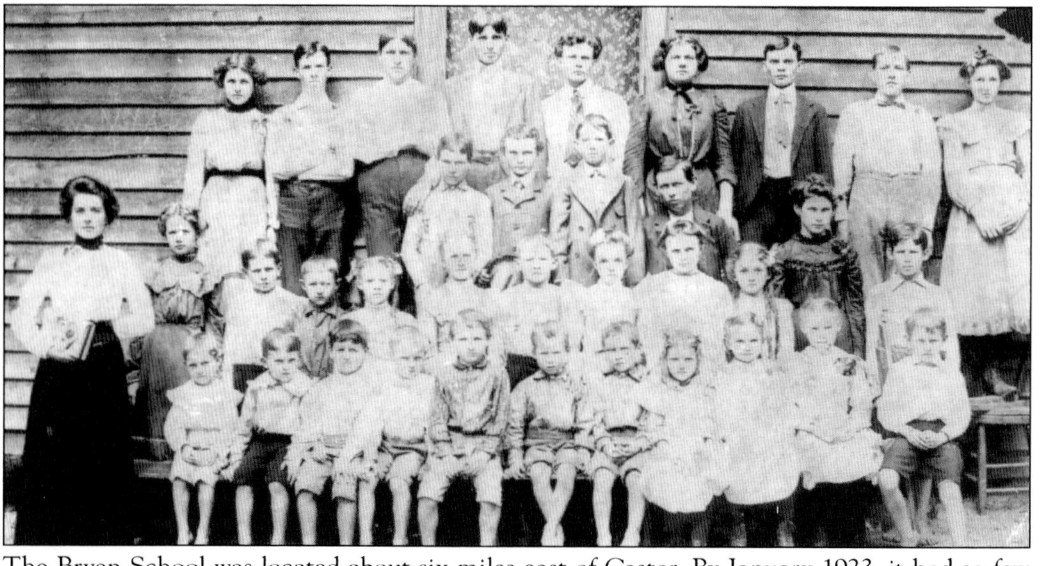

The Bryan School was located about six miles east of Castor. By January 1923, it had so few students that the local citizens petitioned the Bienville Parish School Board to transfer the students to Castor High School. By April 1925, Bryan School had closed, and the building was put up for sale. Spencer Hays purchased the structure and dismantled it for the lumber. (Courtesy of Mary Hamner.)

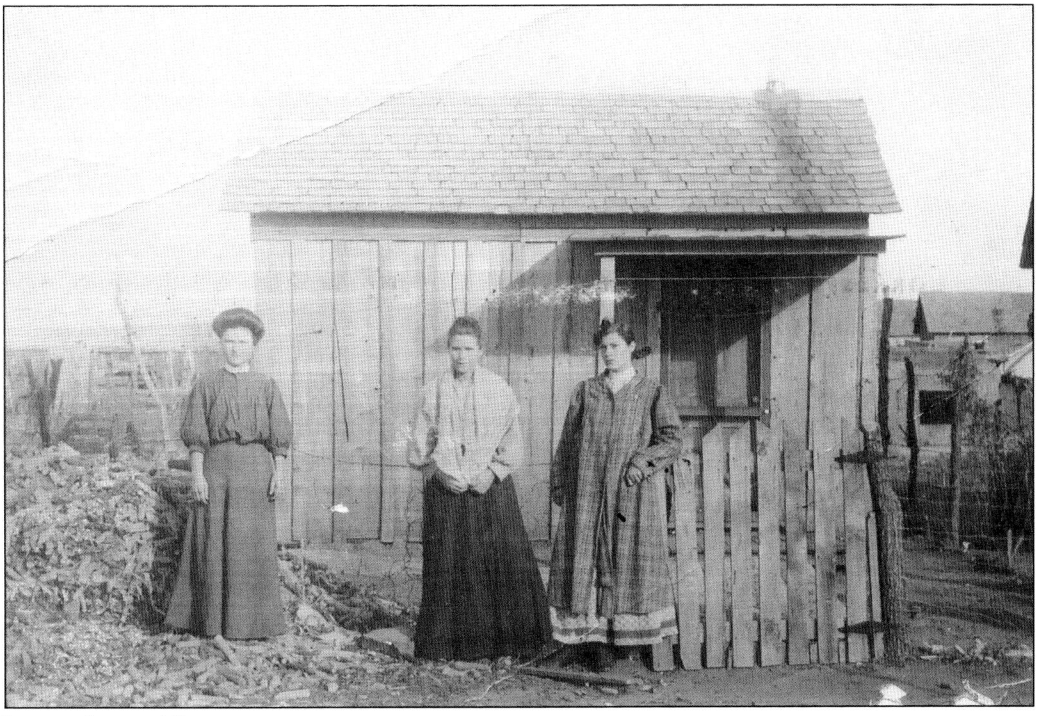

Located near Alberta on Ridge Road, Chandler's Camp was a small community of loggers and their families. In this c. 1920 photograph, Callie (left), Lou (center), and Oma Myers stand outside one of the small houses, which could be easily loaded onto railcars and transferred to the next logging camp. At its peak, seven lines of railroad track connected Chandler's logging camp with Castor. (Courtesy of Mary Hamner.)

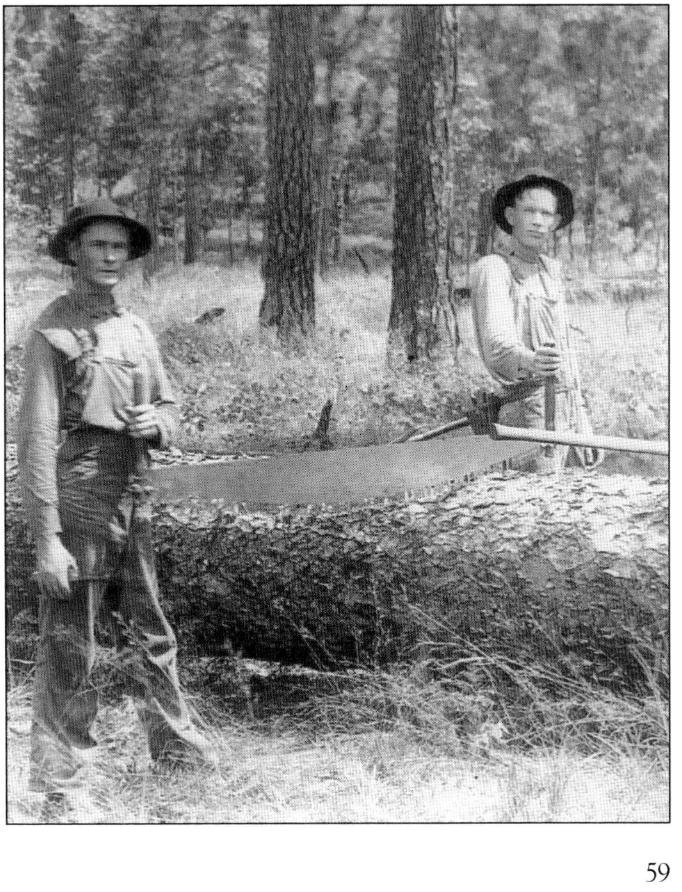

Edgar Myers (left) and Charlie Rogers, a two-man "flathead" team, cut timber near Alberta around 1920. After felling the tree, they cut the virgin pine into sections with a crosscut saw, loaded the sections onto a wagon or tram, and delivered them to the sawmill. (Courtesy of T.S. and Mary D. Myers.)

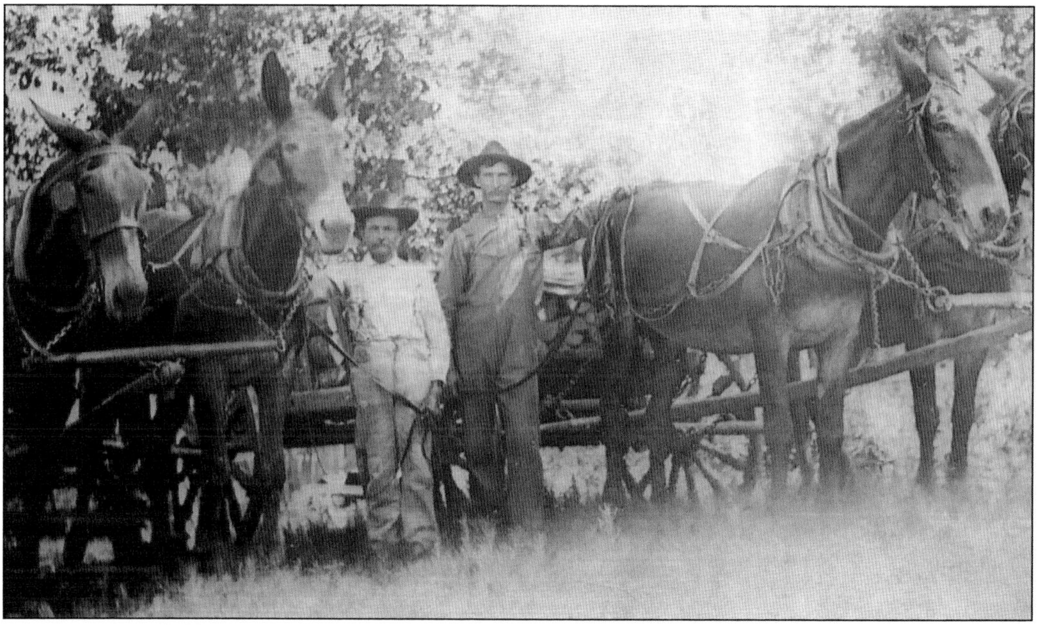

Marion Myers (left) and Lee Goss haul firewood near Chandler's Camp in this c. 1920 photograph. In the early 1900s, wood was the primary fuel for heating homes in Bienville Parish. Farmers and loggers used draft horses, such as the ones shown here, because their tall stature and muscular build made them ideal for hauling heavy loads, plowing fields, and performing many other pulling tasks. (Courtesy of Mary Hamner.)

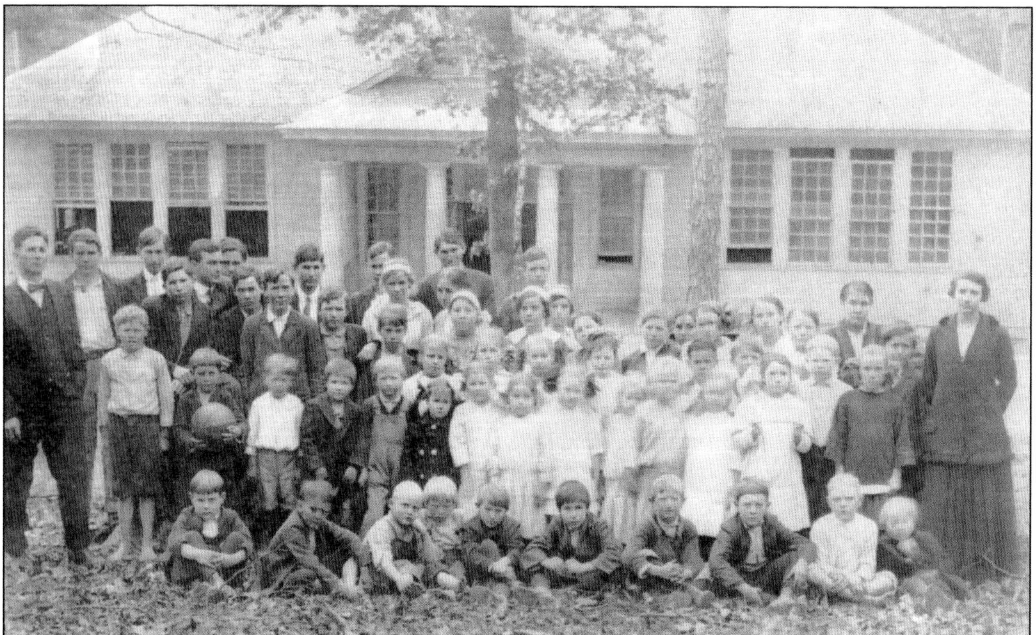

In the early 1900s, Ebenezer was located about four miles south of Castor. The Ebenezer School grew with the influx of loggers who came to the area. As the loggers began moving to other regions for better opportunities, the population of the community and the number of school children began to decline. (Courtesy of Mary Hamner.)

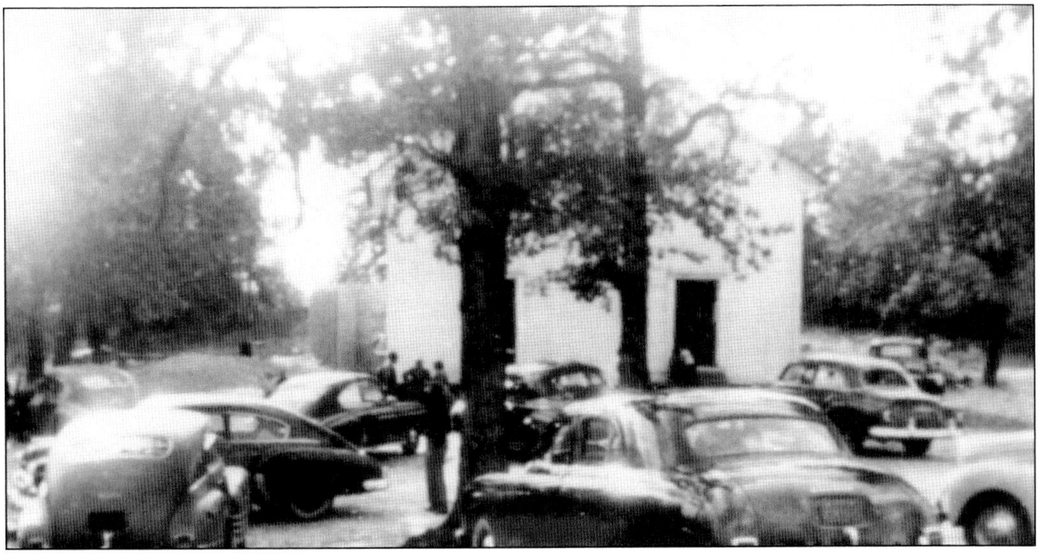

The Ebenezer Church parking lot is filled with automobiles in this late-1940s image. By this point, cars had replaced horses and buggies as the primary mode of transportation. Modern automobiles required better roads, and as roads improved, many families opted for the automobile, which meant they could travel farther and more comfortably. (Courtesy of Mary Hamner.)

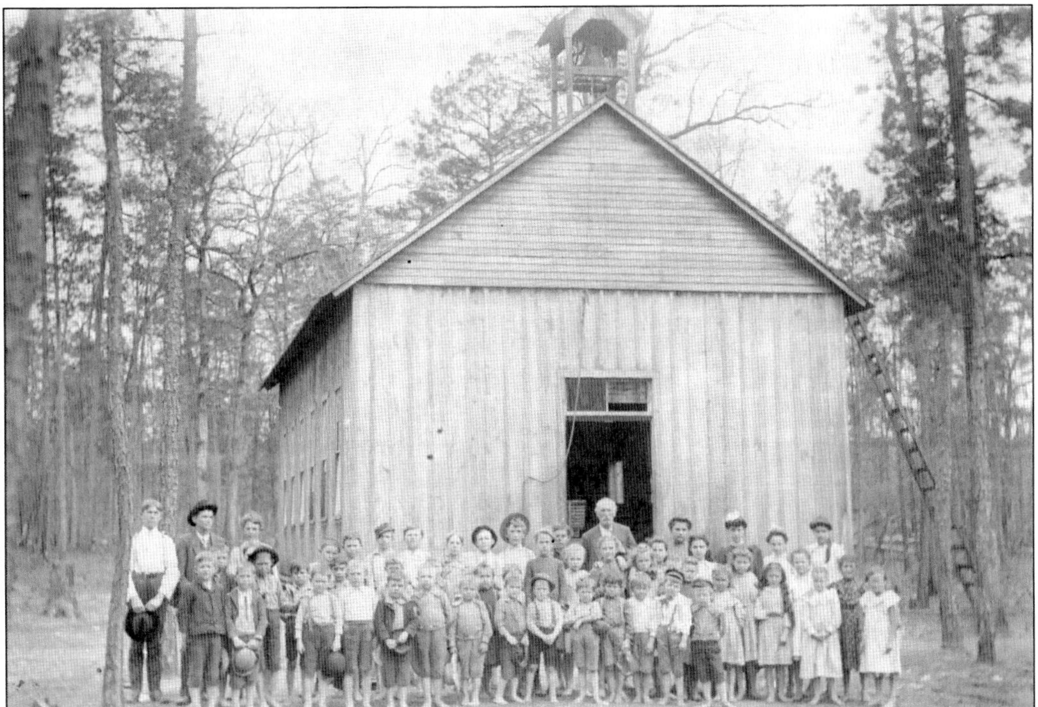

Built around 1840, the Lacy School was located southeast of Castor near Punkin Center Church. "Uncle Bill" Lacy is in the center of the back row, in front of the doorway. On April 3, 1928, the Bienville Parish School Board voted to annex Ebenezer and Lacy Schools to Castor High School. In September 1928, former students of Ebenezer and Lacy Schools began attending Castor High School. (Courtesy of Mary Hamner.)

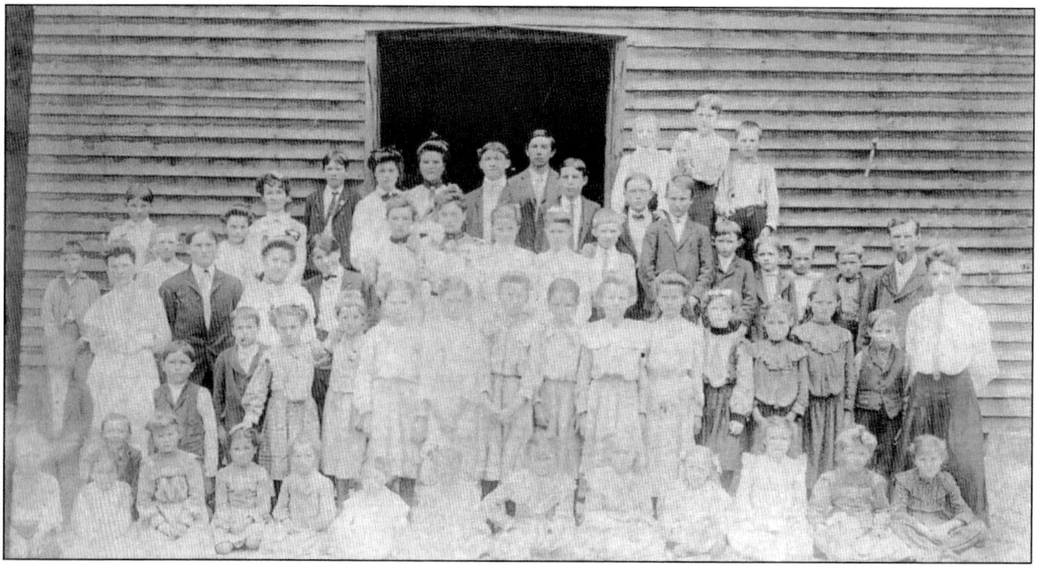

In 1897, the Ridge School and the Ridge Church were housed in the same one-room building. It was located on Ridge Road between Saline and Castor. The head schoolmaster, Mr. Corey (third row, far right), and his assistant, Jennie Corey (second row, far right), taught each child based on his or her individual skill level. (Courtesy of Mary Hamner.)

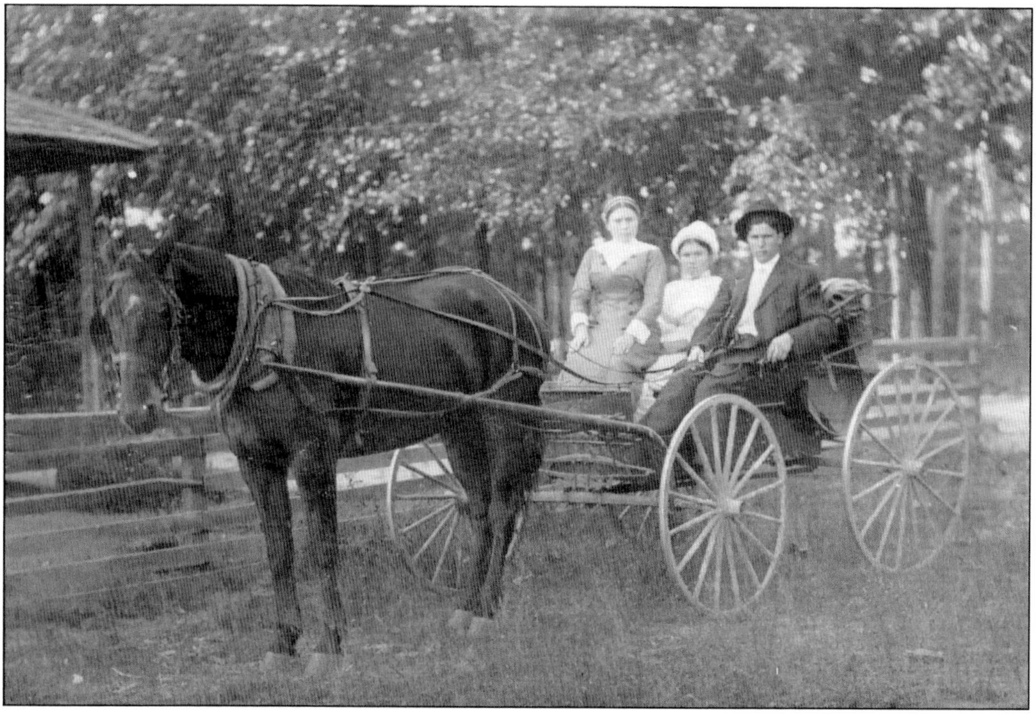

At the turn of the 20th century, residents of Jamestown relied on the horse and buggy as their primary mode of transportation. Horseback riding was less common, because it required more specific skills than driving a buggy. Sears, Roebuck and Company sold buggies for as little as $25. They could easily be hitched to a plowing horse and driven by untrained men, women, and children. (Courtesy of Lavon Sullivan.)

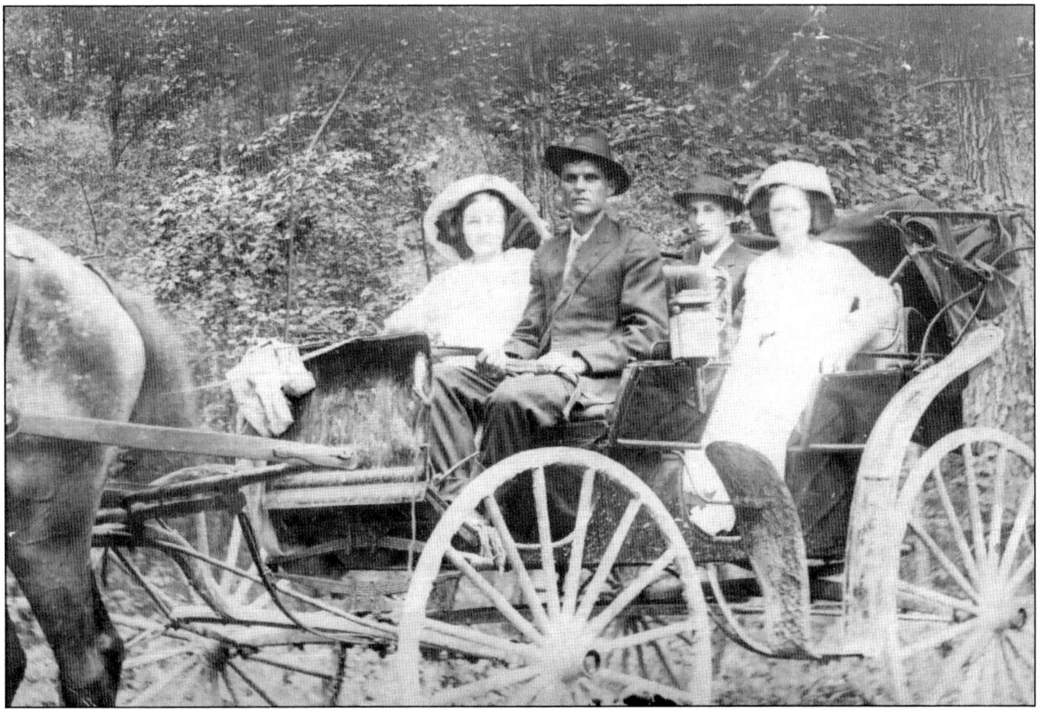

Riding in a double buggy in Jamestown in the early 1900s are, from left to right, Rhodie Herrington, Wiseman Bates, an unidentified male passenger, and Lou Herrington. While a buggy had just one bench seat, a double buggy had two. This upscale model had fenders to keep mud from getting on the passengers. A lamp provided light for nighttime travel. (Courtesy of Lavon Sullivan.)

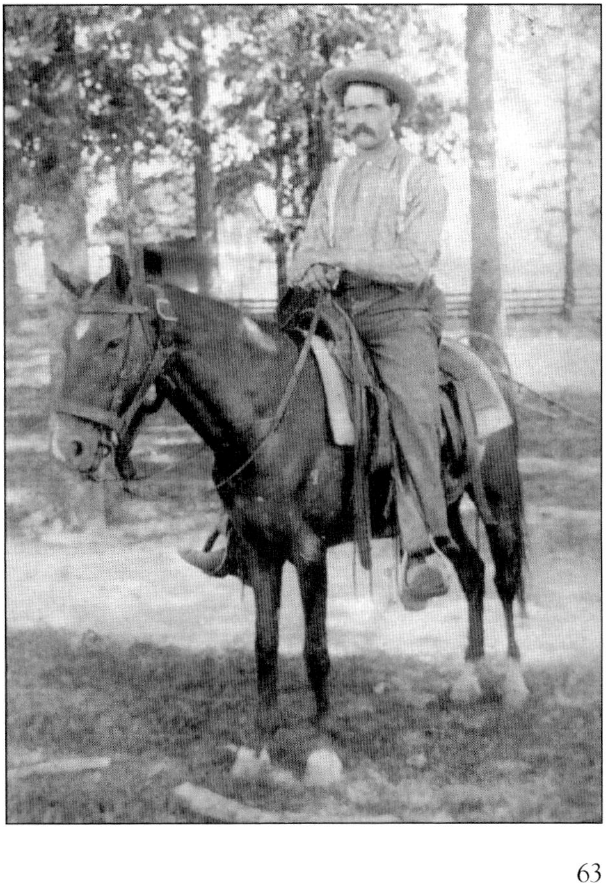

Whereas buggies required at least moderately graded roads, horses were able to travel over almost any terrain. At the turn of the 20th century, farmers, such as Mose Stevens (shown here), used horses for plowing, pulling heavy loads, and for personal transportation. Horseback riding required more skill than driving a buggy. The rider and horse had to train together to ensure that the horse could be safely ridden while performing useful tasks. (Courtesy of Lavon Sullivan.)

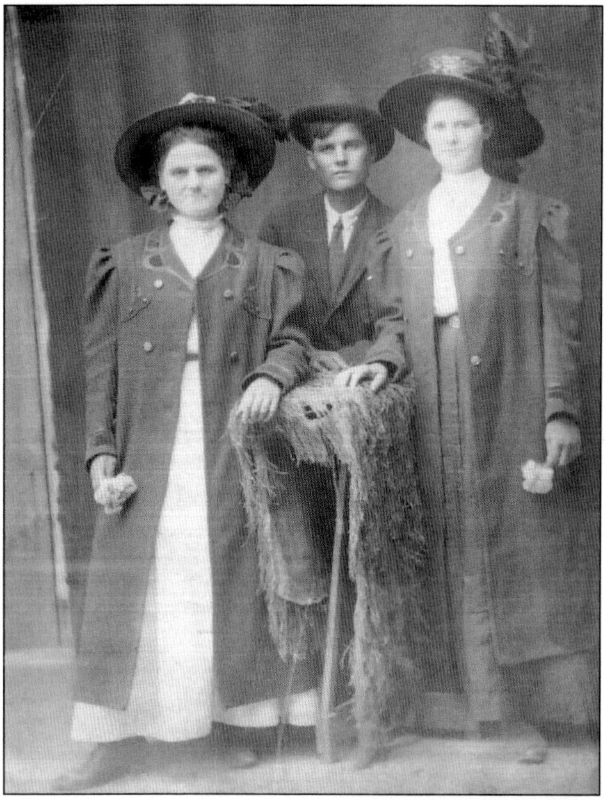

In the early 1900s, Rhodie Herrington (left), Wiseman Bates (center), and Mary Lou Herrington visited a photography studio for this portrait. Long exposure times in early photography required subjects to remain still to reduce the amount of blurring. Photographers had their subjects lean or rest on a "Brady stand" to help keep them still. (Courtesy of Lavon Sullivan.)

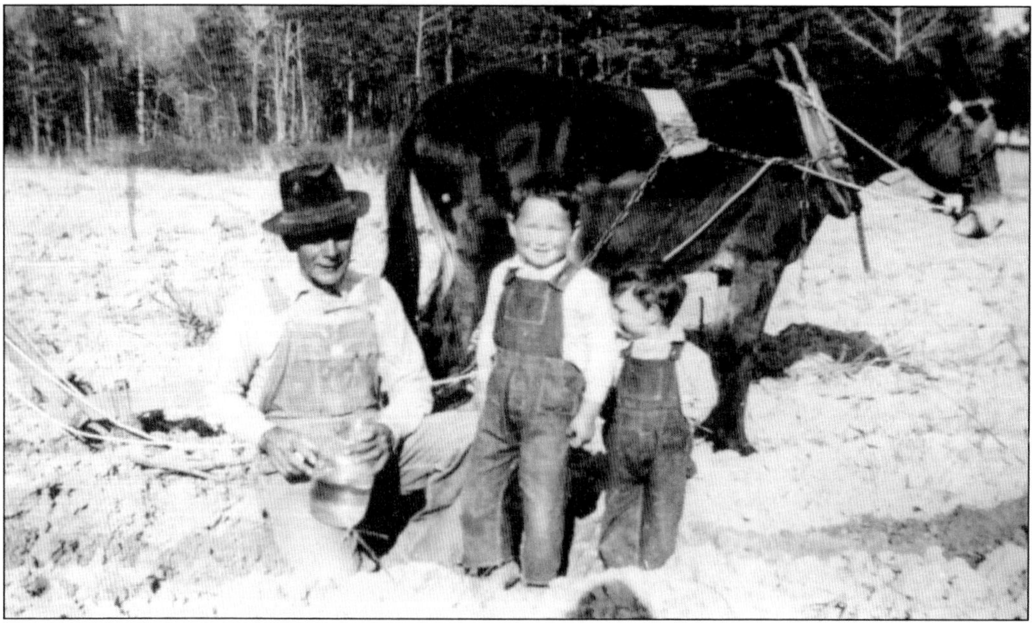

Most rural communities relied on farming for survival. Before tractors were common on rural farms, many farmers hitched their plows to mules. Tilling the land was slow and monotonous. In this 1940s photograph, Pompie Jiles (left) takes a break from plowing to enjoy the cool water that Bobby (center) and Jimmie Chandler have brought him. (Courtesy of Lavon Sullivan.)

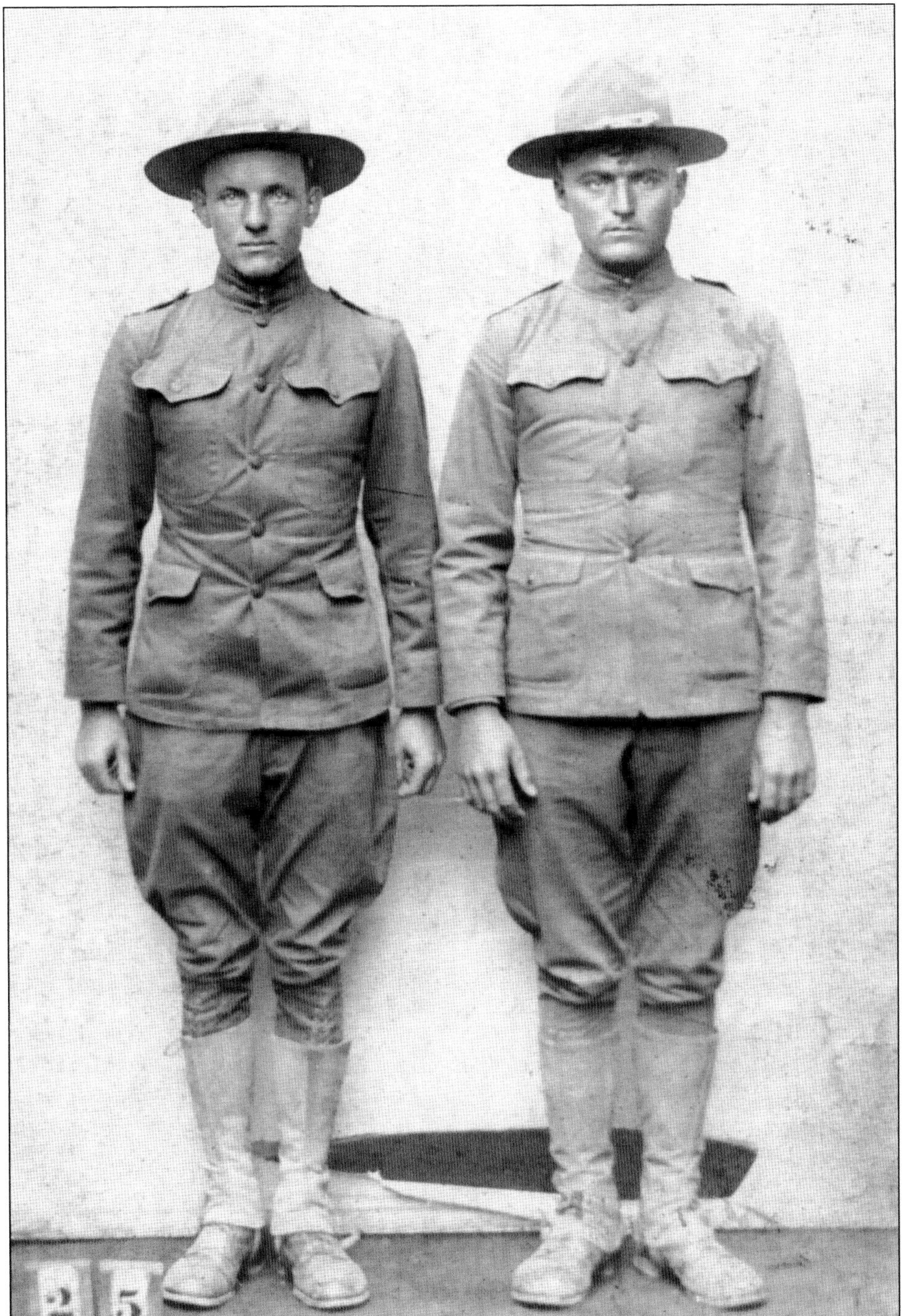

On April 6, 1917, the United States formally entered World War I. Newton Cook (left) and Joseph Herrington (right) were two young men from Bienville Parish who joined the fight. Newton Cook was killed in action on July 26, 1918. On December 31, 1917, Joseph Herrington died from pneumonia at Camp Beauregard, near Alexandria. About a third of all deaths in the war resulted from diseases. (Courtesy of Lavon Sullivan.)

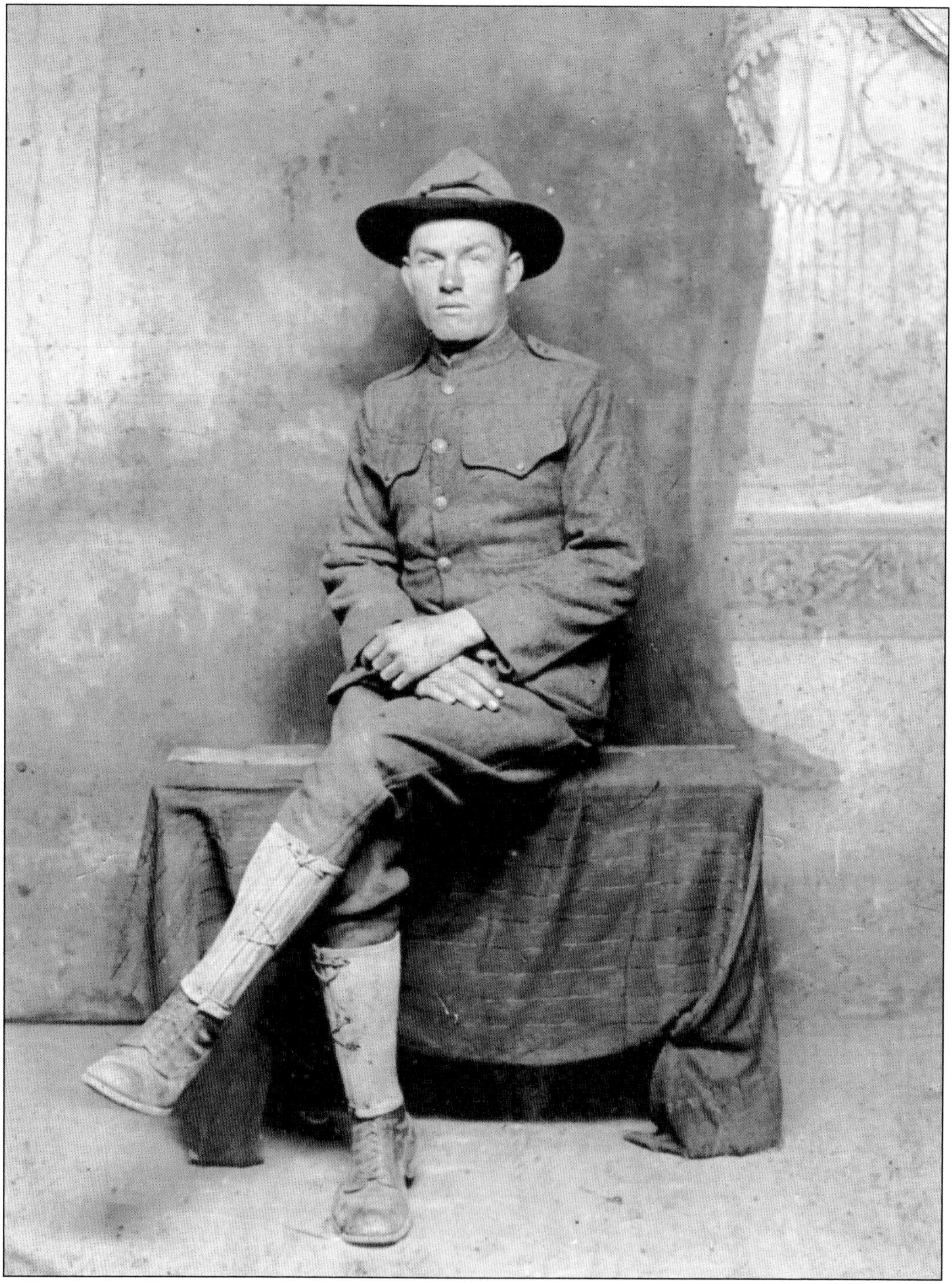

From 1914 until 1917, Pres. Woodrow Wilson attempted to keep America out of World War I. When Germany instituted a policy of unrestricted submarine warfare and sought to build an alliance with Mexico against the United States, Wilson was forced to enter the conflict. Fred Regions of Jamestown was one of the many brave young men who served in what was referred to as the "war to end all wars." (Courtesy of Lavon Sullivan.)

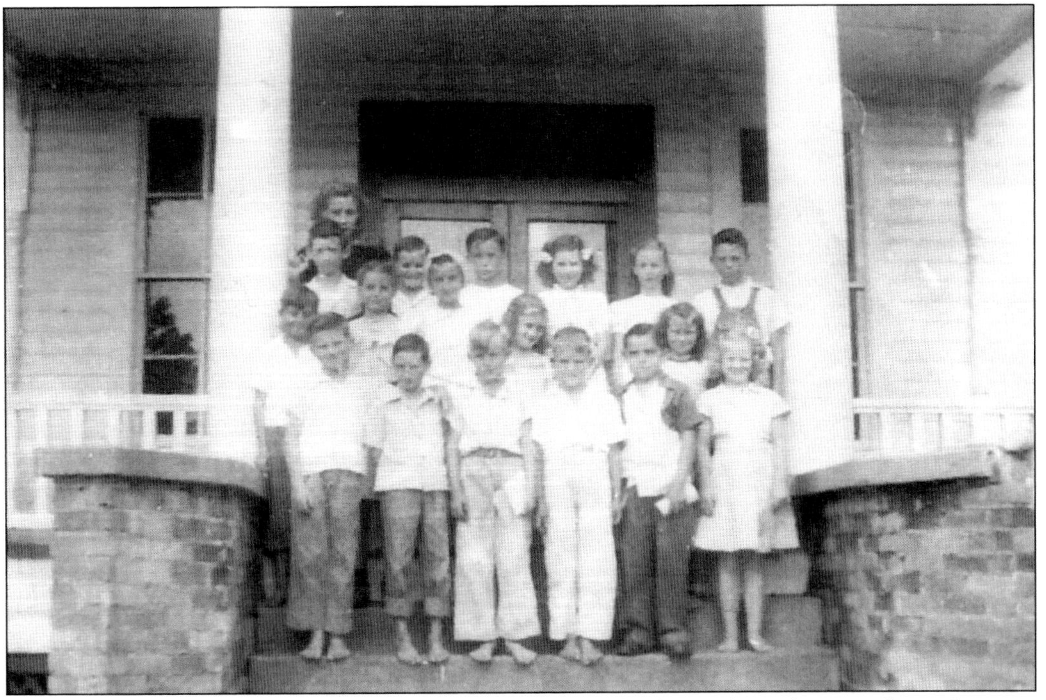

In May 1948, teachers gathered the fourth- and fifth-grade classes for a photograph on the steps of the library at Jamestown High School. Shoes were not a requirement in school and, as this photograph shows, most children did not wear shoes to school in the warm months. (Courtesy of Mary Crochet.)

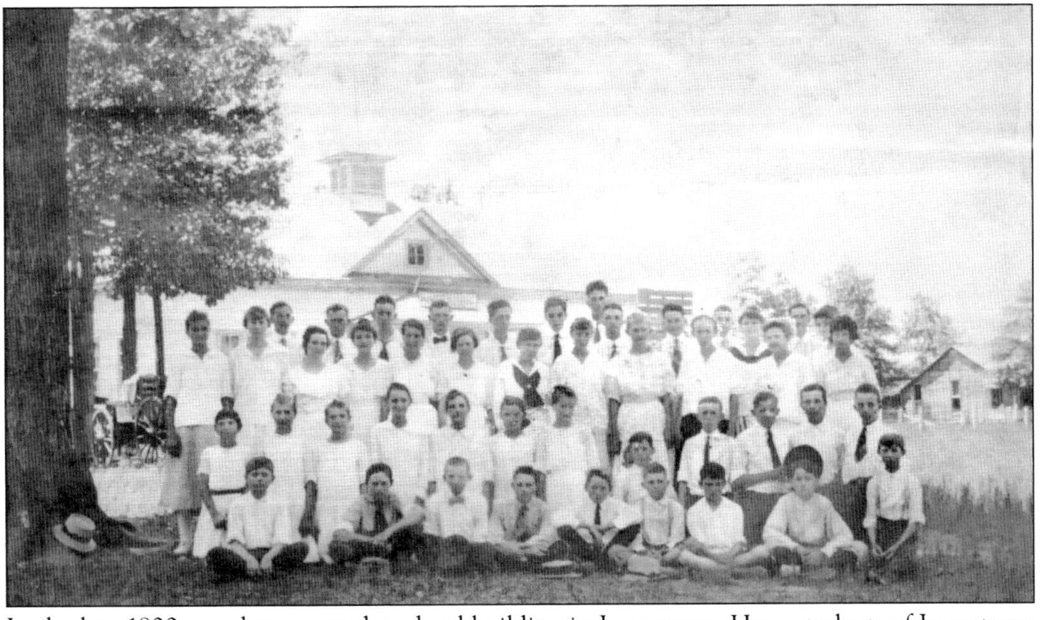

In the late 1800s, workers erected a school building in Jamestown. Here, students of Jamestown High School are gathered on the school grounds in the first decade of the 20th century. On Monday, September 19, 1921, the Bienville Parish School Board officially opened the new, modern Jamestown High School building to students. (Courtesy of Mary Crochet.)

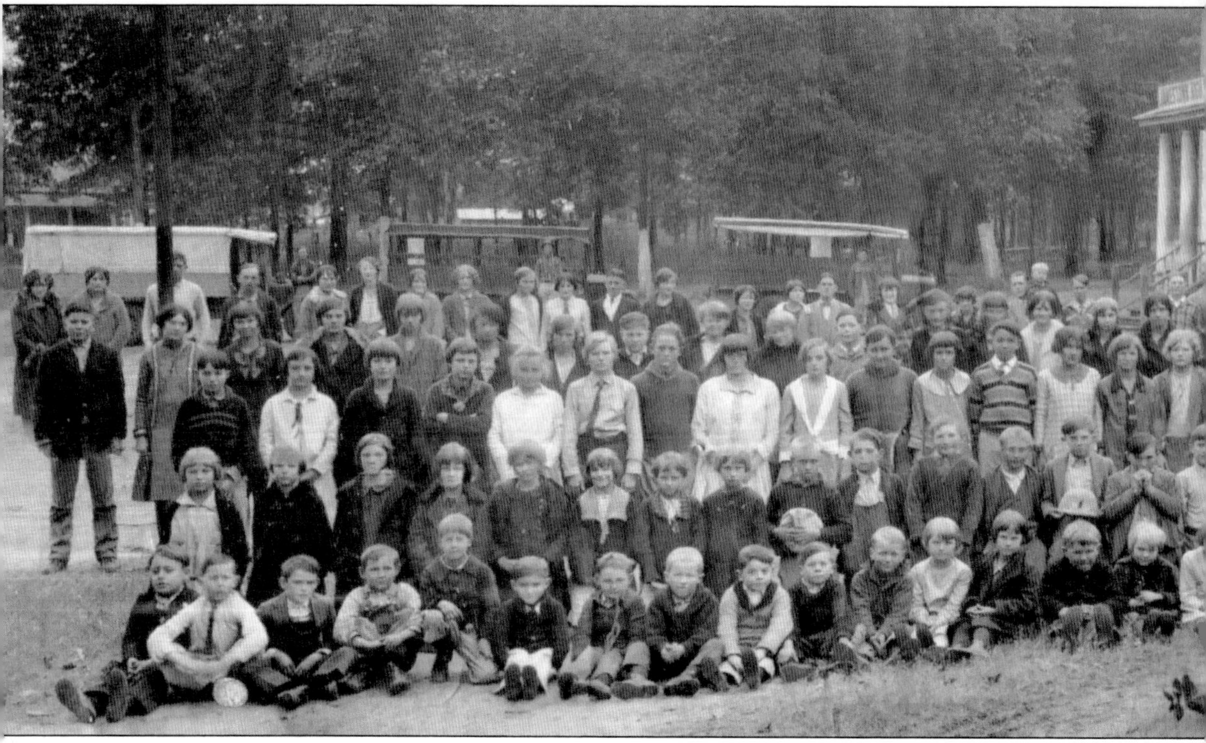

In this c. 1910 photograph, the student body of Jamestown High School gathers on the school grounds. Visible in the background are three school buses. Commonly called kid hacks, such buses had roll-up canvas curtains instead of glass in the windows. Children entered the vehicle from the rear and sat on benches that were mounted to the outside walls of the hack. (Courtesy of Mary Crochet.)

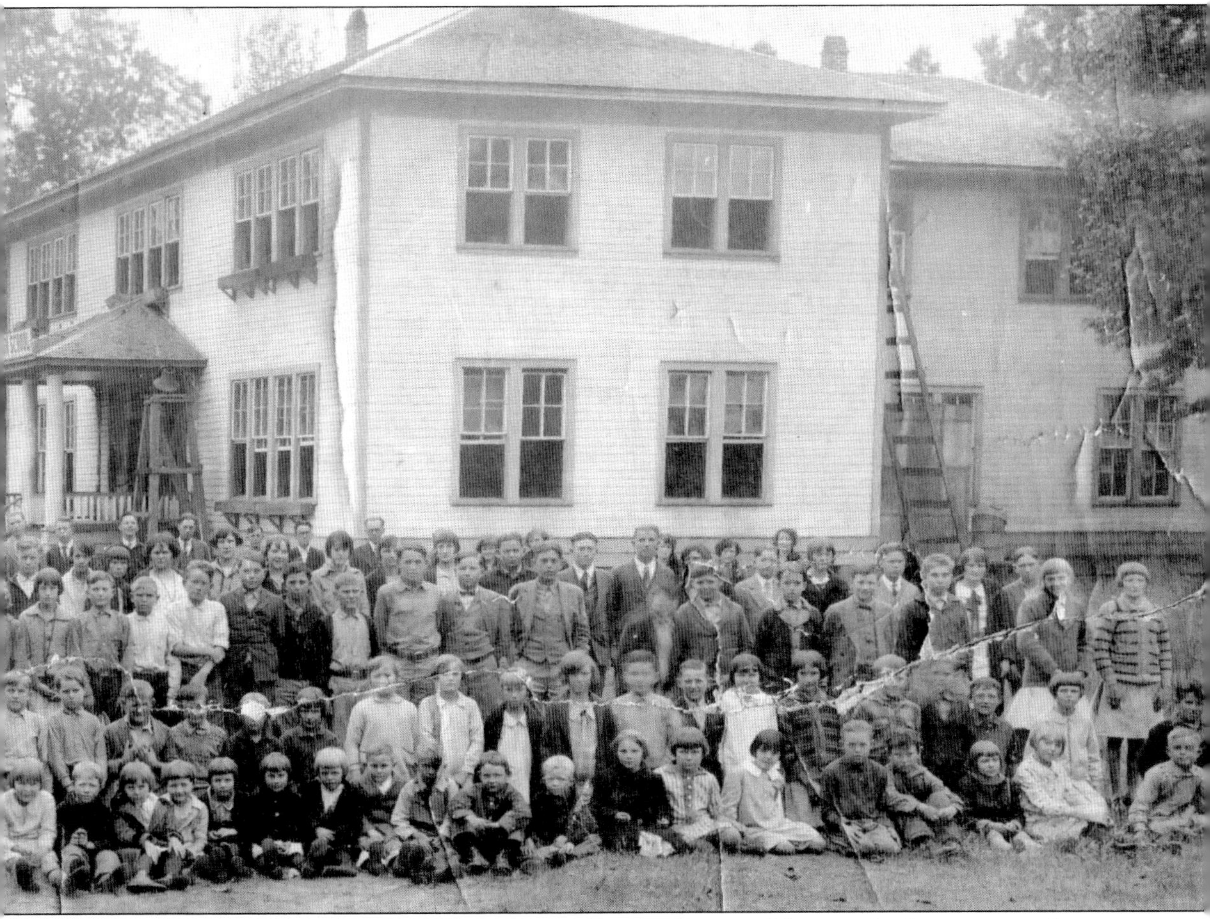

The large number of students shown here required a schoolhouse of this size. In the spring, students planted flowers in the planters that hung from the windows on the front of the building. Although it was a warm day, as evident by the opened windows, the students wear their best clothing for the photograph. (Courtesy of Mary Crochet.)

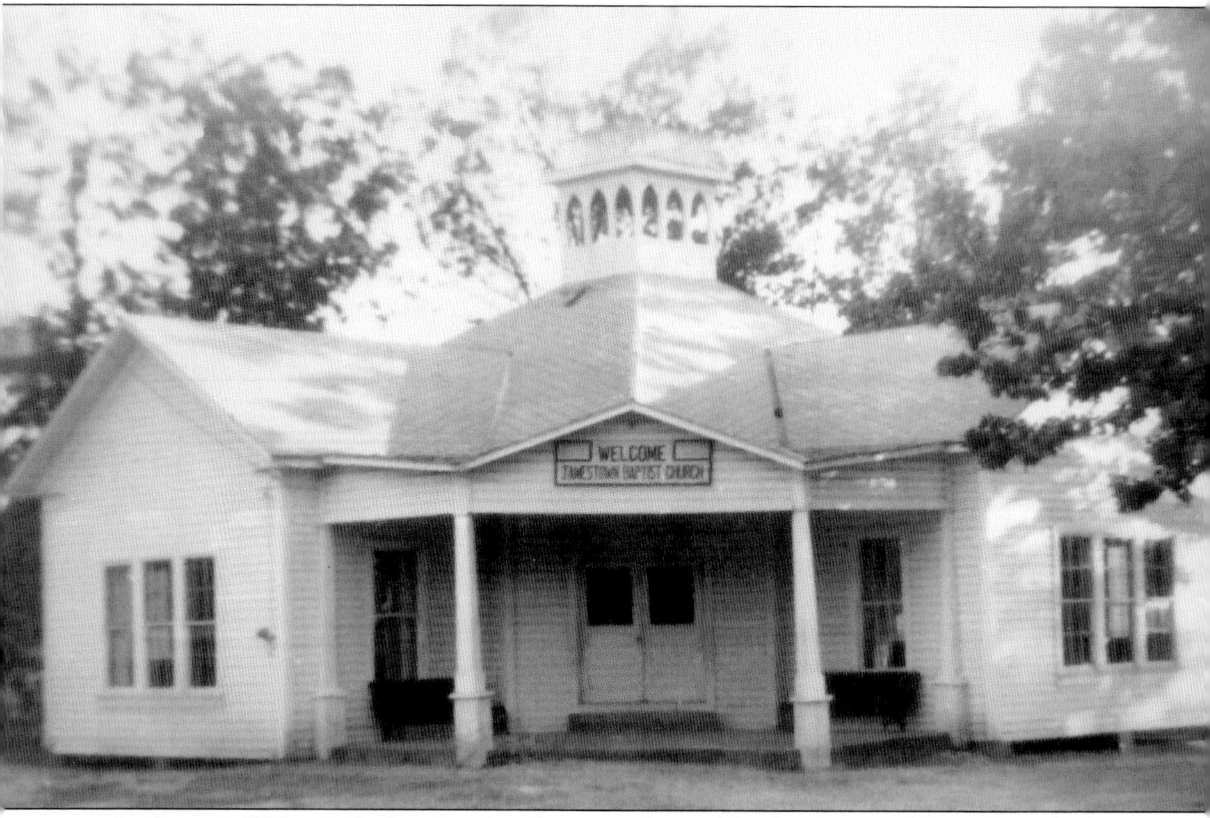

In the early 1920s, the Bodcaw Lumber Company donated land and most of the timber, which was cut and sawed by the Hamner-Smith Sawmill Company, to build the Jamestown Baptist Church. The building was soon completed, and the congregation moved from the school building in the fall of 1922. This structure was torn down in 1957 and replaced by a brick church. (Courtesy of Mary Crochet.)

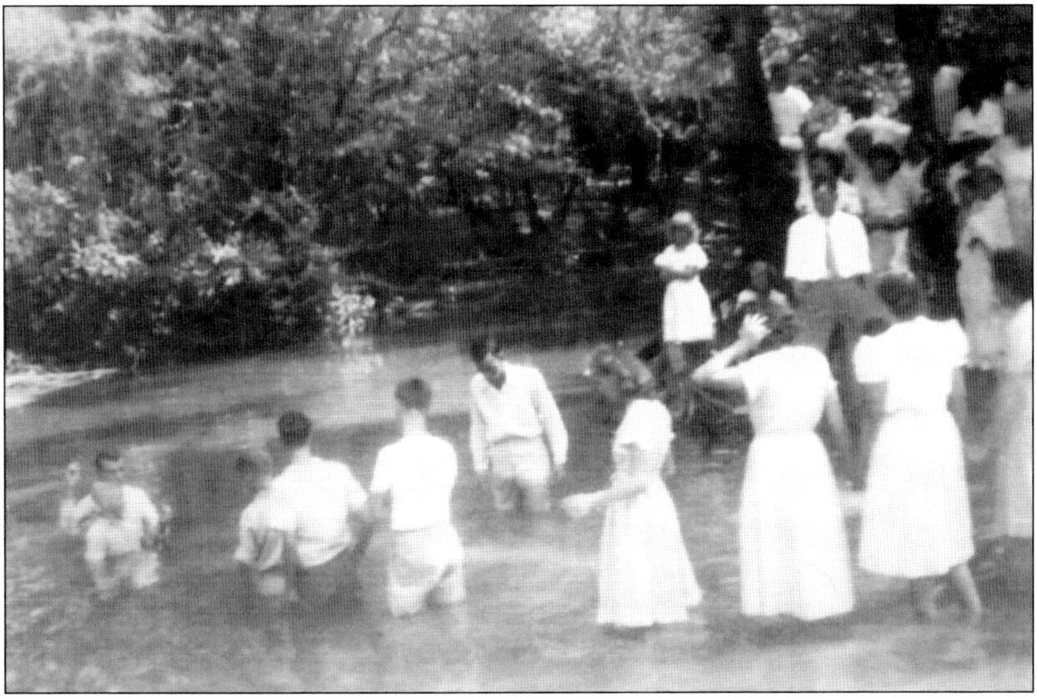

In the summer of 1945, preacher Charles McCullin performs a baptism service at what the locals called the baptizing hole, at Tullis Crossing on Black Lack, just north of Jamestown. The little girl standing on the bank at center right contributed this photograph. (Courtesy of Mary Crochet.)

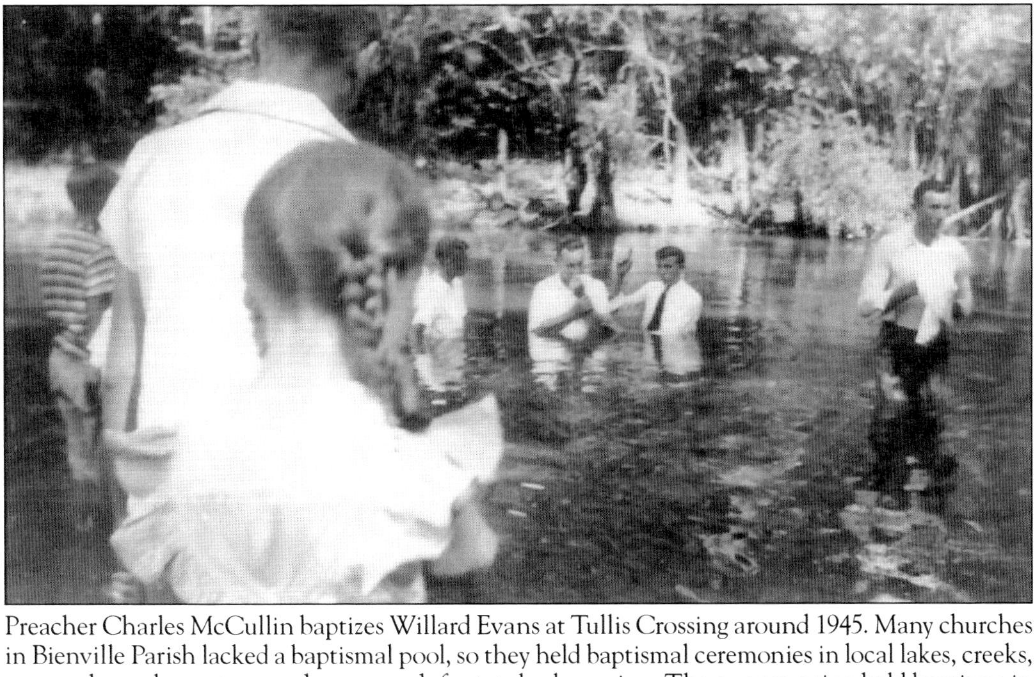

Preacher Charles McCullin baptizes Willard Evans at Tullis Crossing around 1945. Many churches in Bienville Parish lacked a baptismal pool, so they held baptismal ceremonies in local lakes, creeks, or anywhere else water was deep enough for total submersion. The congregation held baptisms in the summer months, when the water was warm. (Courtesy of Mary Crochet.)

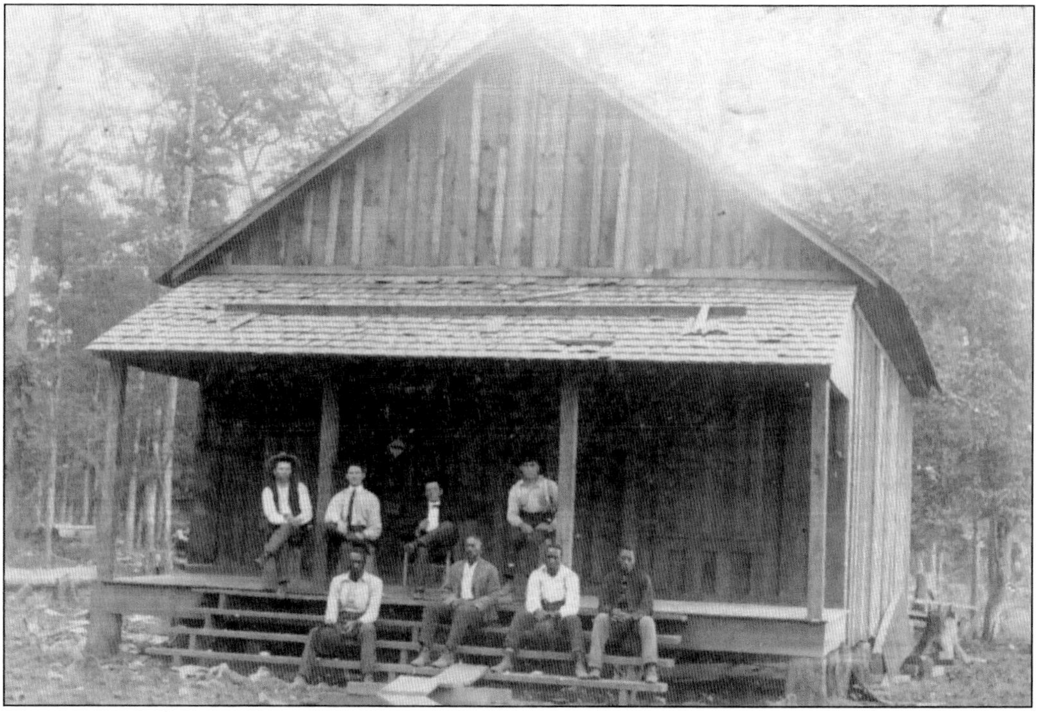

From 1849 until January 1893, Sparta was the parish seat. It was a thriving community with many buildings, such as this newly constructed store. In 1860, Sparta had a population of about 250, but it was located far from a navigable watercourse. Merchants hauled their goods overland from Lake Bistineau, an expensive and time-consuming trip. (Courtesy of Stage Coach Trail Museum.)

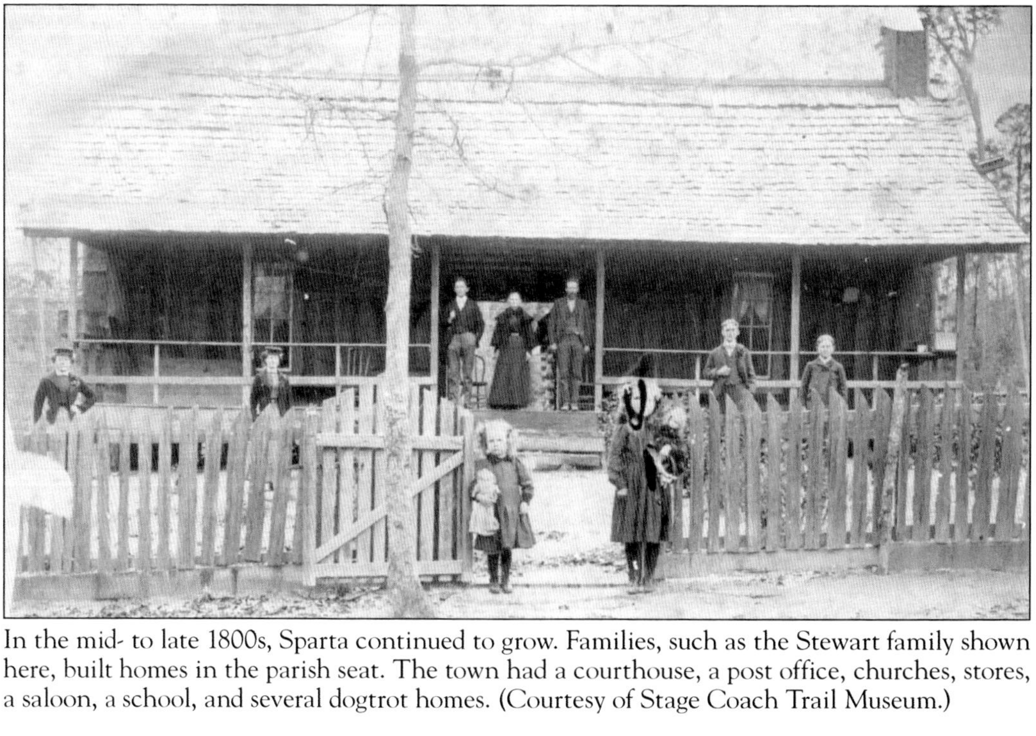

In the mid- to late 1800s, Sparta continued to grow. Families, such as the Stewart family shown here, built homes in the parish seat. The town had a courthouse, a post office, churches, stores, a saloon, a school, and several dogtrot homes. (Courtesy of Stage Coach Trail Museum.)

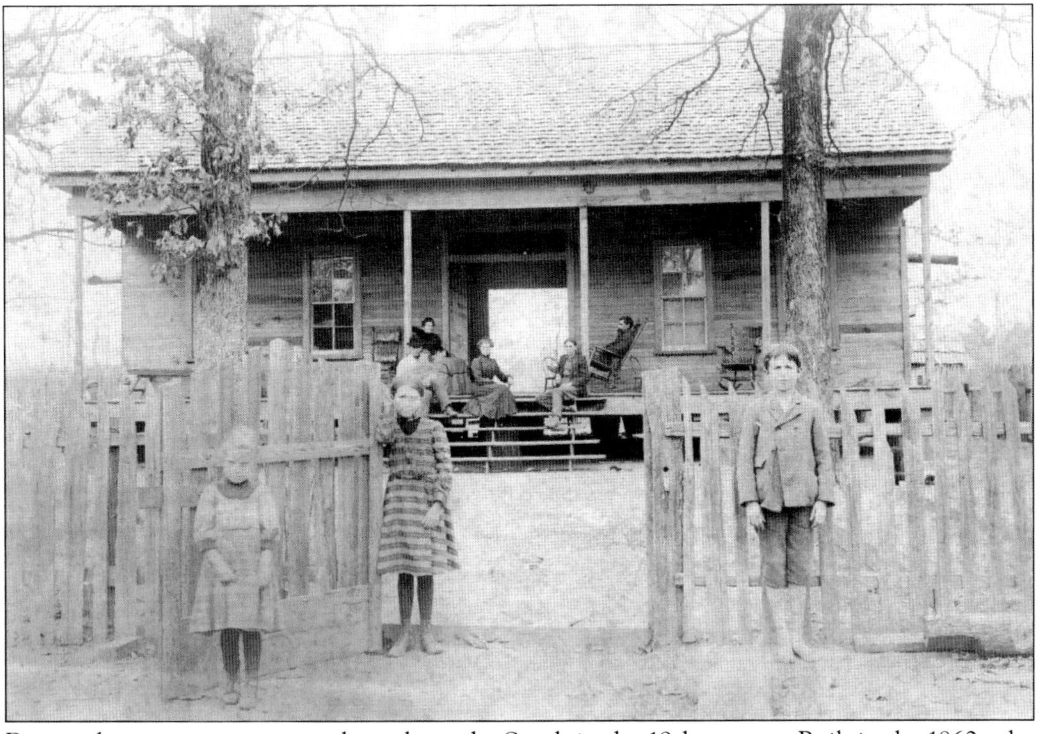

Dogtrot houses were common throughout the South in the 19th century. Built in the 1860s, the Colbert House is listed in the National Register of Historic Places. When built, the Colbert House consisted of two cabins connected by a breezeway, all under the same roof. Dogtrot houses were typically designed with the cooking and dining area in one cabin and bedrooms in the other. (Courtesy of Stage Coach Trail Museum.)

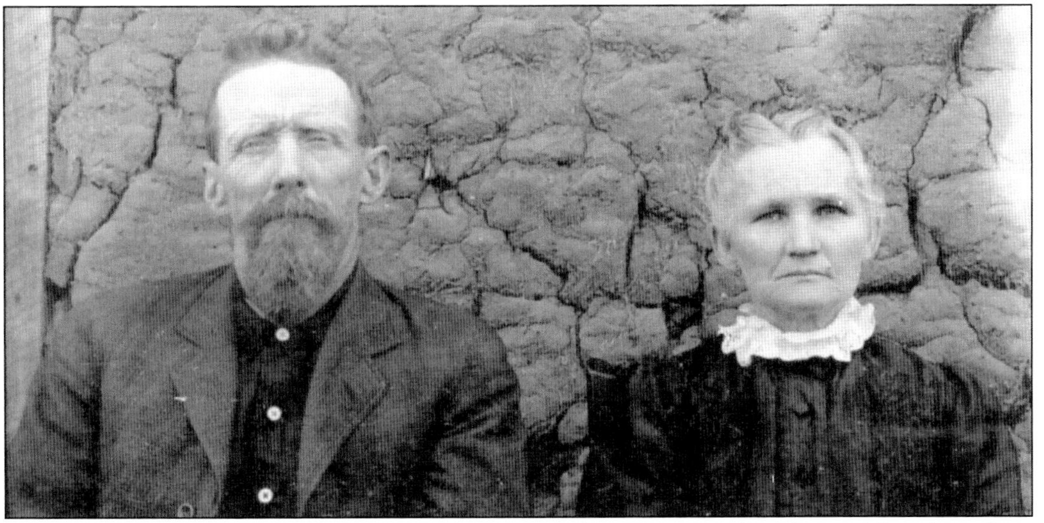

William Stewart and Delilah Huckabay Stewart pose for a photograph in front of their bousillage fireplace in the late 1800s. Bousillage is a mixture of clay and Spanish moss, animal hair, grass, or other types of bonding agents. Colonists in French Louisiana used this construction technique in the 18th and 19th centuries, and the method spread throughout Louisiana. (Courtesy of Stage Coach Trail Museum.)

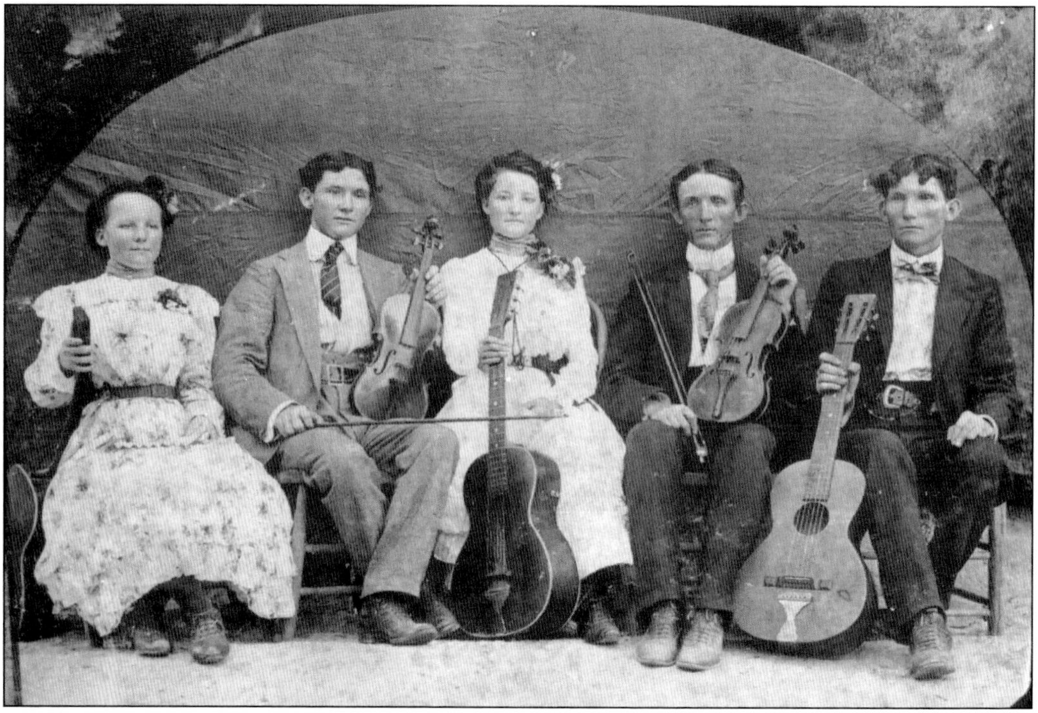

The Stewart Family Band is comprised of Pearlie, Harvey, Daisy, William G. "Billy," and Robert E. Lee Stewart. In the late 1800s, the phonograph and the radio were in the experimental stage. Live music was one of the most popular forms of entertainment. People traveled great distances to hear the Stewart Family Band play a mixture of hymns and folk songs. (Courtesy of Stage Coach Trail Museum.)

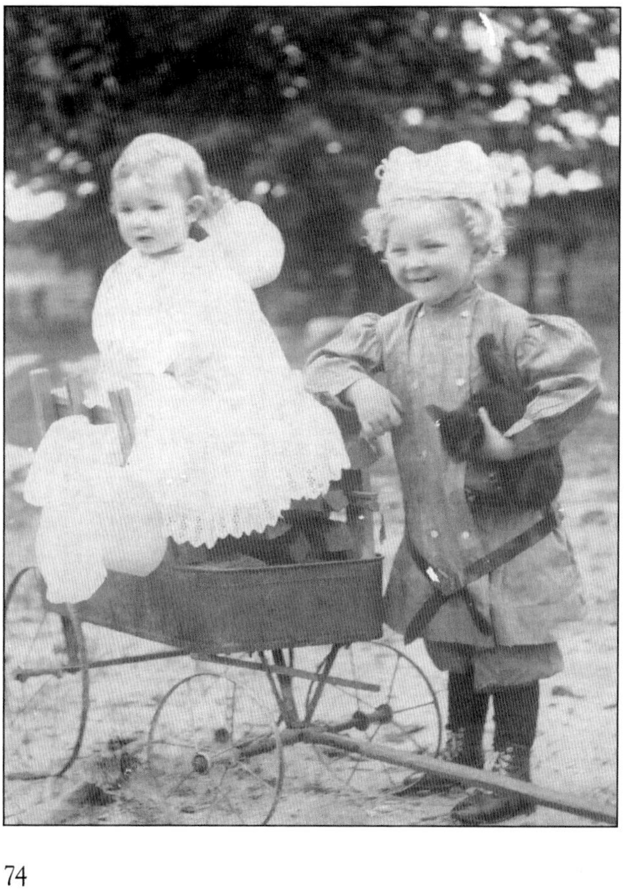

The Stewart family children pose for a photograph on a dirt street in Sparta. The town was built in a sandy region, which made farming difficult. In the 1880s, workers completed the Vicksburg, Shreveport & Pacific Railroad, which crossed Bienville Parish. The railroad passed through Arcadia and Gibsland, but it bypassed Sparta, and the town began to decline. (Courtesy of Stage Coach Trail Museum.)

Civic leaders and elected officials proposed that the parish seat be relocated. Even loyal citizens of Sparta, including Dr. W.L. Huckabay, understood that the change was necessary. In 1893, the Bienville Parish Police Jury held an election to decide between Arcadia, Bienville, and Gibsland as the new parish seat. In a runoff, Arcadia beat Bienville by a vote of 1,323 to 1,258. (Courtesy of Stage Coach Trail Museum.)

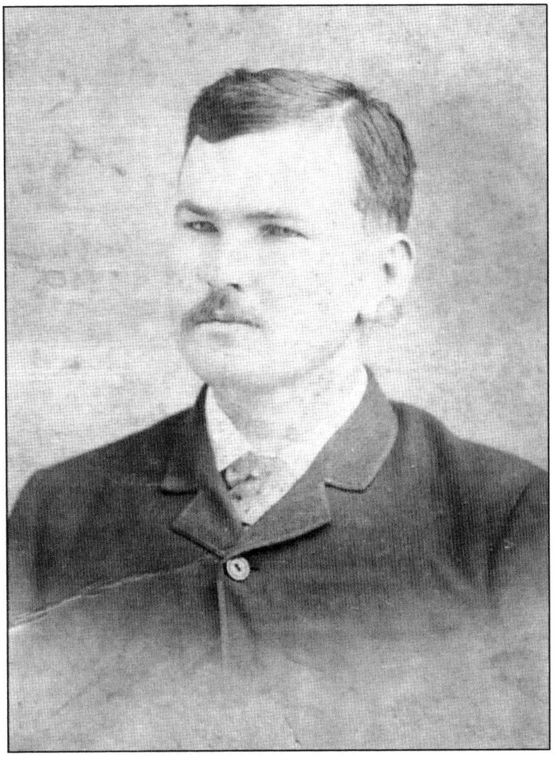

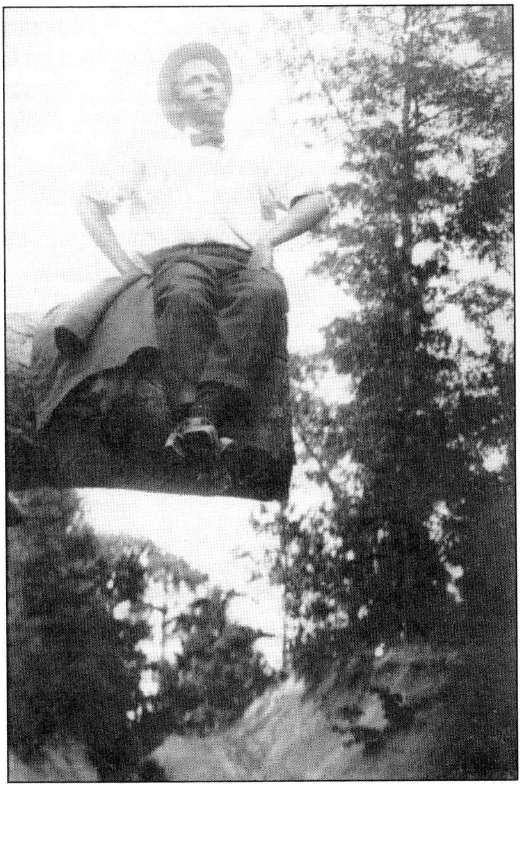

On the night of the election, about half an hour after the votes were counted, six wagons appeared from the woods. Without incident, the drivers entered the courthouse, removed the record books, threw them haphazardly into the wagons, and left for Arcadia on the road seen in this photograph. For the rest of his life, Virgil Day, the last surviving witness to the event, remained bitter about the night "they stole the parish seat." The man in this photograph is unidentified. (Courtesy of Stage Coach Trail Museum.)

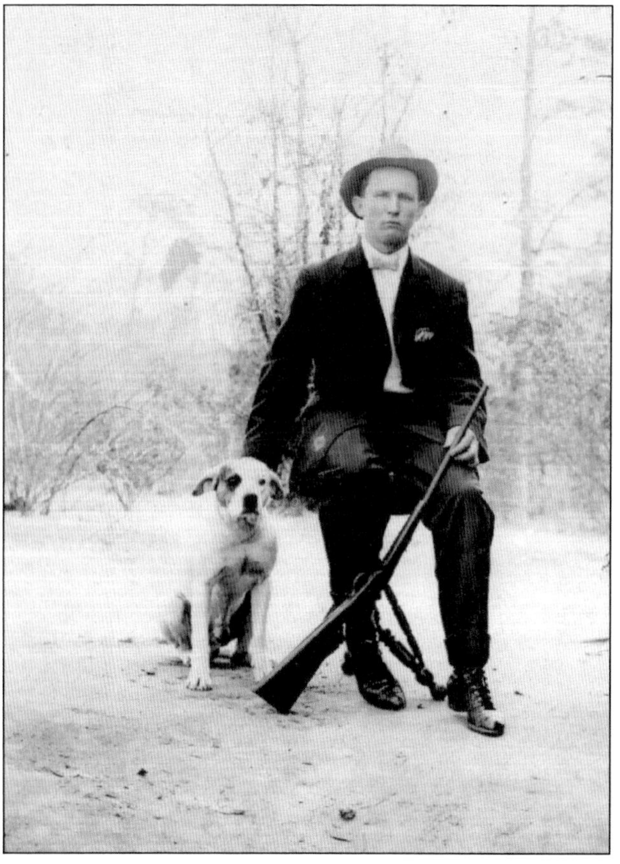

When the record books were moved to Arcadia, many citizens in the southern part of the parish were ready to take up arms to retrieve the documents. Most citizens, however, felt that the move was a mistake that would be worked out. Over 100 years later, the parish seat remains in Arcadia, although citizens are quick to tell about the "midnight raid" and "the night the wagons came" and "stole the government." (Courtesy of Stage Coach Trail Museum.)

Family members gather at W.G. Stewart's home at Sparta in 1905. By this time, many citizens of Sparta had moved to Arcadia or one of the other towns along the route of the railroad. Several families disassembled and moved their homes, leaving little behind. (Courtesy of Stage Coach Trail Museum.)

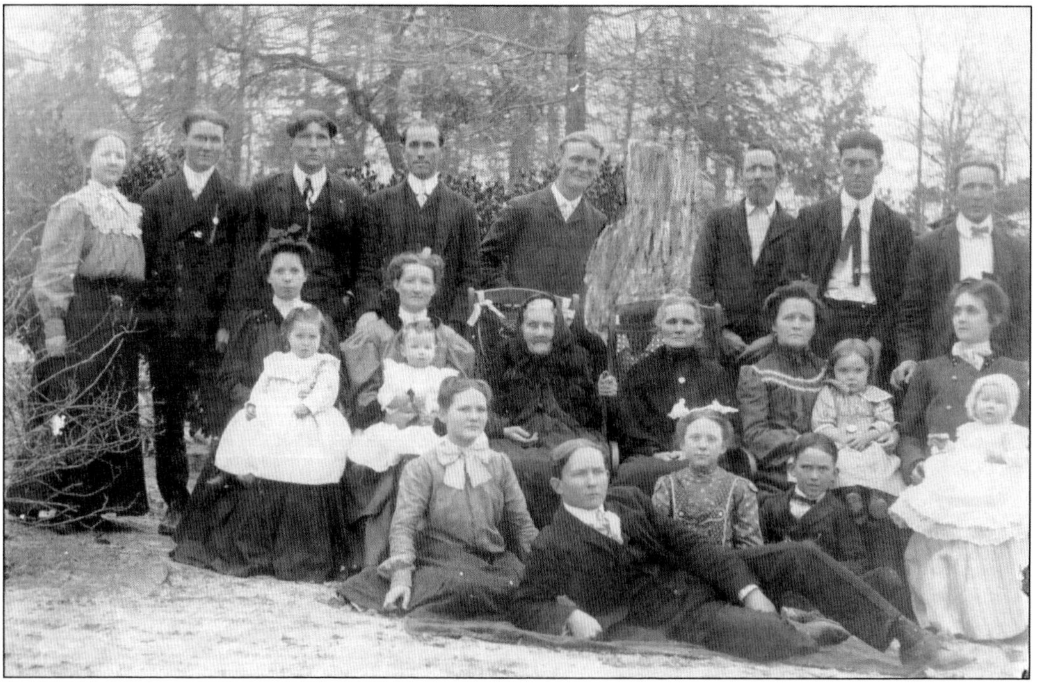

Four

South Bienville Parish

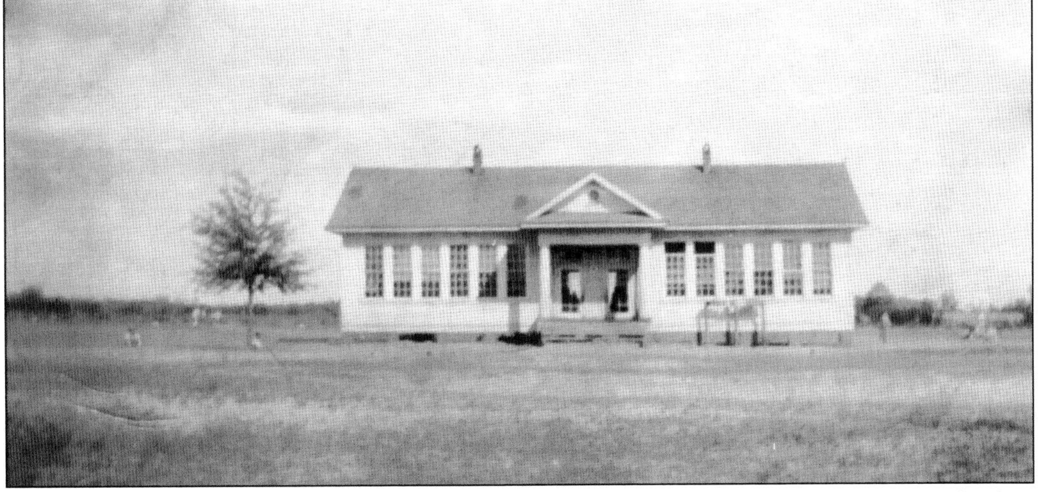

The Brown community, commonly called Brown Town, is located about six miles west of Saline on Highway 155. In September 1844, some 61 Baptists, including George Brown, for whom the town was named, met under an oak tree in Brown Town and decided to build a Baptist church in the area. The young oak shown to the left of the school still survives and has grown into a massive tree. (Courtesy of Muriel Sullivan.)

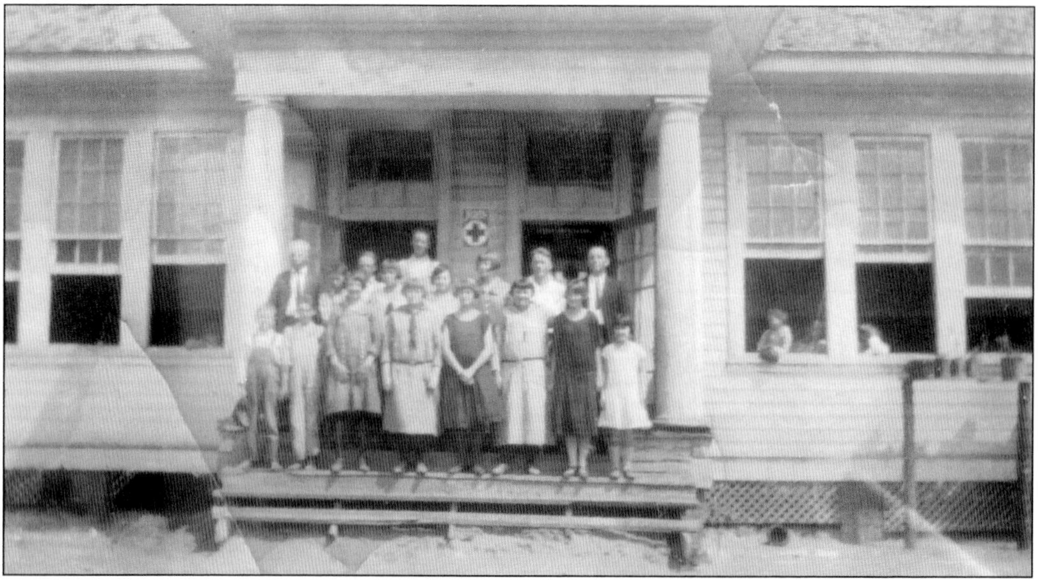

In 1925, the students and teachers at Brown Town school supported the humanitarian efforts of the Red Cross. Students who donated time or money to the Red Cross received small, white metal clip-on pins with a red cross, resembling the sign in the center of this photograph. (Courtesy of Muriel Sullivan.)

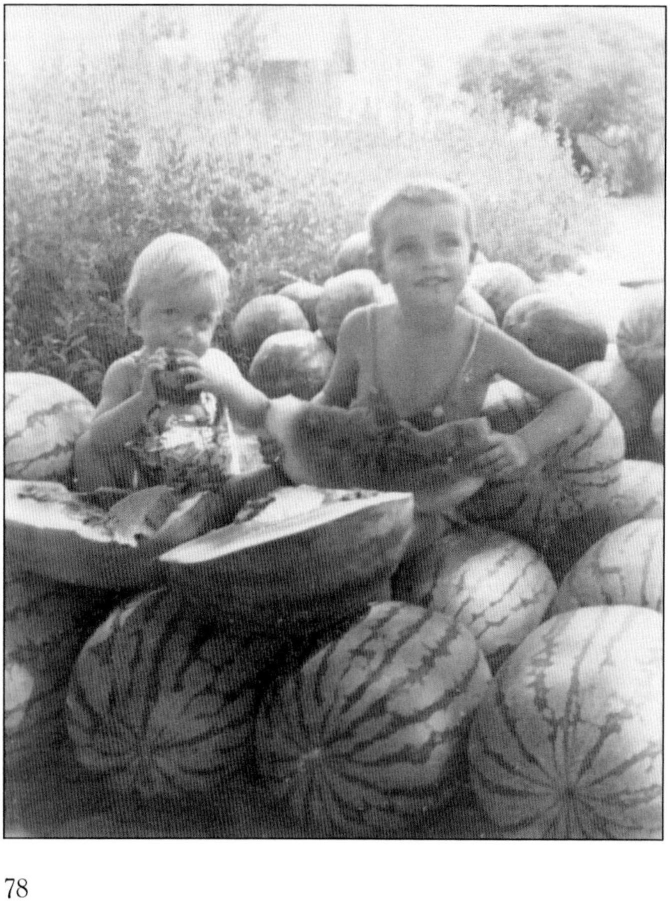

On this hot summer day in the early 1940s, Bernice and C.H. Cheatwood Jr. sample a portion of their dad's striped watermelon crop. The watermelon harvest was an exciting time, as the product was only available during the summer months. Watermelons were a featured treat at most summer gatherings. Countless articles in the *Bienville Democrat* end with "ice cold watermelons were served." (Courtesy of Muriel Sullivan.)

Eva Dell Cheatwood poses at the water well that was the source of water for the family. They drew water by lowering a bucket into the well, allowing it to fill with water, and pulling the full bucket back up. This well was uncommonly deep, based on the amount of rope used to draw the bucket from the depths of the well. (Courtesy of Muriel Sullivan.)

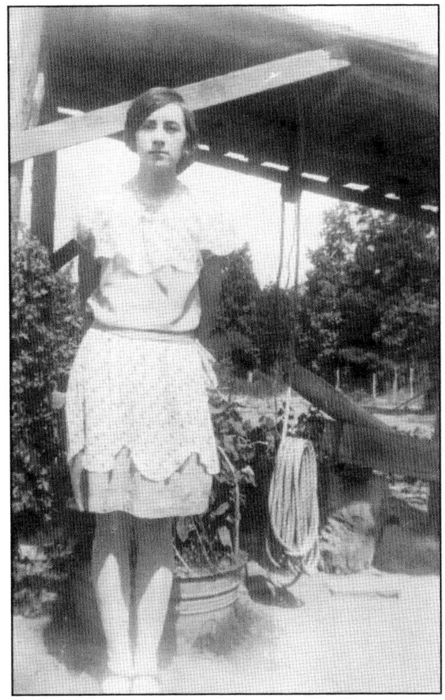

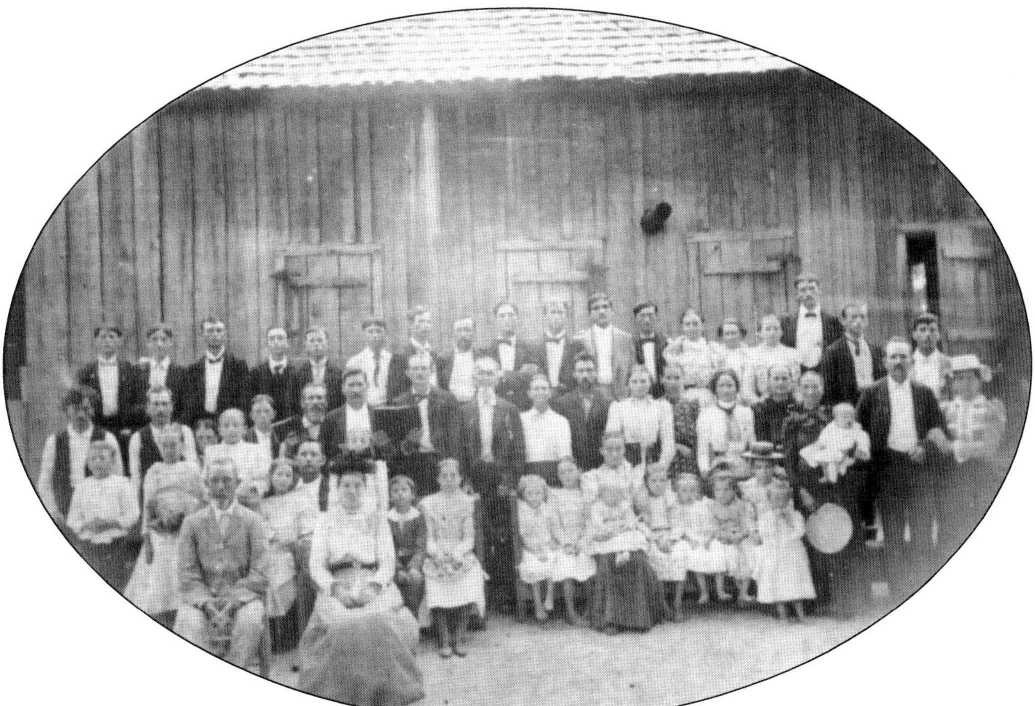

In 1842, settlers from the Carolinas arrived and acquired a donation of land from one of the local families to build a church and burial grounds. Carolina Baptist Church was named after these Christian settlers. Taken in the late 1800s, this photograph shows the congregation in front of the building that served as a school during the week and a church on Sundays. (Courtesy of Cheryl Babers.)

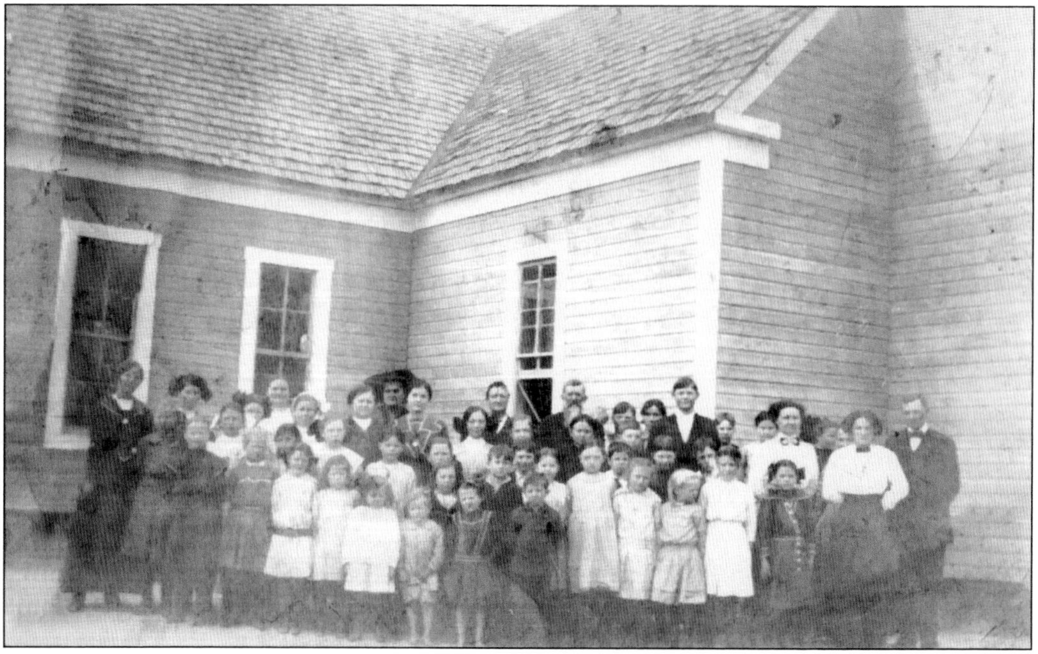

Since 1842, there have been three buildings on the Carolina Baptist Church site. The pews in the first church building were made from split logs. On January 2, 1912, the church congregation poses for a photograph in front of the second Carolina Church building. Worshipers walked or rode horses to services. In 1992, Joe Harper wrote that his parents walked and carried him to worship at Carolina Church. (Courtesy of Lavon Sullivan.)

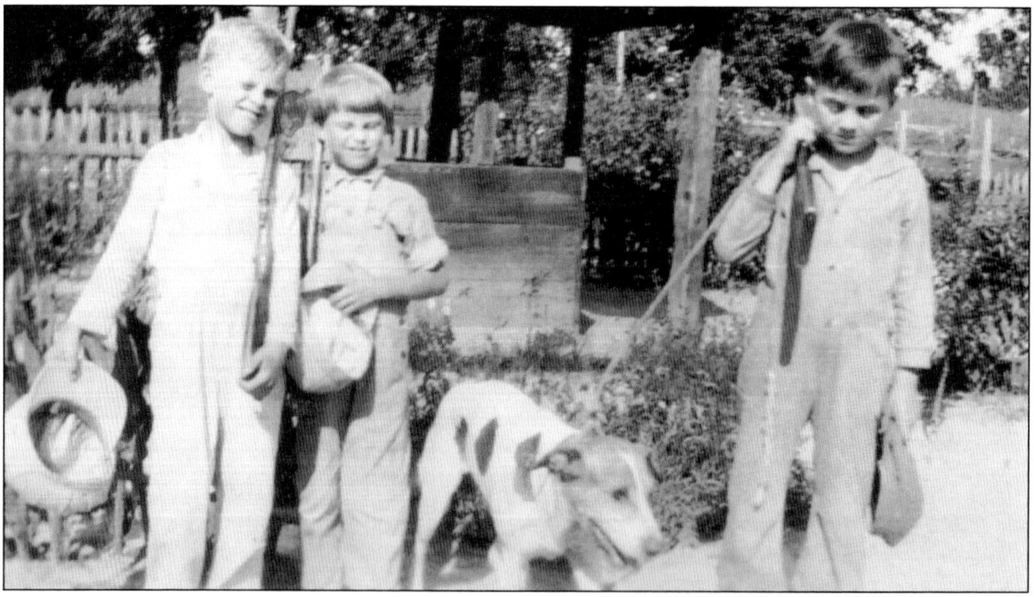

A.W. "Shorty" Rogers (left), Charles Rogers (center), and Joe Harper were best friends as kids. They went to church together, played together, and, with the help of Joe's dog, Sput, hunted together. In the 1930s, they set off on another hunting expedition with Sput. In 1992, Joe remembered one day, as a child, Charles was singing off-key loudly in church. When Charles asked how he was doing, they burst into laughter. (Courtesy of Lavon Sullivan.)

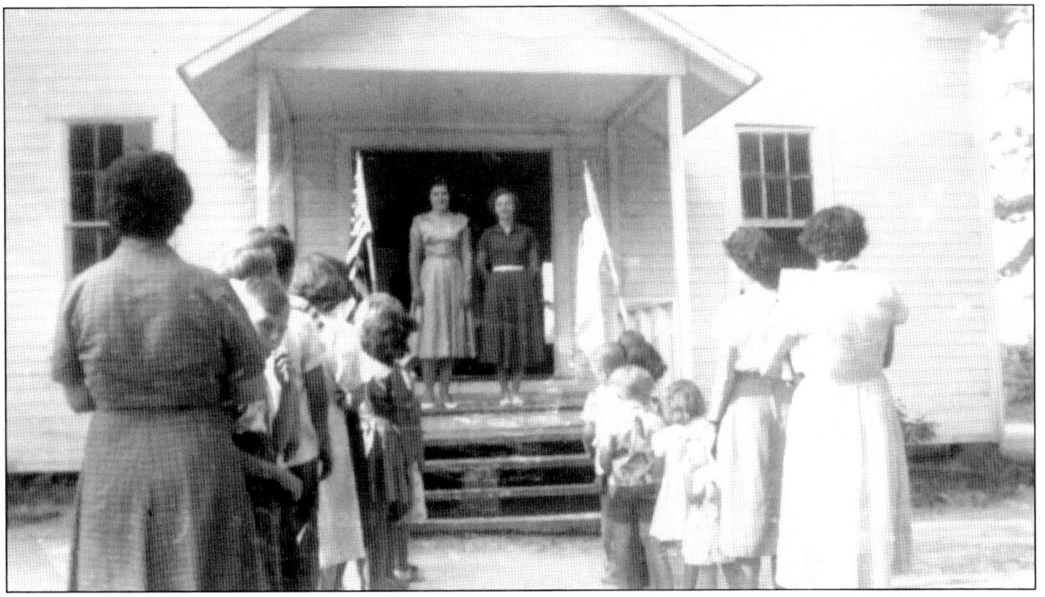

In August 1953, members of Carolina Baptist Church attended Vacation Bible School. Always held in summer, the Bible school was a highly anticipated form of religious service for children. This photograph shows the third Carolina Church building. The congregation literally erected the third church. The men tore the old building down, while the women and children removed the nails and stacked the lumber. They then used the old lumber to build the new church. (Courtesy of Lavon Sullivan.)

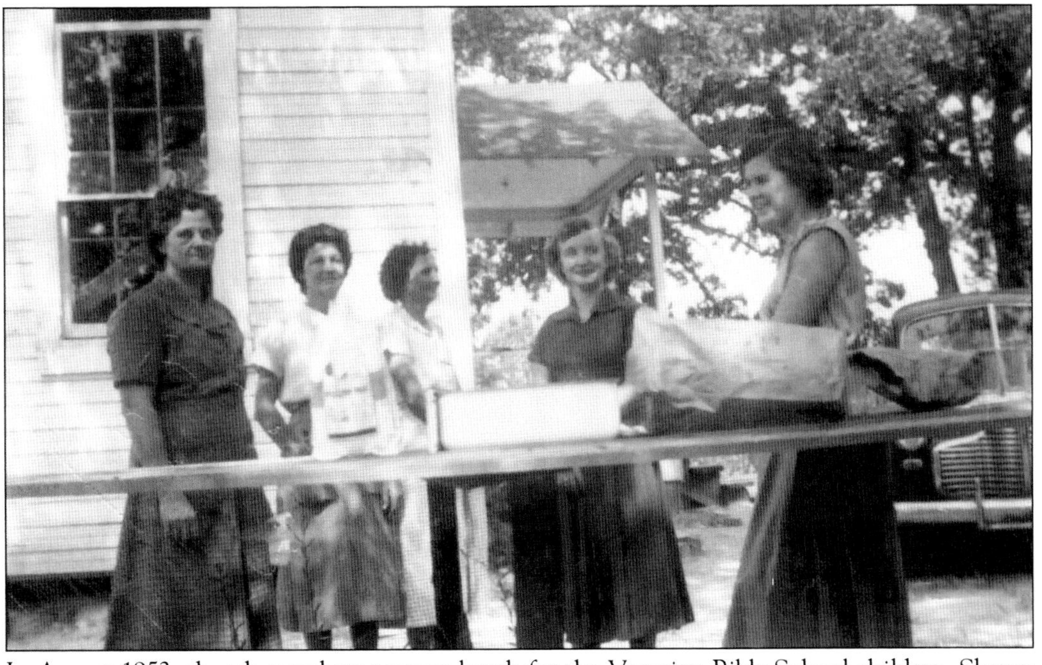

In August 1953, church members prepare lunch for the Vacation Bible School children. Shown here are, from left to right, Gusta Thomas, Virta Sanderland, Irma Thomas, Laura Bell Thomas, and Patsy Kelly. The school began as a way to teach children about the Bible on a daily basis, which is why it was held during one or two weeks during the summer. (Courtesy of Lavon Sullivan.)

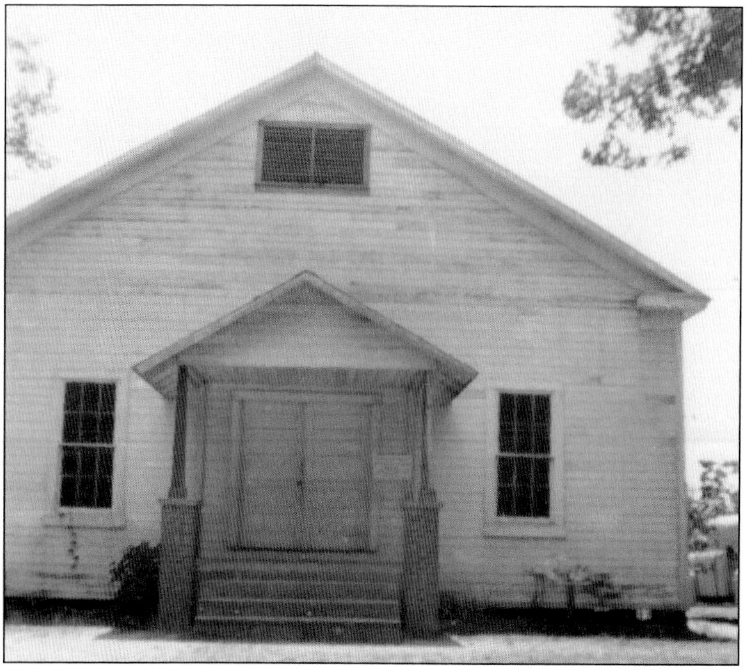

The structure of the current Carolina Baptist Church is the same as it was when this photograph was taken in August 1959, though the exterior was bricked in the 1980s. A board between two oak trees in front of the church was used as a footstep to help women mount their horses or enter their wagons. The board still exists today. (Courtesy of Wanda Culpepper.)

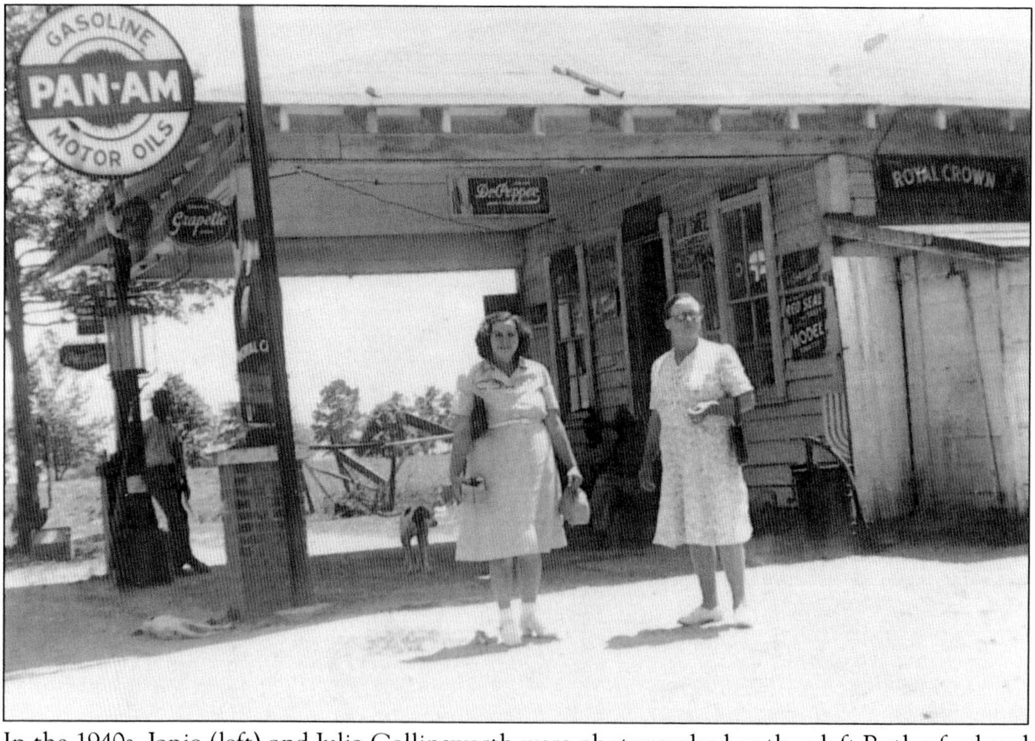

In the 1940s, Janie (left) and Julia Collinsworth were photographed as they left Rutherford and Ruby Robinson's store in Danville. Many people in the area remember Ruby as a very giving person. "If you bought 5¢ worth of candy, you left with 25¢ worth of candy, because she wanted the children to test out her newest candy." The store was located across from Burns Forrest Products office. (Courtesy of Wanda Culpepper.)

In 1914, workers built a new school in Danville. Friendship High School was completed a decade later, and the Danville school closed. The school board donated the building, which was renovated and used as the Danville Church. Tyson Collinsworth (left), J.P. Collinsworth (center), and H.T. Collinsworth pose in front of the church in the 1940s. In 1957, the congregation built a new church. (Courtesy of Wanda Culpepper.)

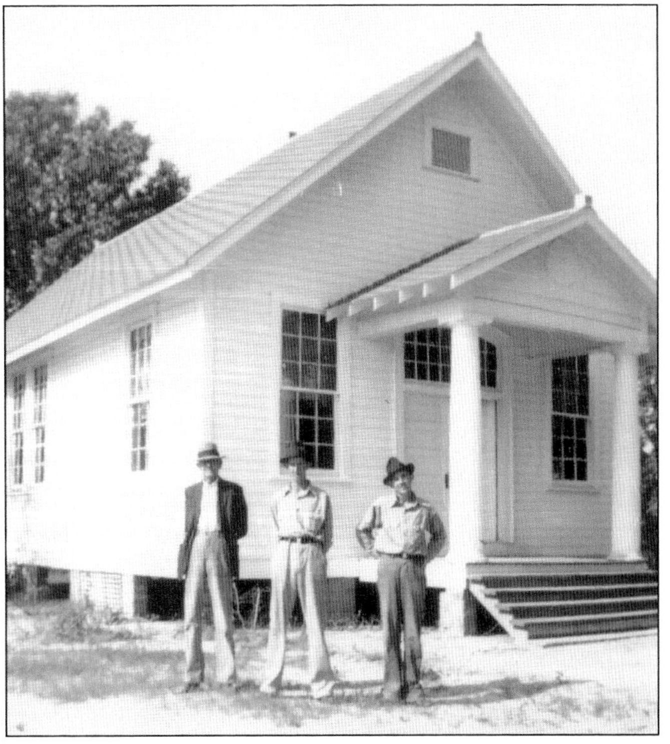

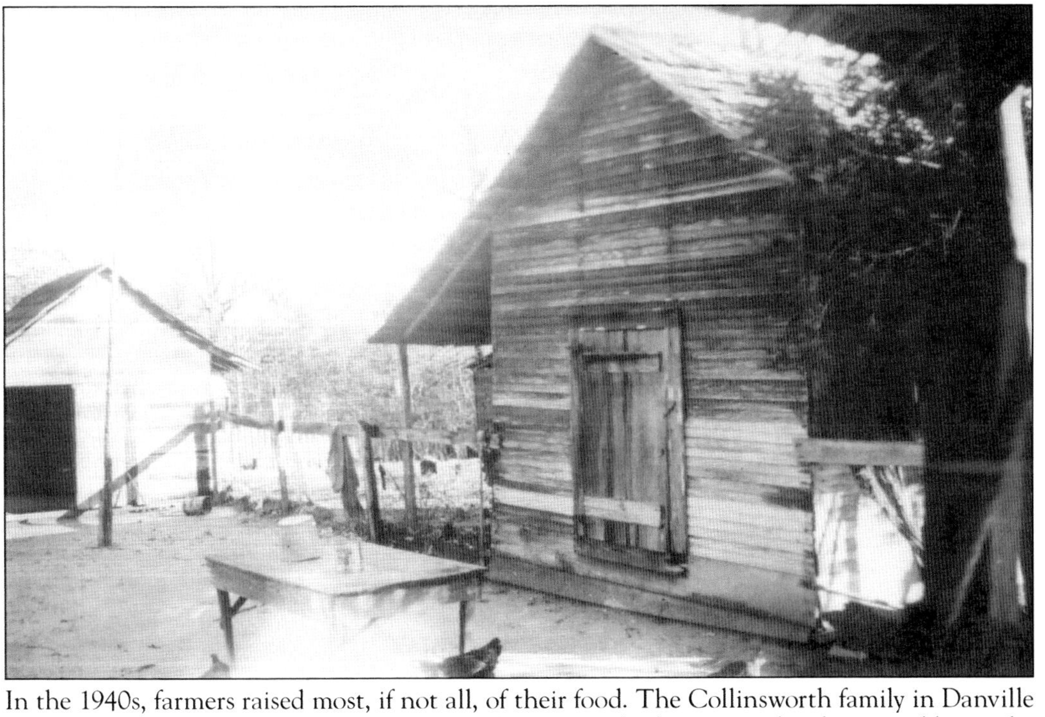

In the 1940s, farmers raised most, if not all, of their food. The Collinsworth family in Danville was no exception. They had a chicken coop for raising chickens, a garden for vegetables, and a smokehouse for smoking and preserving meats. The meat table shown here was used for cutting up the meat. (Courtesy of Wanda Culpepper.)

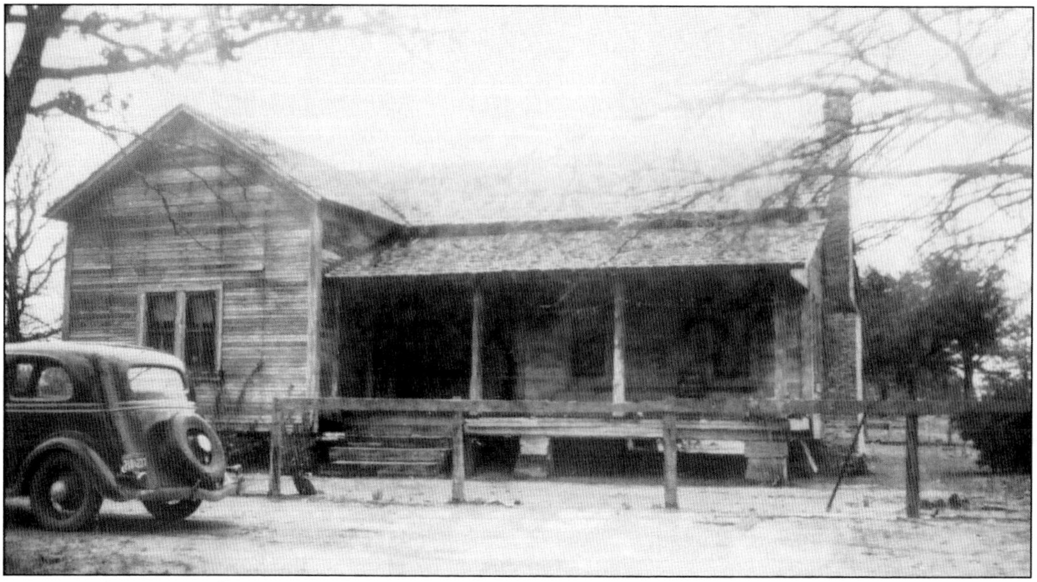

Tyson and Bettie Collinsworth's house in Danville, seen here in the 1940s, was originally a dogtrot house. It was common to renovate dogtrot houses as more rooms were needed. When Bettie decided that she wanted a living room, Tyson boxed in the left portion of the house. (Courtesy of Wanda Culpepper.)

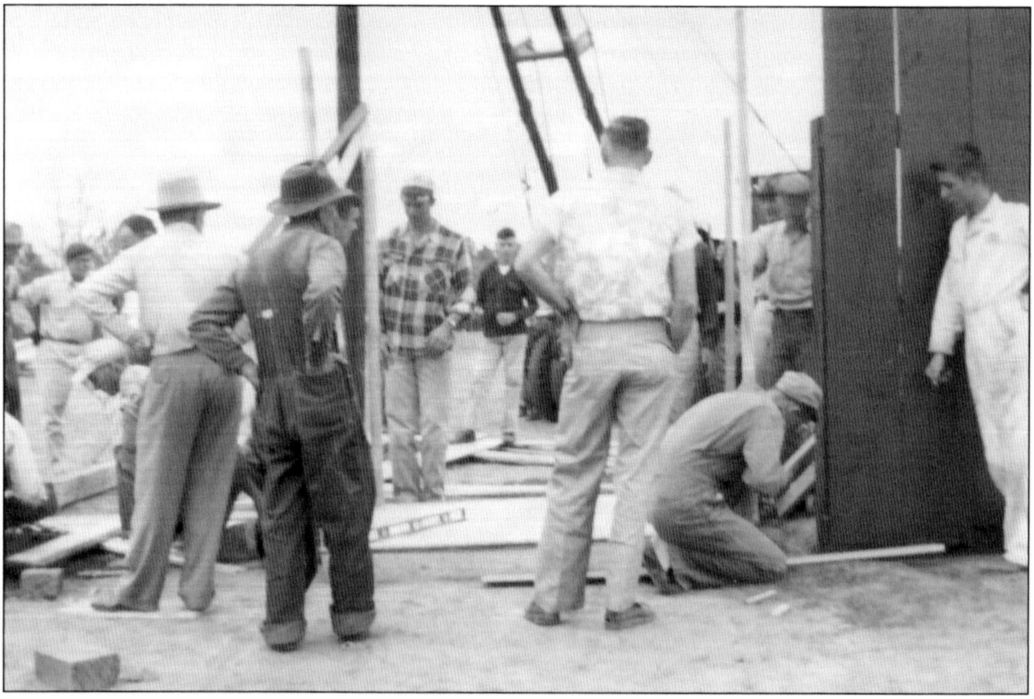

The 1950s are commonly referred to as the golden age of baseball. The sport drew large crowds all across America. Danville's baseball team played its home games at the baseball diamond at Friendship High School. In October 1951, the community gathered and began building a new baseball park on a field adjacent to Bud and Averil Robinson's home in Danville. (Courtesy of Wanda Culpepper.)

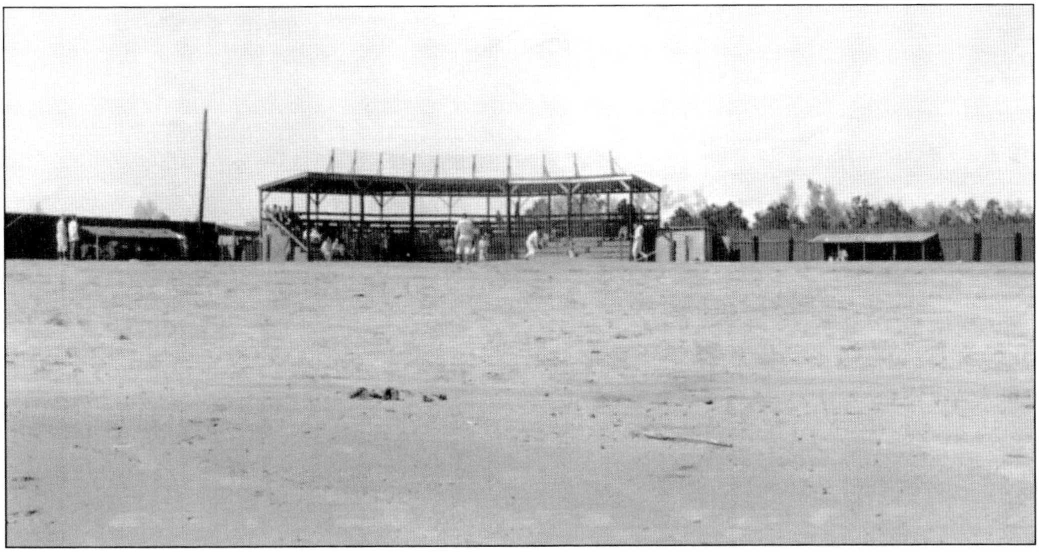

From 1950 through 1956, the Danville ballpark was the home of the Danville Deacons. The Deacons were one of the best teams in the area. It won either the regular-season title, the playoff championship, or both, of the Jackson-Bienville Baseball League all seven years of its existence. The Deacons were the team to beat. (Courtesy of Wanda Culpepper.)

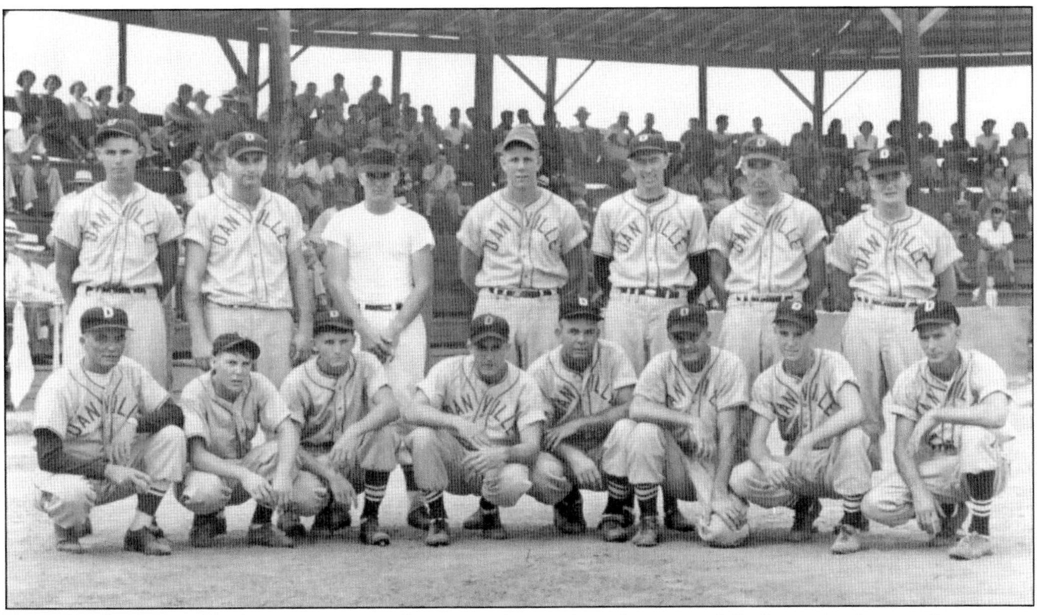

In 1952, the Danville Deacons sported new uniforms, but the team failed to win the regular-season title, as it had the previous two years. The Ansley Trojans won the title by winning 13 of their 14 games. Danville finished the season with a record of 11-2. (Courtesy of Wanda Culpepper.)

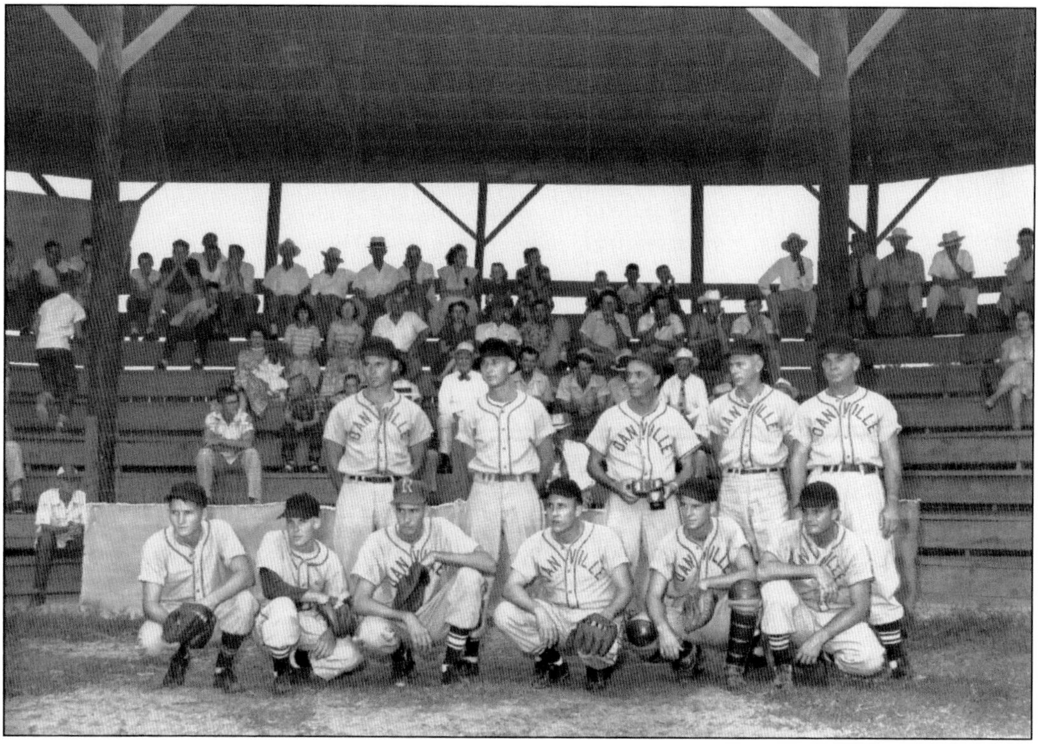

In 1953, the Danville Deacons won the Western Division title with an 8-0 season record. In 1954 and 1955, the Deacons won both the regular season and playoff championships. In 1956, the team finished first in the regular-season standings for the fourth consecutive year, but lost the championship to Dubach. All attempts to organize the league for the 1957 season failed, and the Deacons disbanded. (Courtesy of Wanda Culpepper.)

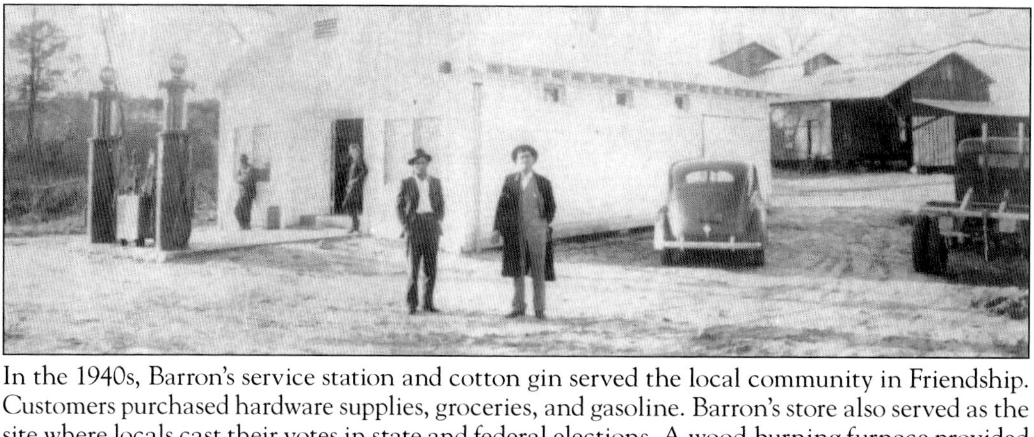

In the 1940s, Barron's service station and cotton gin served the local community in Friendship. Customers purchased hardware supplies, groceries, and gasoline. Barron's store also served as the site where locals cast their votes in state and federal elections. A wood-burning furnace provided the power for the cotton gin. Shown here in the foreground are Cleve (left) and Lawrence Barron. (Courtesy of Pat Mathews.)

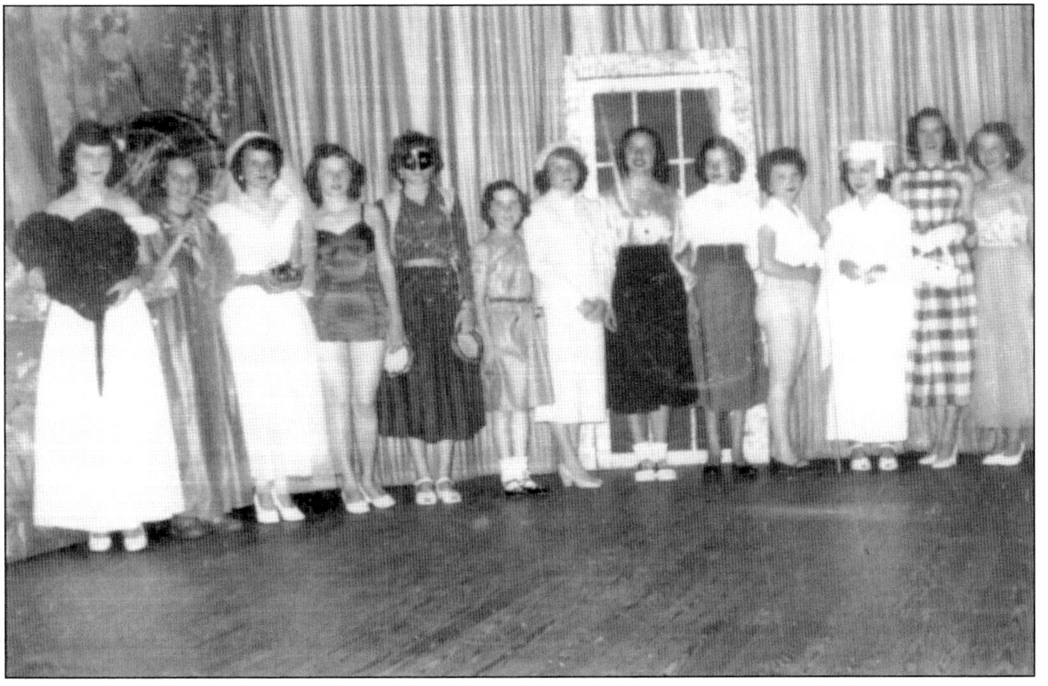

In the early 1950s, the ladies of Friendship High School held a play to entertain the community. A large crowd watched as the students acted, sang, and danced. Characters included a graduate, nurse, bride, valentine, and a character from the movie *Singin' in the Rain*. (Courtesy of Pat Mathews.)

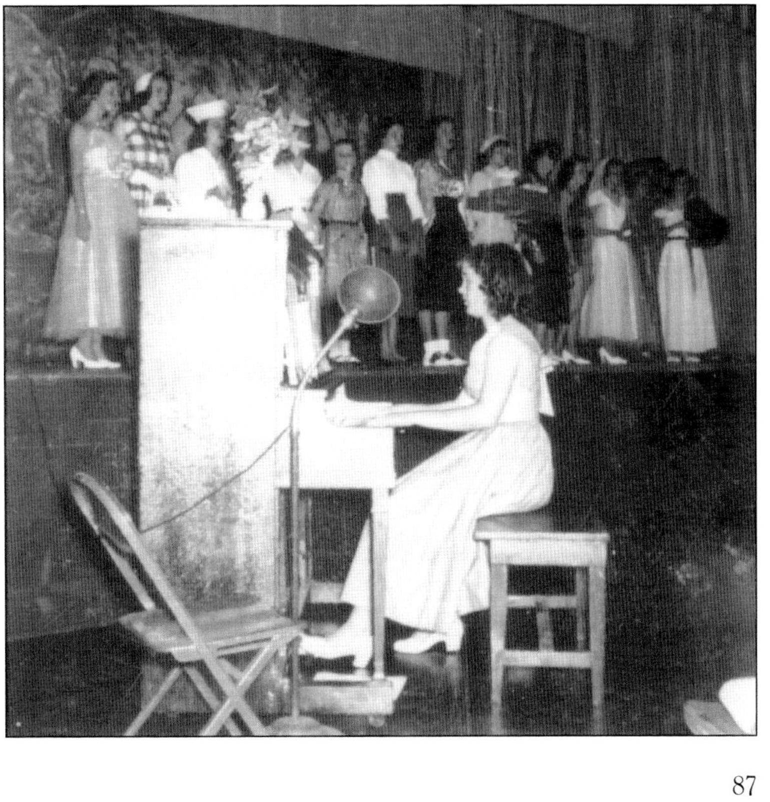

The ladies sing as Patty Smelly plays the music on piano for the program. Friendship High School's gymnasium doubled as the auditorium. Local artist Arnold Bail hand-painted the detailed backdrop visible in this photograph. (Courtesy of Pat Mathews.)

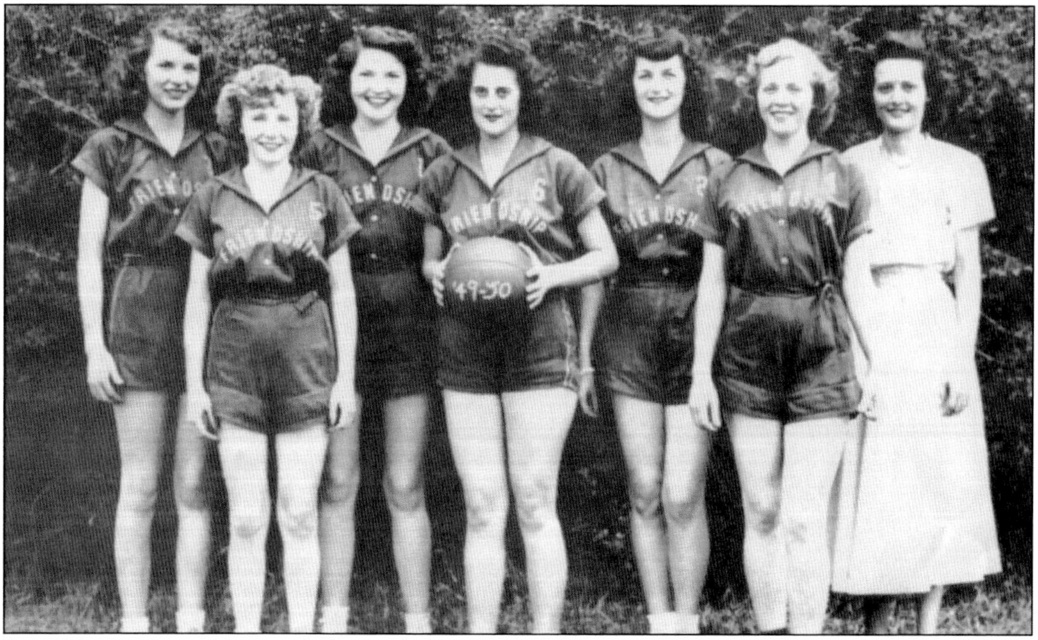

In 1950, the Friendship girls' basketball team won first place in the Class C state basketball tournament. Basketball became a popular sport for high school athletes, as it required little investment for equipment. The 1950 girls' team consists of, from left to right, Belva Collinsworth, Katie Lou Parker, Emma Roy Lindsey, Arlena Toms, Glennie Rae Sandlin, Polly Hines, and Margie Barron. (Courtesy of Pat Mathews.)

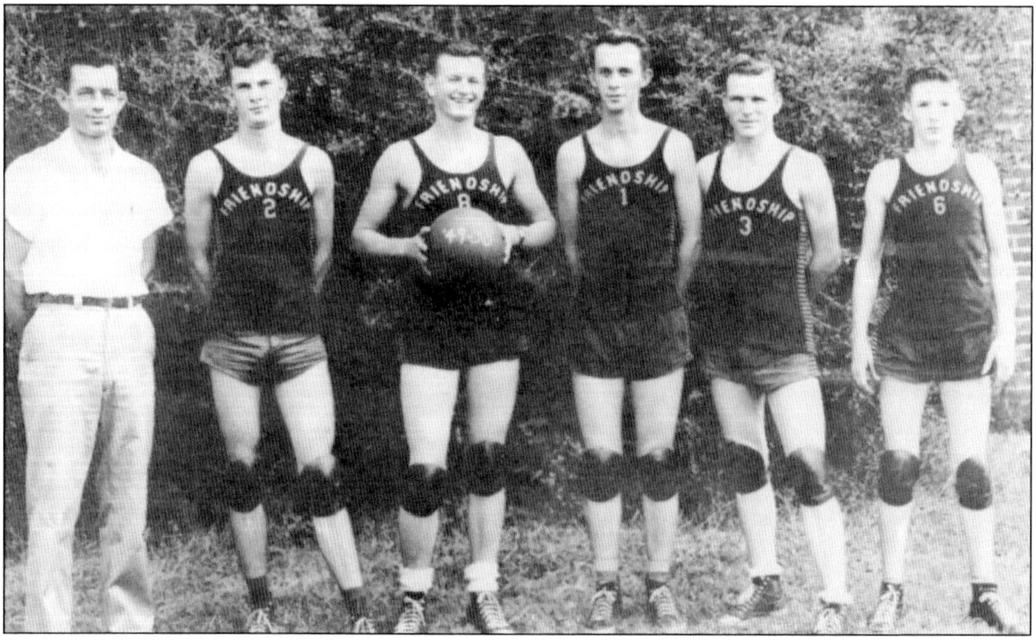

The Friendship boys' basketball team won second place in the 1950 Class C state championship. In small communities before the era of televised sports, basketball games drew large crowds. The team consists of, from left to right, Harold Parks, Robert Odell Thomas, Glen Roy Robinson, Robert Williams, Edwin McConathy, and Buddy Parker. (Courtesy of Pat Mathews.)

In the 1953–1954 school year, the last boys' basketball team at Friendship High School poses for this photograph. Since 1924, Friendship High School educated the children of Friendship and Danville. The last team's members are, from left to right, Jessie Knotts, Raymond Lindsey, Travis Lindsey, Laurice Hines, and Lloyd Knotts. (Courtesy of Pat Mathews.)

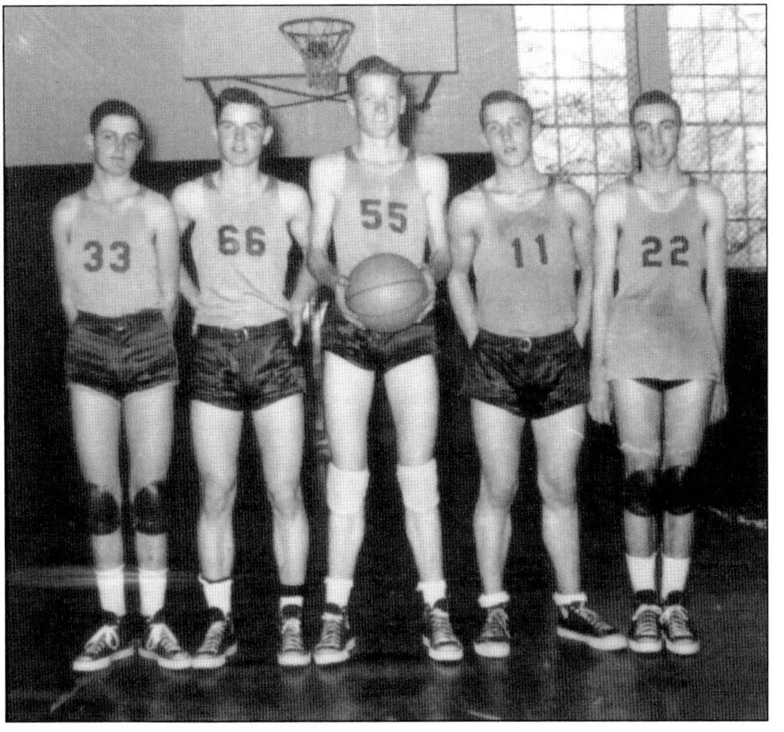

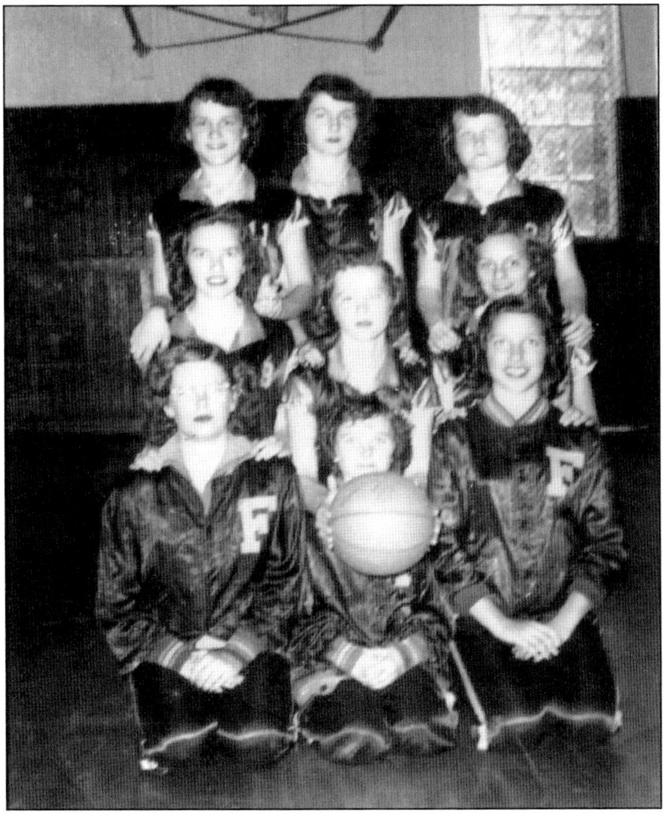

In 1953–1954, the last girls' basketball team at Friendship High School has gathered for this photograph. In 1954, Friendship High School closed, and students transferred to other schools. Shown here are, from left to right, (first row) Elba Pratt, Mary Roden, and Carol Autrey; (second row) Marta Beth Autrey, Patsy Mathews, and Virginia Collinsworth; (third row) Jo Ann Robinson, Jackie Usrey, and Betty Jean Robinson. (Courtesy of Pat Mathews.)

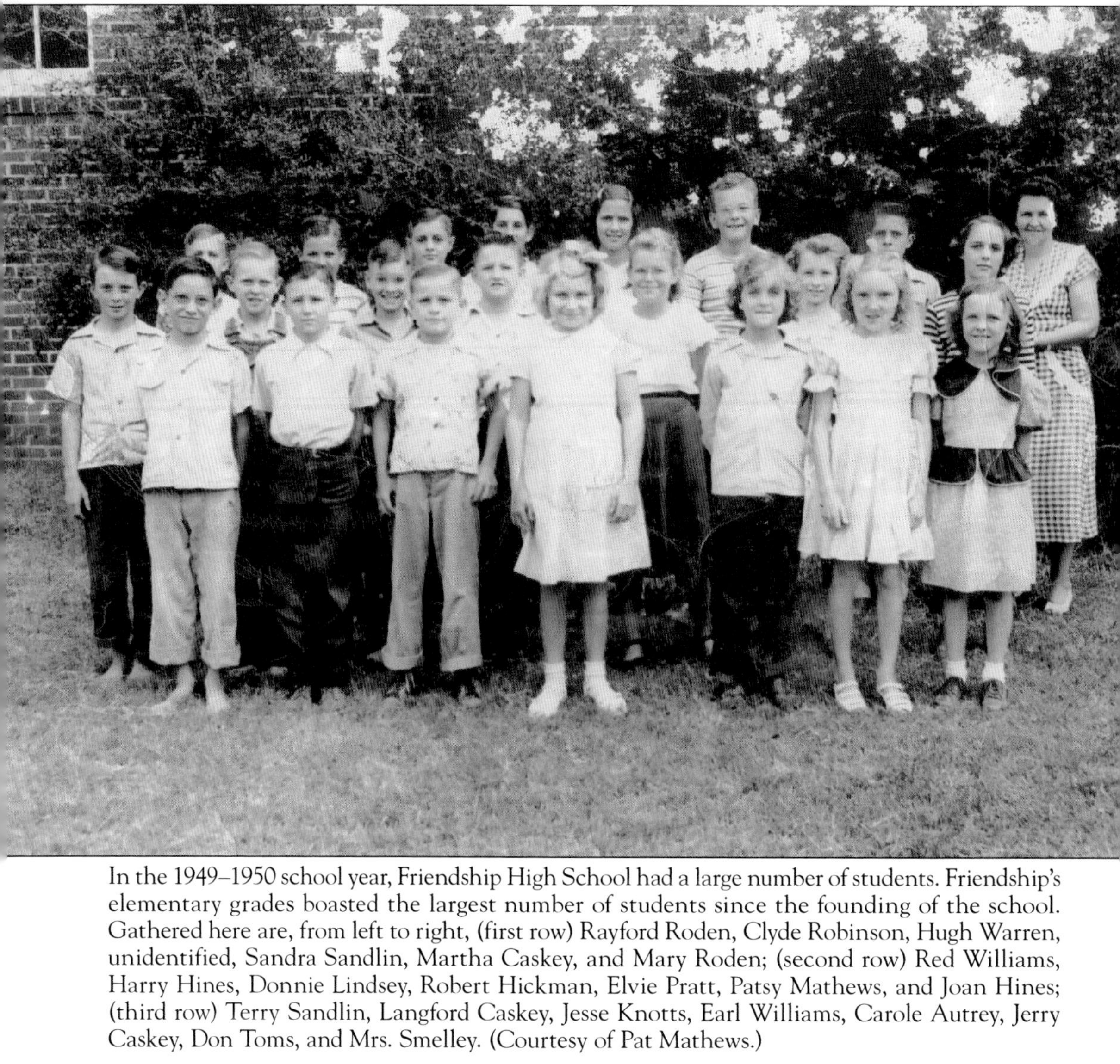

In the 1949–1950 school year, Friendship High School had a large number of students. Friendship's elementary grades boasted the largest number of students since the founding of the school. Gathered here are, from left to right, (first row) Rayford Roden, Clyde Robinson, Hugh Warren, unidentified, Sandra Sandlin, Martha Caskey, and Mary Roden; (second row) Red Williams, Harry Hines, Donnie Lindsey, Robert Hickman, Elvie Pratt, Patsy Mathews, and Joan Hines; (third row) Terry Sandlin, Langford Caskey, Jesse Knotts, Earl Williams, Carole Autrey, Jerry Caskey, Don Toms, and Mrs. Smelley. (Courtesy of Pat Mathews.)

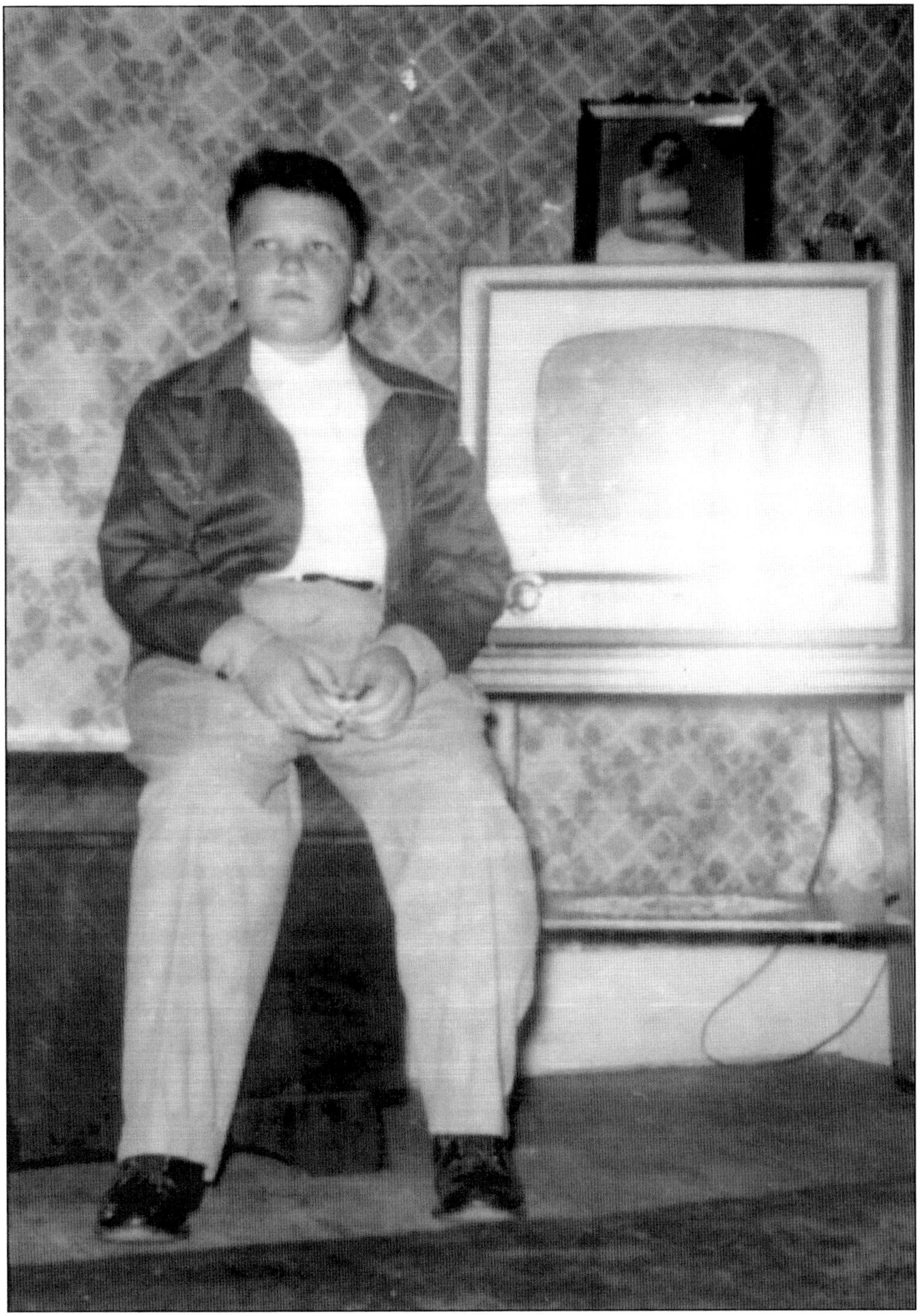

From 1920 until the early 1950s, radio was the primary home entertainment medium. By 1951, there were approximately 12 million television sets in American homes. Around 1953, William "Butch" Mathews sits beside the family's new Sylvania television that they bought from Buddy Hall's store in Friendship. Popular shows in 1953 included *I Love Lucy*, *Arthur Godfrey Time*, *Amos 'n' Andy*, and *Howdy Doody*. (Courtesy of Pat Mathews.)

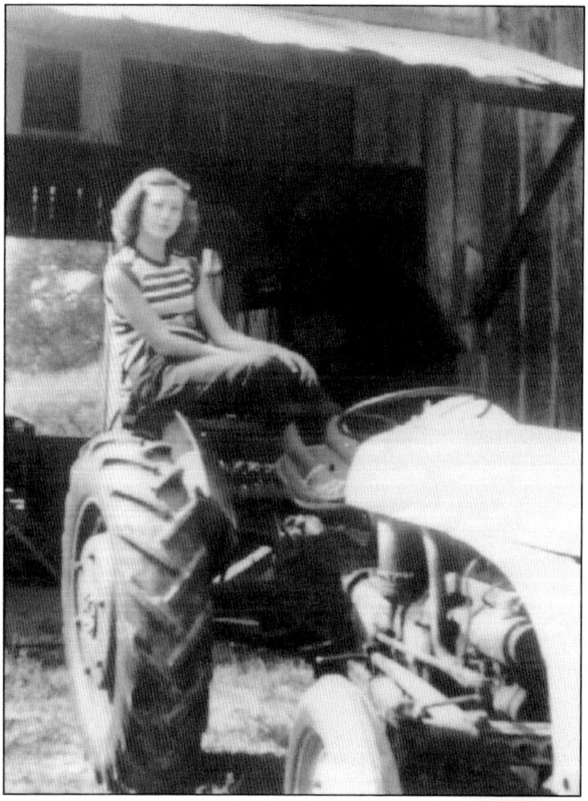

In the early 1950s, Pat Mathews poses on a tractor at Barron's Cotton Gin. Workers unloaded the trucks filled with cotton in a drive-through fashion. Trucks were driven into the gin, a vacuum system pulled the cotton up, and the empty trucks exited through the doorway where the tractor was parked. (Courtesy of Pat Mathews.)

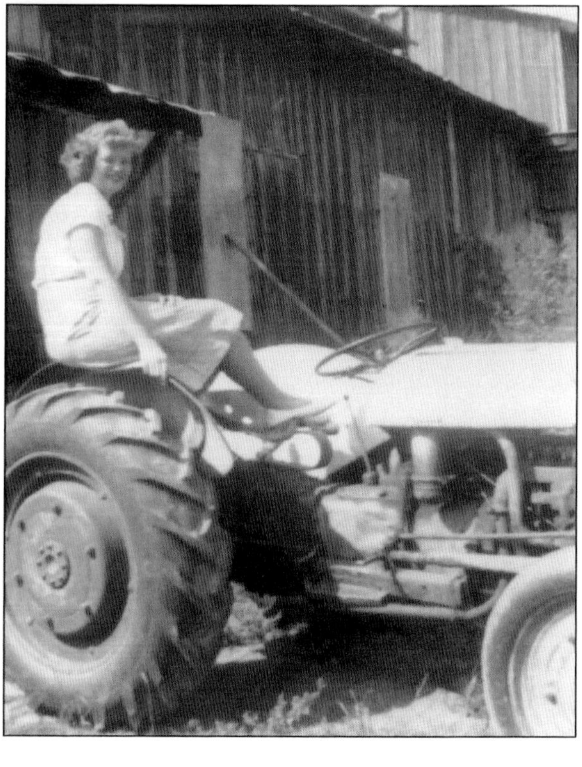

In the 1950s, Mary Ann Toms visited Pat Mathews at Barron's Cotton Gin, and they took turns posing for photographs. A gin (short for engine) separates the cotton fiber from the seeds. Until Eli Whitney's invention of the cotton gin in 1793, workers removed the seeds by hand. This photograph gives a better idea of the size of Barron's Cotton Gin. (Courtesy of Pat Mathews.)

The New Ramah community was located about a mile north of the parish line on Highway 153. In the 1880s, Ela Parker, a member of the community, poses with her guitar. In the early 1920s, the New Ramah School was consolidated with Ashland's school, and the community declined. New Ramah Road, also called Parish Road 620, marks the location of the New Ramah community. (Courtesy of Muriel Sullivan.)

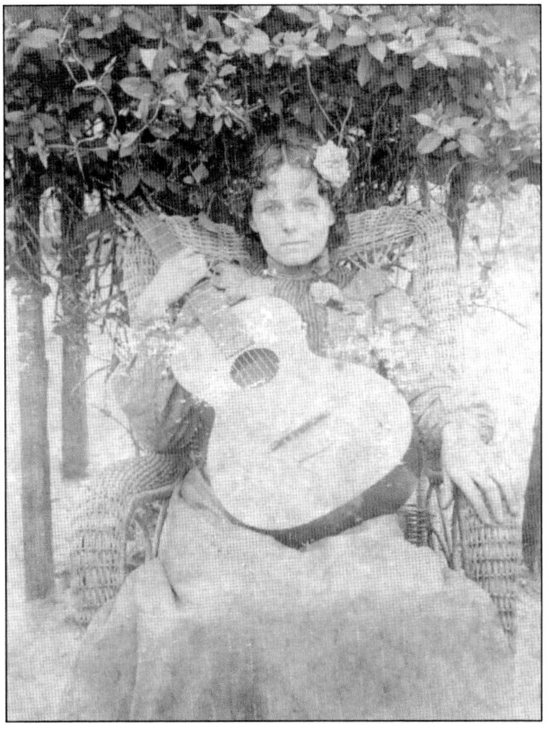

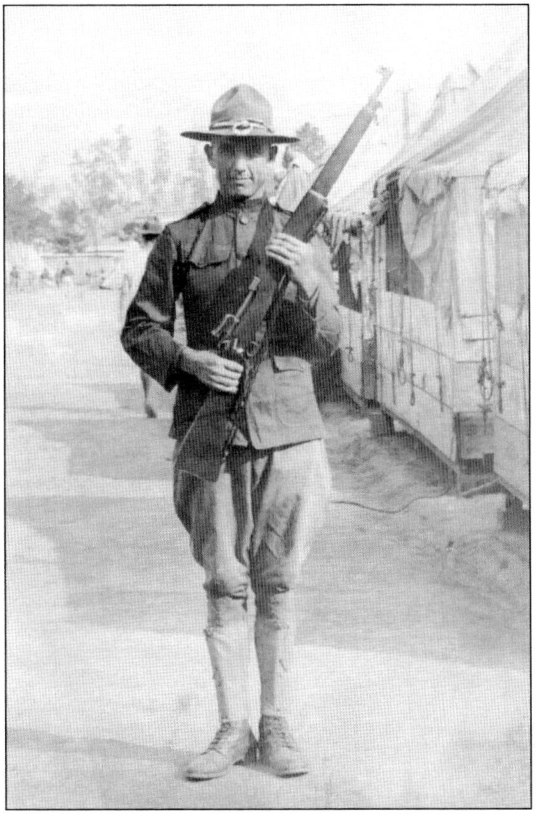

Young men from most small communities in Bienville Parish, including New Ramah, joined the military during World War I. At least two million soldiers died from diseases during the war. John Sullivan (pictured), a soldier from New Ramah, died from pneumonia while in basic training. (Courtesy of Muriel Sullivan.)

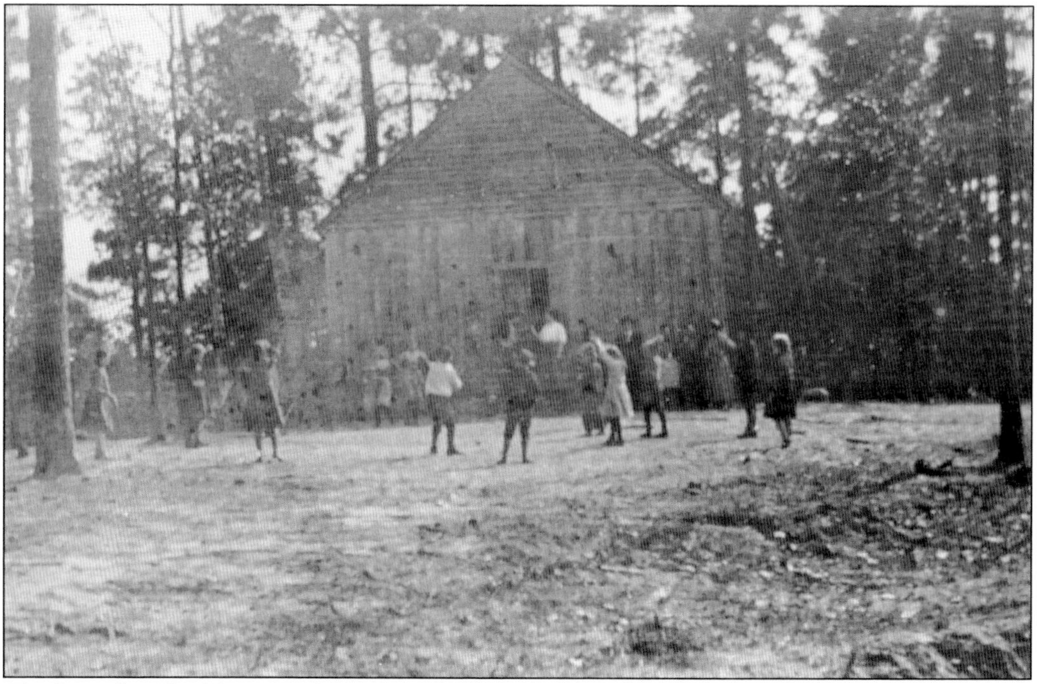

The first school building in Saline contained just two rooms. All students shared a single classroom, but they studied lessons based on their individual levels of education. E.S. Richardson, the first teacher at Saline, went on to become the superintendent of schools in Webster Parish. It would be another five years before Saline had a state-recognized school. (Courtesy of Bruce Evans.)

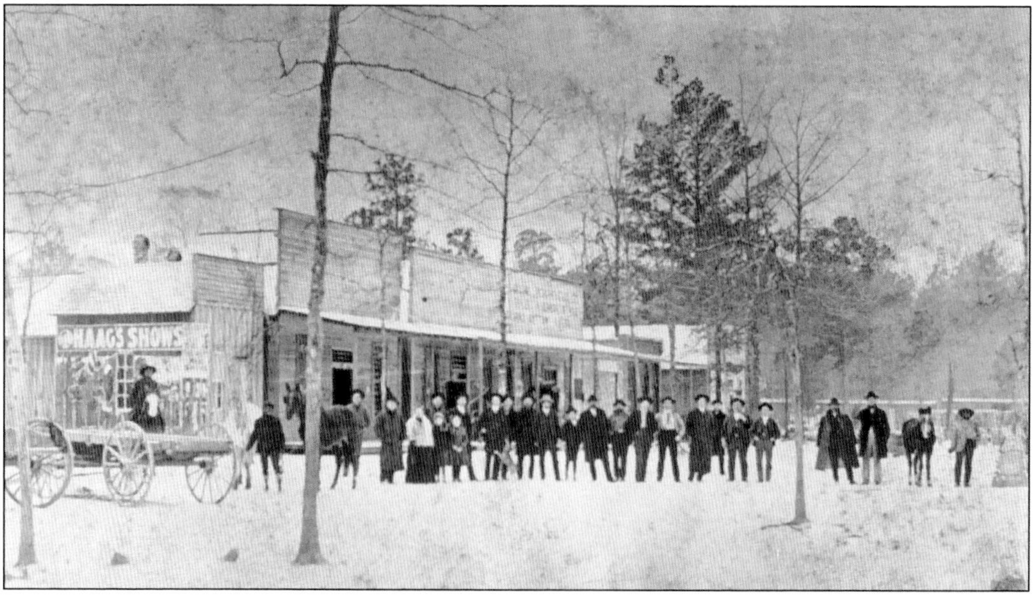

In 1903, settlers founded Saline along the path of the Louisiana & North West Railroad (L&NW). By 1904, businesses on the south side of Main Street include, from left to right, Jack Bishop's Barber Shop, Saline Post Office (Wiley Dorman, postmaster), Dr. McDonald's office, Saline Mercantile Company (Edgar Brown, manager), Bank of Saline, and McCoy & Frey Mercantile Store. L&NW boxcars are visible in the background. (Courtesy of Bruce Evans.)

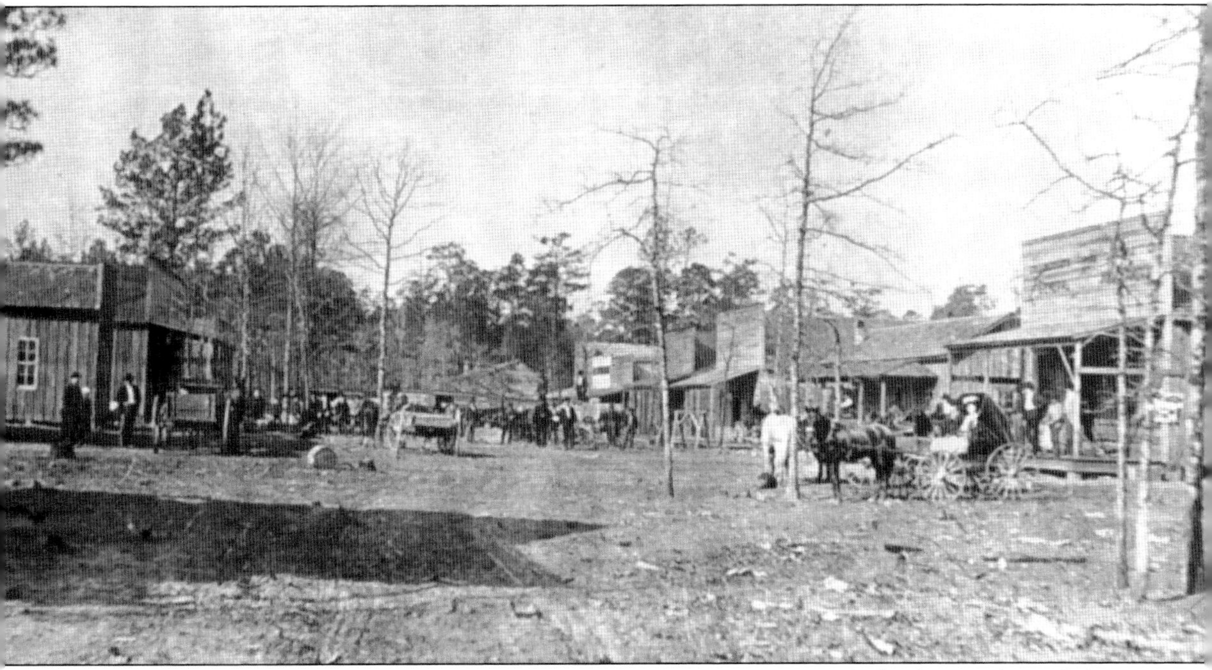

In the spring of 1905, businesses on the north side of Main Street include, from right to left, Rogers & Collingsworth Mercantile Company, Vance Hotel, Lewis Babers Mercantile Company, Tom Harper Mercantile Company, Lucky & Cooper Mercantile, Dr. Moore's office and drugstore, Jack Readhimer Drug Company, and McCoy's Gin (across the railroad tracks). John Black's livery stable is located on the south side of Main Street. (Courtesy of Bruce Evans.)

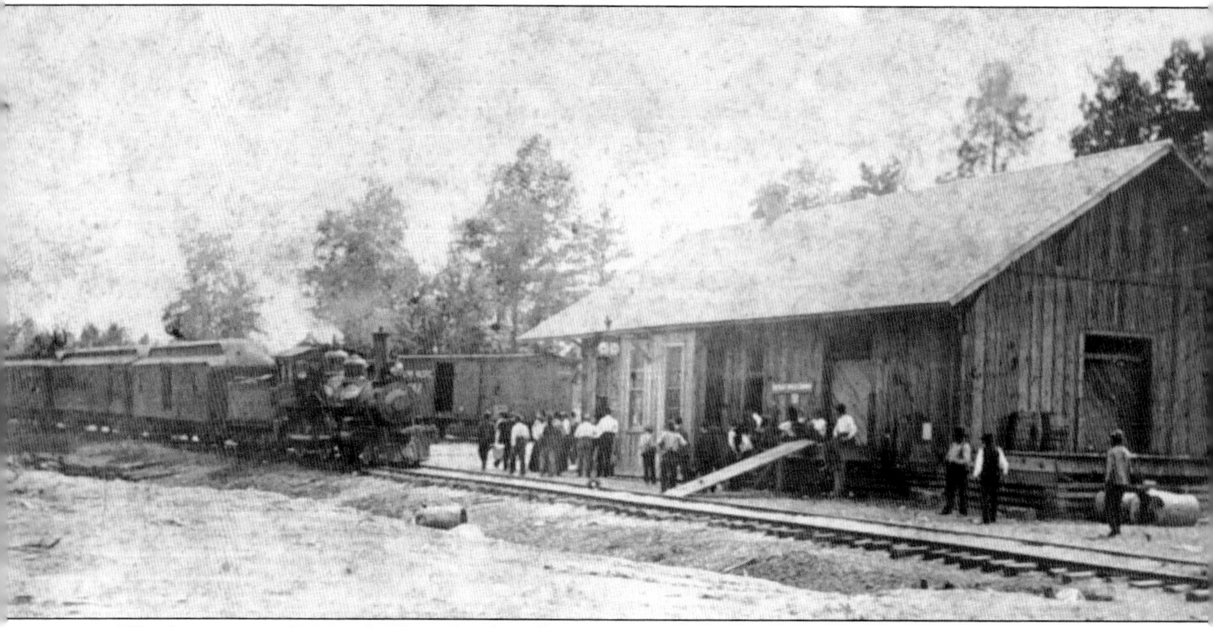

The Louisiana & North West Railroad transported passengers and freight to towns along the line, including Natchitoches, Grand Ecore, Hagen, Caspari, Howell, Creston, Chestnut, Strange, Saline, Lucky, Blume, Bienville, Bear Creek, Brice, Pratt, Gibsland, Darley, Athens, Mulnix, Homer, Camp, Haynesville, Arkansas State Line, Mohawk, Emerson, Brister, Kerlin, Magnolia, and McNeil. Many of these early railroad towns no longer exist. (Courtesy of Bruce Evans.)

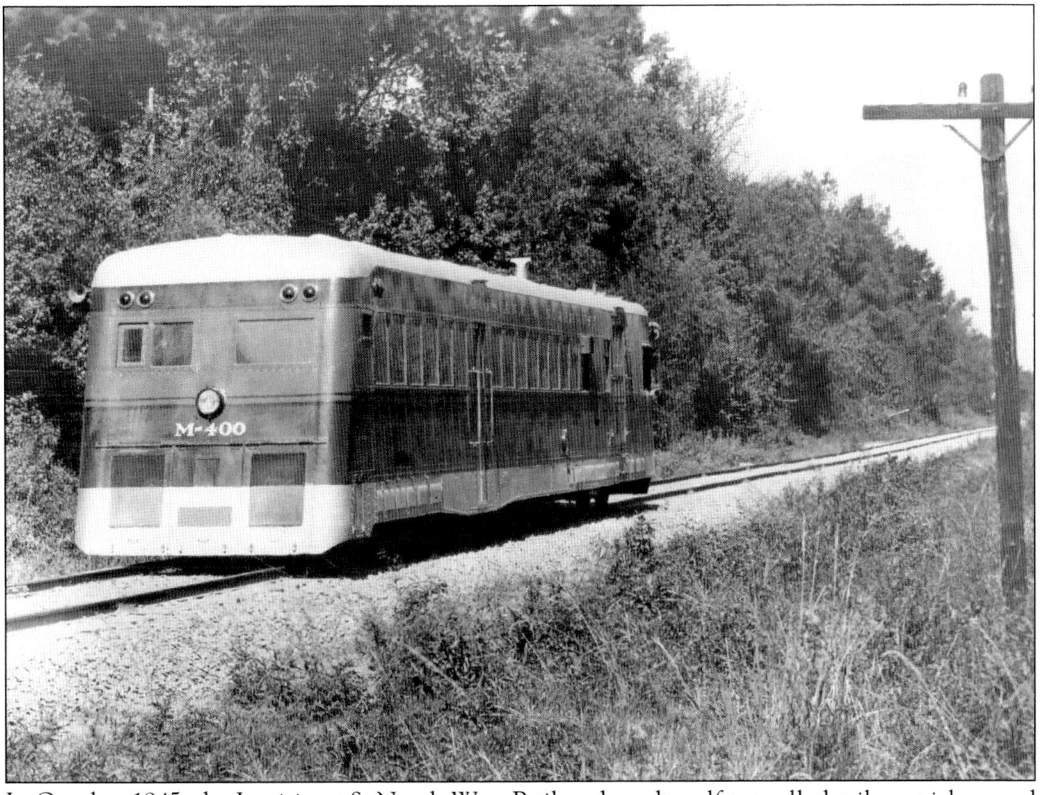

In October 1945, the Louisiana & North West Railroad used a self-propelled railcar, nicknamed the "Doodle" or "Doodlebug," as an inexpensive alternative to conventional multicar trains for transporting passengers and mail. In the 1940s, large passenger trains struggled to remain profitable as automobiles became the most popular method of transportation. The railcar's nickname derived from its similarity to the doodlebug insect. (Courtesy of Louisiana & North West Railroad.)

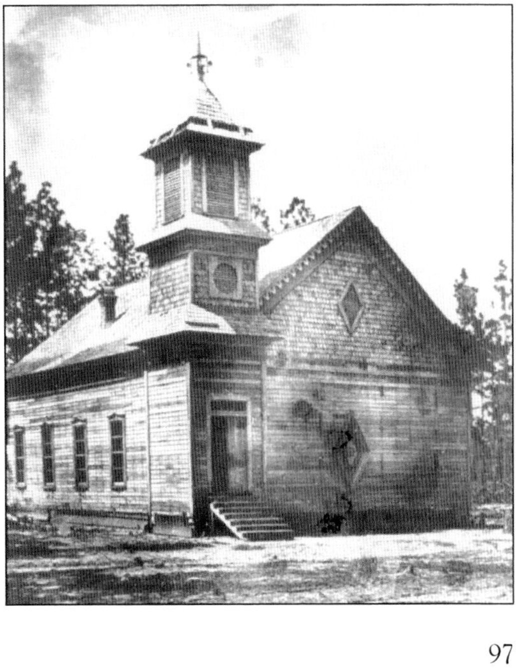

Early in 1904, the citizens of Saline formed Magnolia Baptist Church in an attempt to bring the community together, beyond what the local fraternal organizations achieved. Rev. J.H. Crosby, who was also a carpenter, completed the church building two years later. The congregation began with just 18 members, but by July 1932, it boasted a membership of around 300. (Courtesy of Bruce Evans.)

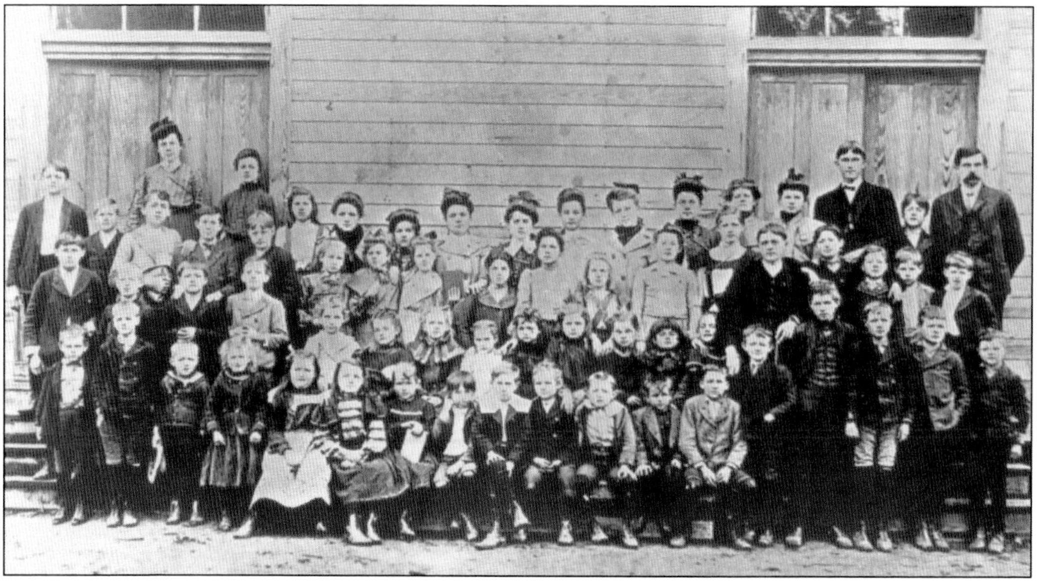

Less than five years after the first settlers built homes and businesses in Saline, the number of students in this 1906 photograph of Saline High School is evidence that the town was growing. Glass was a difficult product to transport on trains and wagons because of its fragile nature, which made it expensive. This is one possible explanation for the broken window in this photograph. (Courtesy of Bruce Evans.)

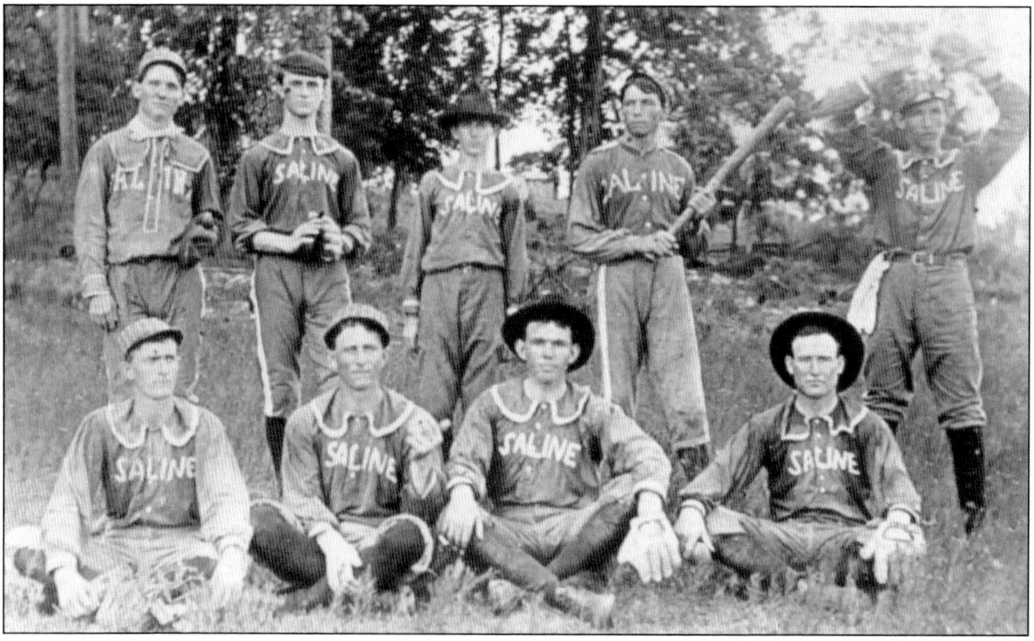

In 1907, during baseball's so-called dead-ball era, the Saline High School team includes, from left to right, (first row) Jim Madden, Less McChristian, A.D. Smith, and an unidentified player; (second row) Harvey Stewart, Will Cooper, D.Q. Madden, Bob Shively, and George Tait. At this time, baseballs were so expensive that only one was used per game. By the end of the game, the ball would be stained, misshapen, and lumpy—what players referred to as a "dead ball." (Courtesy of Bruce Evans.)

In 1903, J.T. Vance built the Vance Hotel. By 1907, the time of this photograph, Clarence Thomas owned the establishment, renamed the Thomas Hotel. It was destroyed by fire in 1913. Shown here are, from left to right, (on the steps) Percy, Eva, and Ezelle Thomas; (lower porch) unidentified boarder, Ruby Enloe, Eudie Enloe, A.H. Enloe, Zelma Enloe, Mr. and Mrs. Clarence Thomas, and unidentified boarder; (upper porch) George Lucky, Will Cooper, and Jack Keasler. (Courtesy of Bruce Evans.)

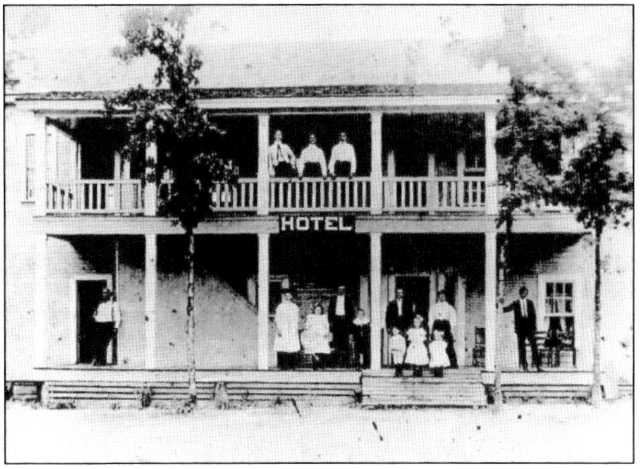

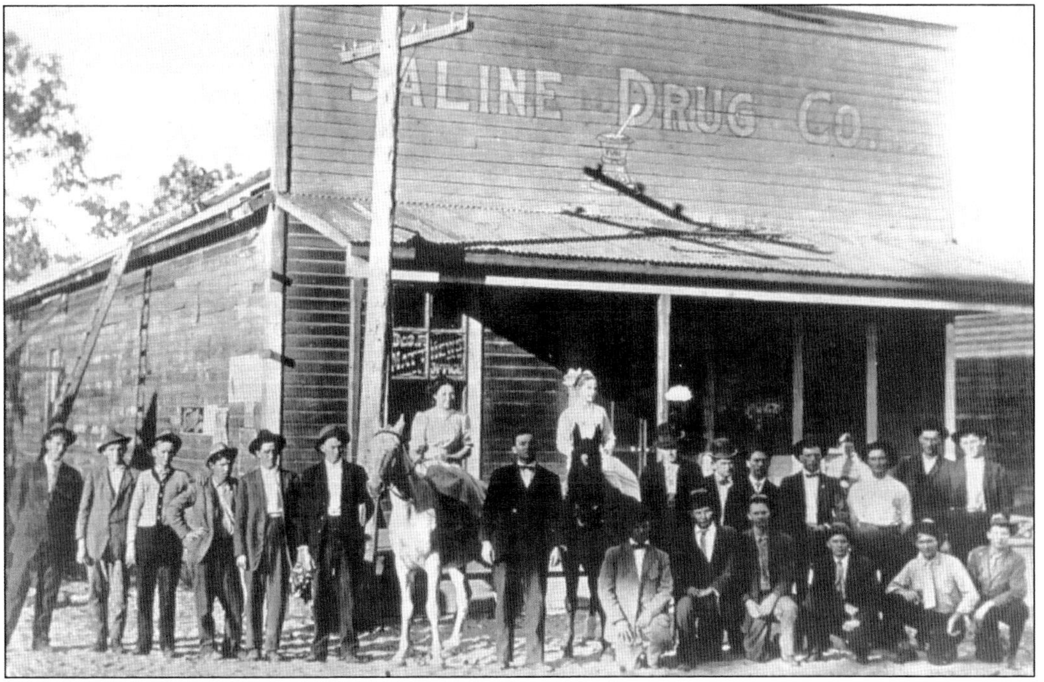

Located on the north side of Main Street, Dr. Matthews's office was inside the Saline Drug Company. Shown here are, from left to right, (kneeling) Wallace Rogers, A.I. Rhodes, T.B. Hood, Fed Hood, Willie Bishop, and Will Stinson; (standing) unidentified, Oscar Salter, Tal Mitchell, Alvin Bishop, Charlie Holman, Huey Thomas, Tom Godfrey, Dr. McDonald, owner Eugene Roger, Dr. O.F. Matthews, Joe Pullin, unidentified, C.C. Dison, and Lucius Corbitt; (on horseback) Ora Michael and Verta Moore. (Courtesy of Bruce Evans.)

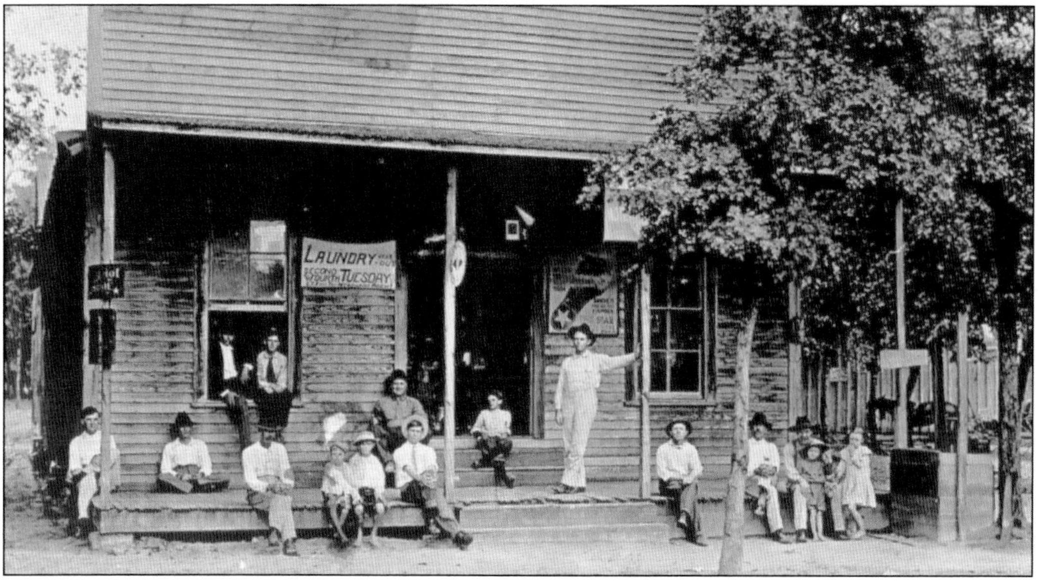

Seen here in 1909, L.T. Frey's Store sold general merchandise and offered a send-out laundry service. Dr. Matthews and Doyle Frey are seated in the window. The other adults include, from left to right, M.O. Collingsworth, George Smith, J.B. Still, Wiley Pullin, Harold Pullin, Emmett Moore, W.F. Frey, Mason McCody, A.D. Smith, Mr. Whittington, L.T. Frey, Mr. Jackson. The names of the children are not known. (Courtesy of Bruce Evans.)

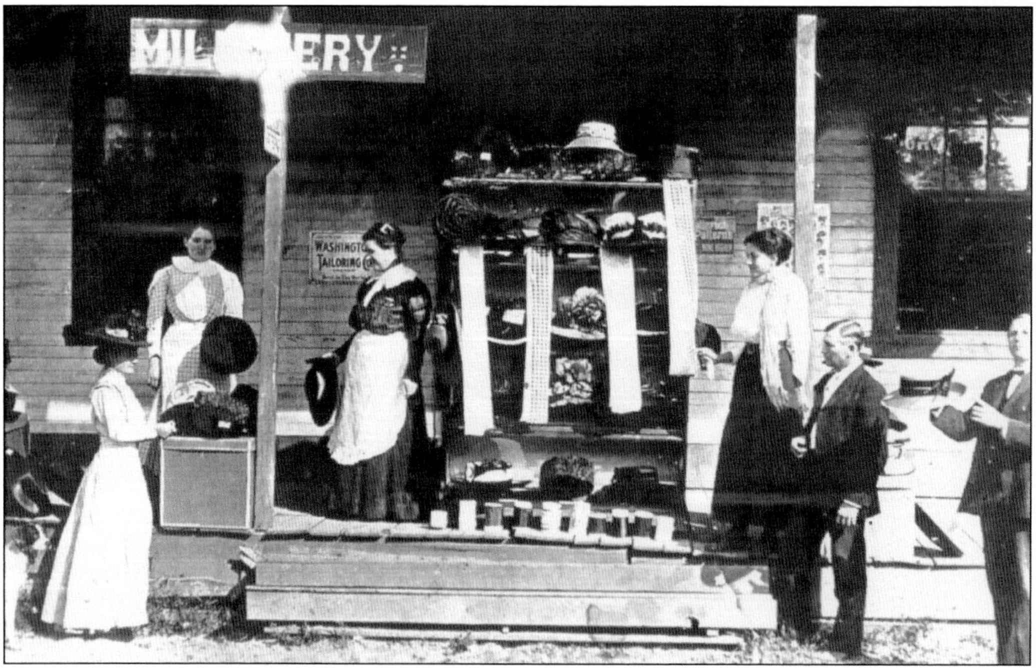

Mrs. Clarence Thomas operated a millinery shop on the south side of Main Street in Saline until it burned down on December 2, 1920. On this afternoon in 1909, Mrs. Thomas displays her wares to prospective customers. Millinery shops were almost always owned by women, who used fabrics and other items sold in the shop to create shirts, aprons, neckerchiefs, caps, hats, cloaks, hoods, and trim for gowns. (Courtesy of Bruce Evans.)

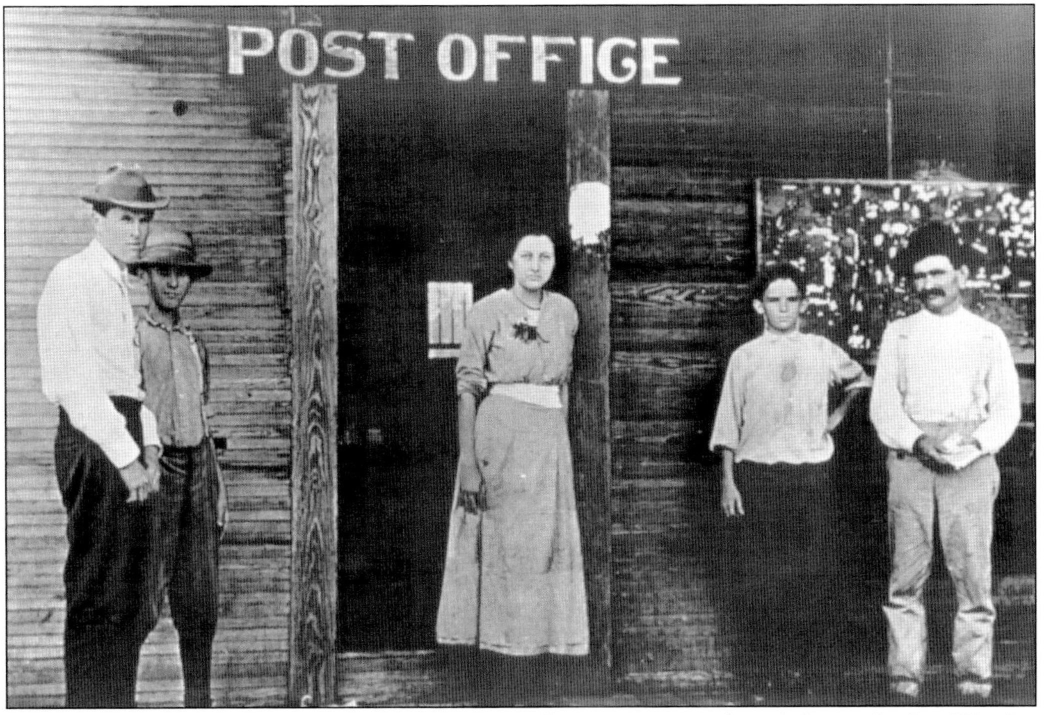

Posing for a photograph outside the Saline Post Office in 1909 are, from left to right, Jim Wright, Bob Terrell, postmistress Nena Evans, Mason McCoy, and Sam Hennigan. Evans married Billy Montgomery four years later. He was the postmaster at Saline from 1940 to 1963. The post office was located on the north side of Main Street in Saline. (Courtesy of Bruce Evans.)

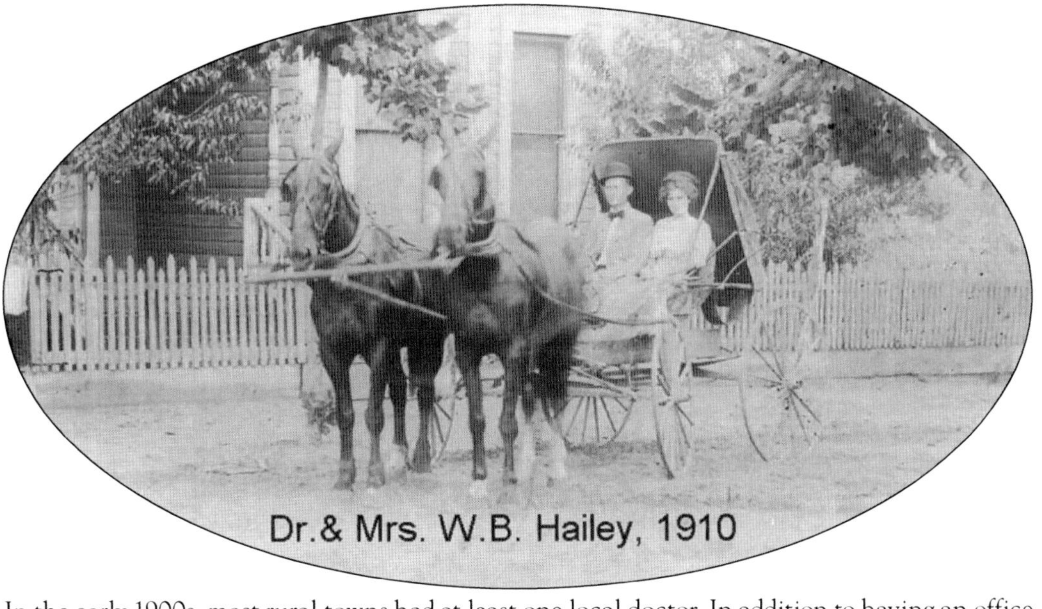

In the early 1900s, most rural towns had at least one local doctor. In addition to having an office in town, Dr. W.B. Hailey made house calls to tend to the sick, deliver babies, set broken bones, and perform minor surgeries. Being the doctor in a rural town meant that he was always on call. (Courtesy of Bruce Evans.)

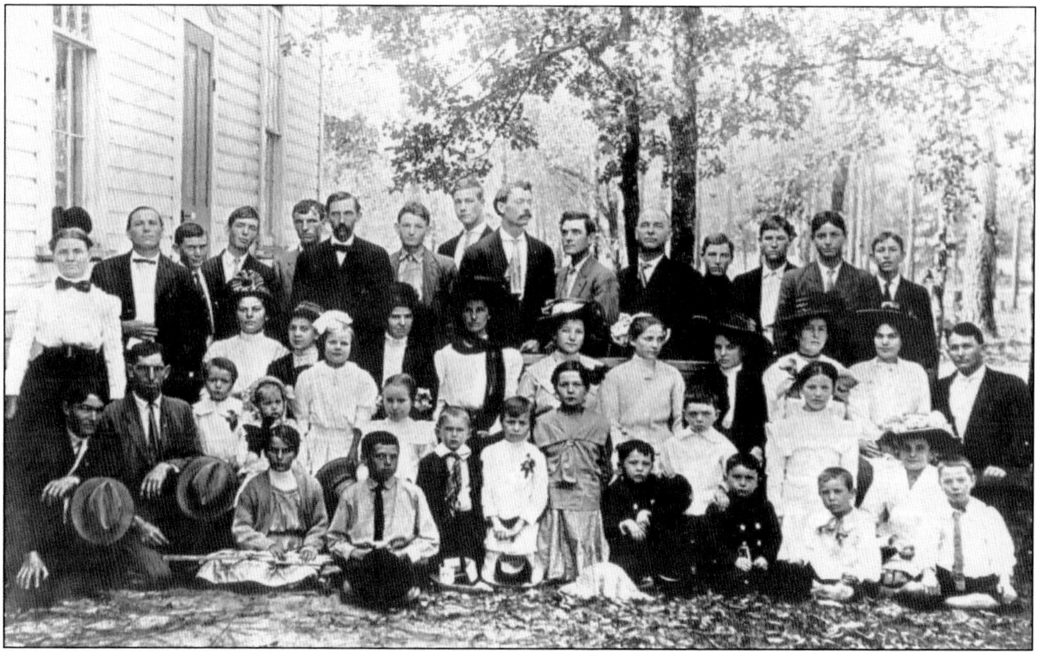

Magnolia Baptist Church's Sunday school classes has gathered for this photograph six years after the church was completed. Regardless of the clothes they wore during the week, churchgoers reserved their best clothing for Sunday. For women, Sunday best meant dresses and hats. Men wore full suits and hats. Children also wore their best clothing to church. (Courtesy of Bruce Evans.)

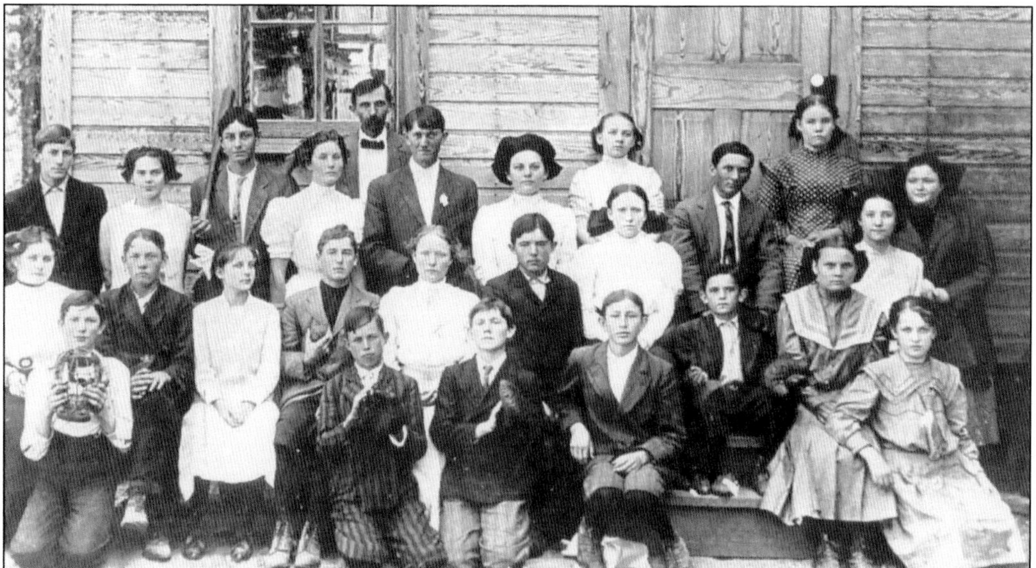

The last full school year for the original school building was 1911. The student body had grown to a point that the one-room school was no longer practical. Most of the boys participated in baseball, as is evident by the equipment many are shown with here. (Courtesy of Bruce Evans.)

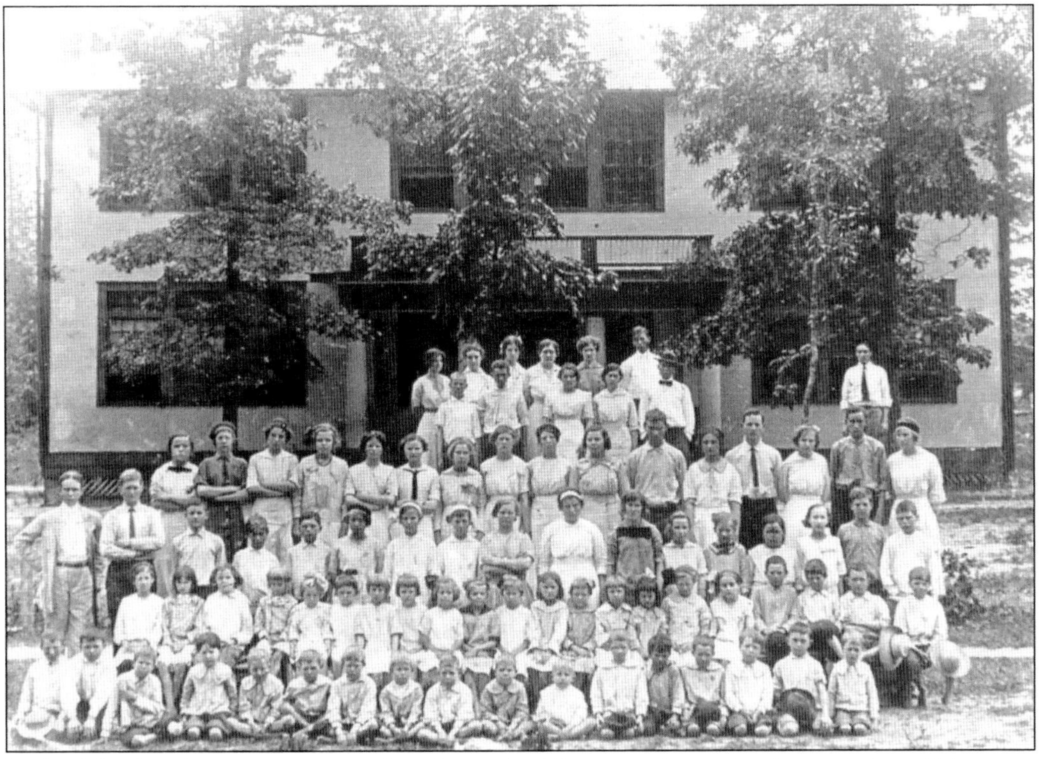

In the fall of 1911, construction workers began building a modern school, consisting of 11 rooms. By the fall of the 1912–1913 school year, when this photograph was taken, the new school was in full operation. This building served the community until it was destroyed by fire in November 1927. (Courtesy of Bruce Evans.)

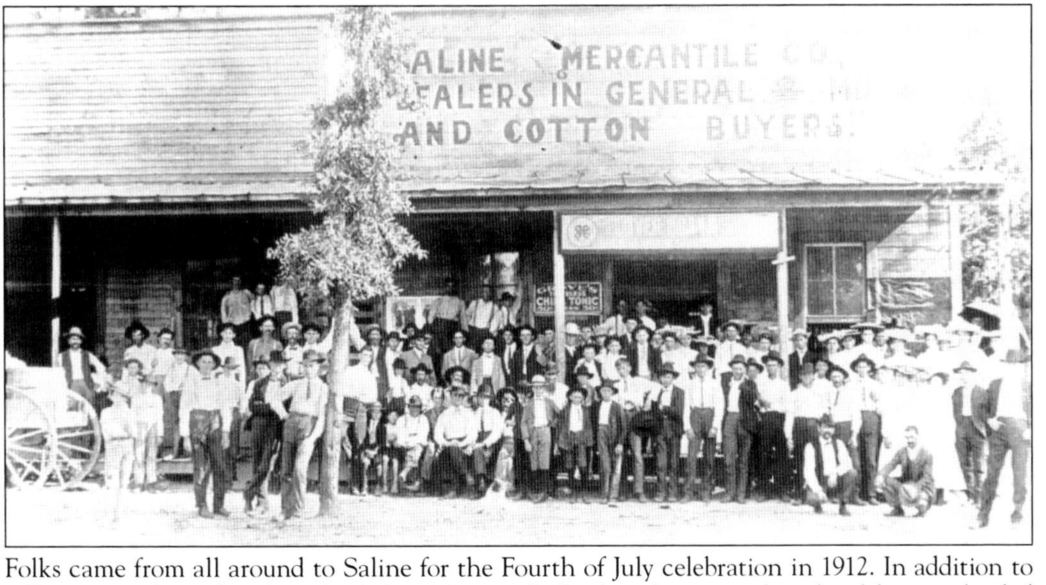

Folks came from all around to Saline for the Fourth of July celebration in 1912. In addition to selling general merchandise, the Saline Mercantile Co. bought cotton from local farmers, loaded it onto trains, and shipped it to large cotton centers like New Orleans and Atlanta. From there, it was transported to textile factories around the world. (Courtesy of Bruce Evans.)

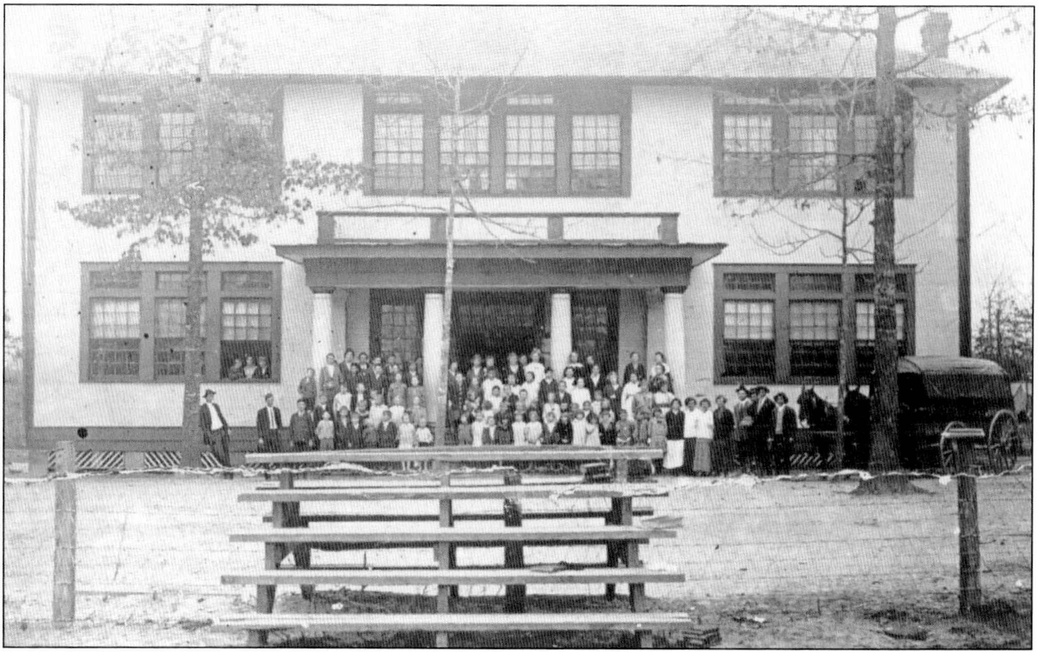

Saline High School students pose for a photograph in front of the school around 1915. The school was enclosed by a fence to keep livestock out, but students had a hard time keeping the front gate closed. School officials solved the problem when they removed the gate and built steps, which enabled students and faculty to safely climb over the fence, but kept livestock out. (Courtesy of Bruce Evans.)

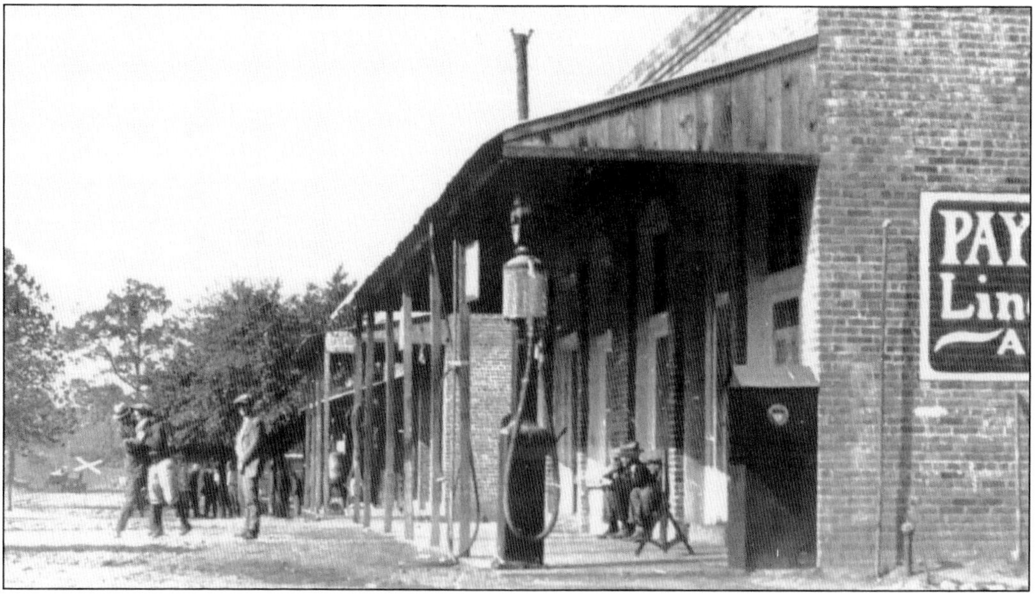

In 1923, most roads in Bienville Parish were in bad condition. The quality of roads improved as automobiles became more affordable and, thus, more numerous. With a small deposit, customers of Payton Motor Company ordered their cars from the factory in Detroit, Michigan. The automobiles were transported to Saline on the L&NW Railroad. In 1923, the price of Ford automobiles ranged from $269 to $595. (Courtesy of Bruce Evans.)

The Payton Motor Company sold Lincoln and Ford automobiles, auto parts, and gasoline on Main Street in Saline. Payton Motor also had a full-service shop to repair automobiles. In 1923, one of the Payton children waits to help the next customer. Whereas Fords sold for as little as $269, Lincoln custom automobiles cost as much as $7,200. (Courtesy of Bruce Evans.)

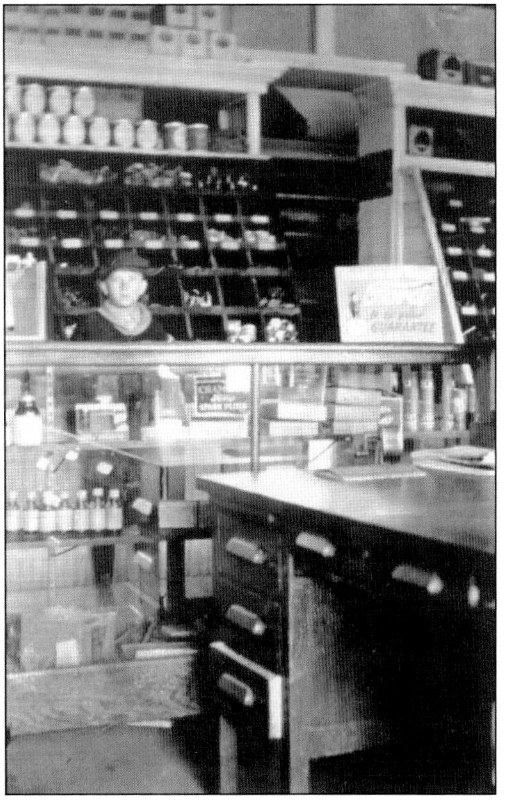

By 1923, the time of this photograph, automobiles were common in Saline, but they had not yet completely replaced horses. In the distance, a farmer who had not yet converted to the automobile can be seen driving his horse and wagon away from town. Dirt roads made automobile travel difficult. Cars struggled through the muddy roads following rains. When the streets were dry, enormous dust clouds surrounded automobiles. (Courtesy of Bruce Evans.)

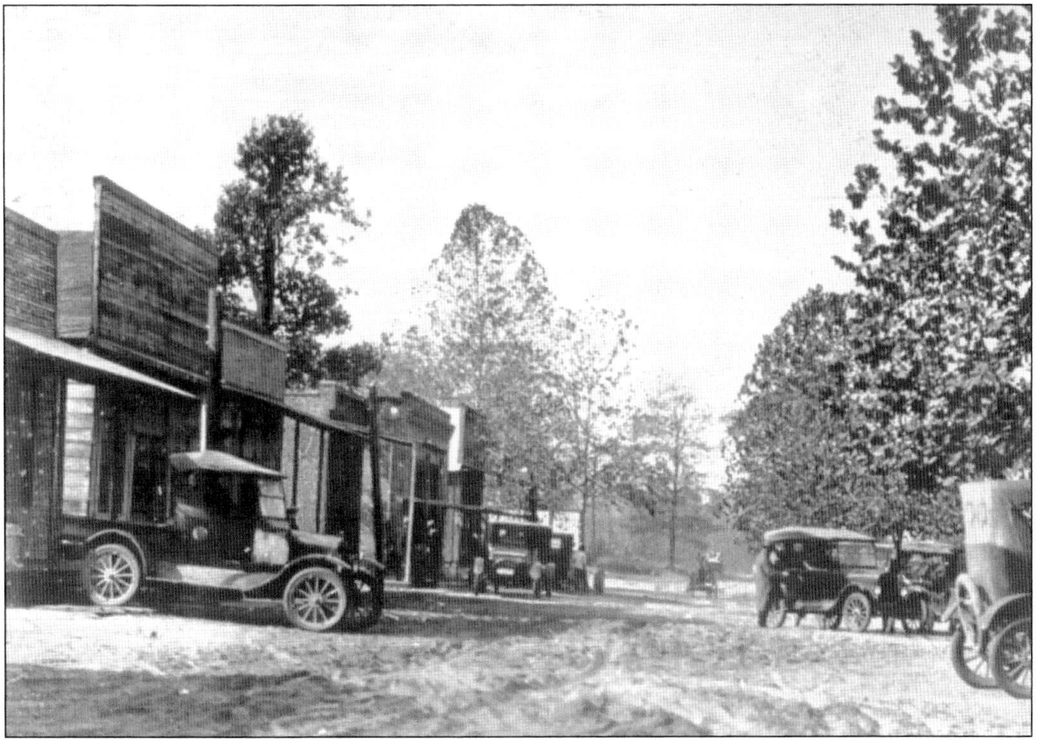

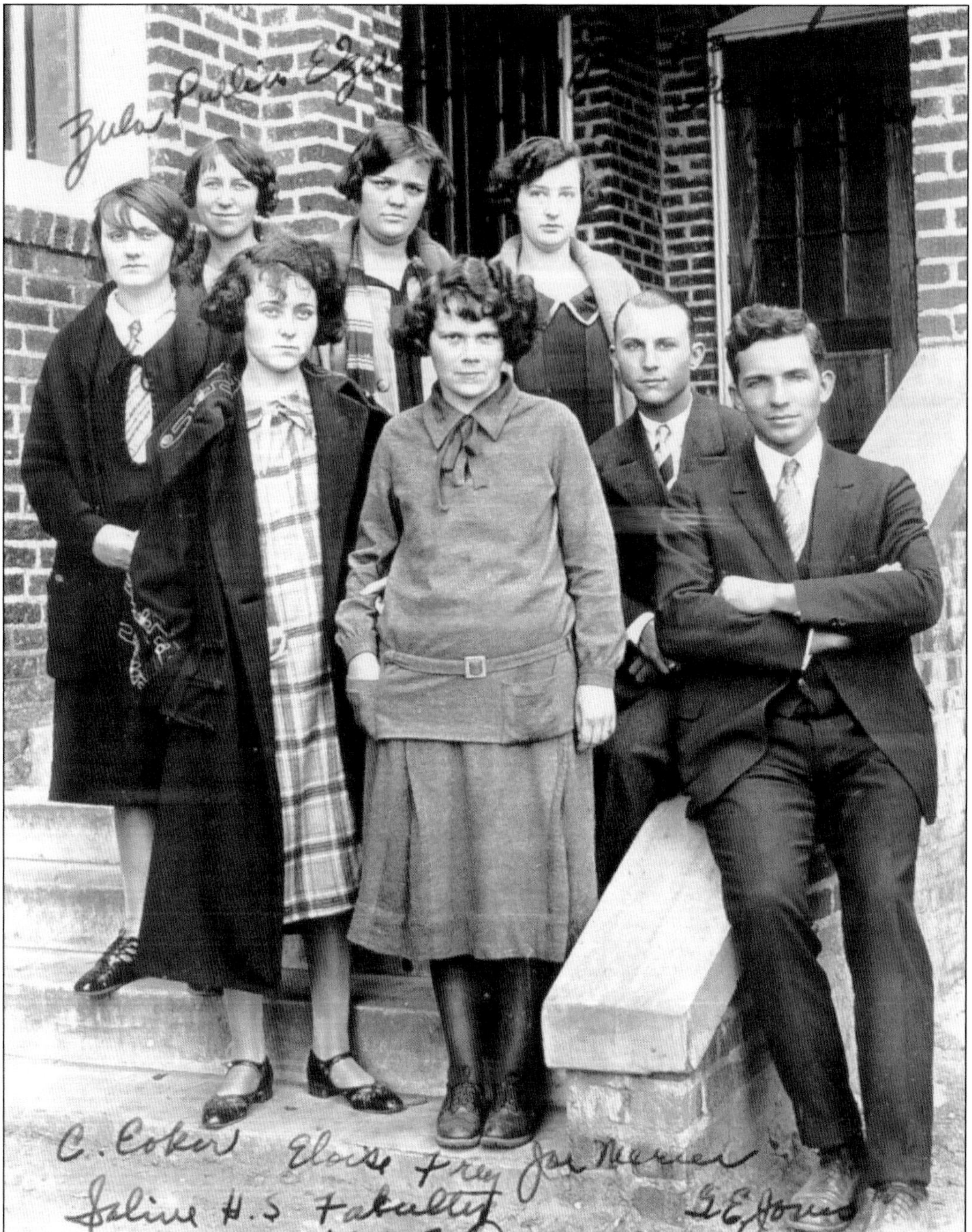

The 1925–1926 Saline High School faculty includes, from left to right, (front row) Constance Coker (primary school), Eloise Frey (foreign language and science), Joe Mercer (history and English), and principal G.E. Jones; (back row) Zula Pullin, Eselle King (second and third grades), Josephine "Jo" Houck (fourth and fifth grades), and Gladys Bayes. In addition to serving as Saline's principal from 1925 to 1934, Jones taught mathematics. (Courtesy of Bruce Evans.)

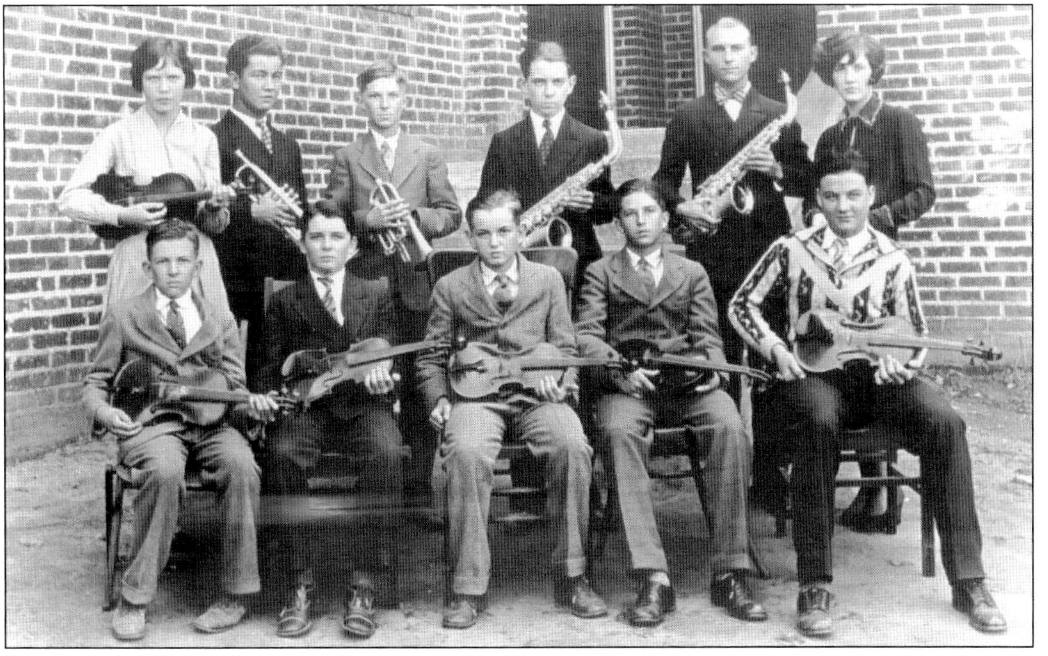

Photographed in 1927, the Saline High School orchestra consists of, from left to right, (seated) Claude Montgomery, Wilburn Rogers, A.D. Smith Jr., Wilson Payton, and Edwin Payton; (standing) Flora Mae Singleton, Earl Weaver Jr., Mason Payton, George Rogers, Joe Mercer, and Irene Lucky. Rogers later served as principal at Saline High School, from 1938 to 1966. (Courtesy of Bruce Evans.)

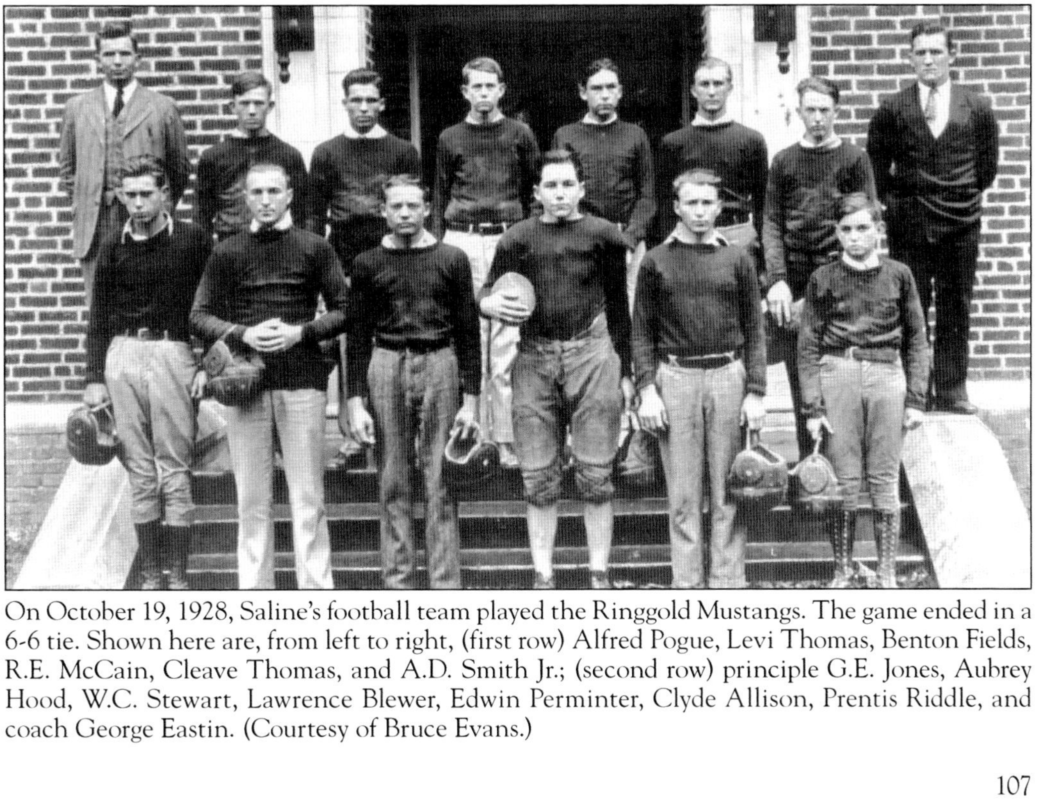

On October 19, 1928, Saline's football team played the Ringgold Mustangs. The game ended in a 6-6 tie. Shown here are, from left to right, (first row) Alfred Pogue, Levi Thomas, Benton Fields, R.E. McCain, Cleave Thomas, and A.D. Smith Jr.; (second row) principle G.E. Jones, Aubrey Hood, W.C. Stewart, Lawrence Blewer, Edwin Perminter, Clyde Allison, Prentis Riddle, and coach George Eastin. (Courtesy of Bruce Evans.)

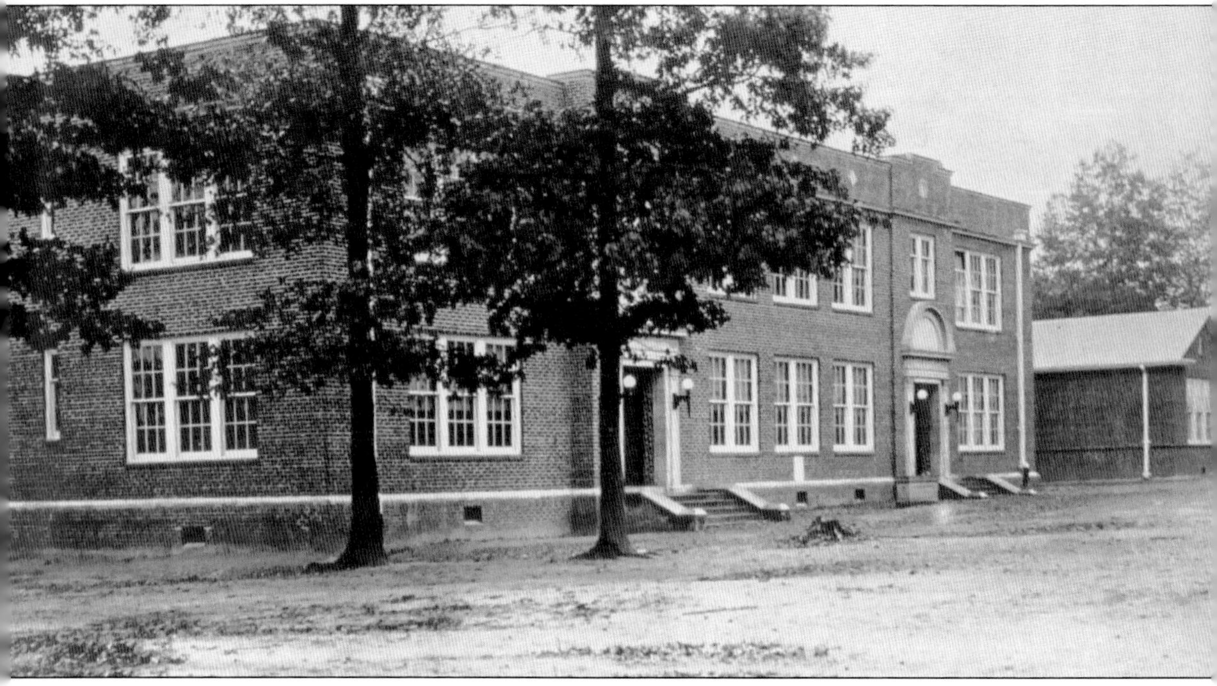

The newly constructed high school, shown here in 1928, replaced the one destroyed by fire. It served the community until 1974, when it too was consumed by fire. The building at right had been attached to the previous school by a covered walkway. While the fire was consuming the school, a concerned citizen connected a cable to the covered walkway and his truck. He continued to pull until the buildings were disconnected, thus saving the smaller structure from the flames. It is still used as a classroom today. (Courtesy of Bruce Evans.)

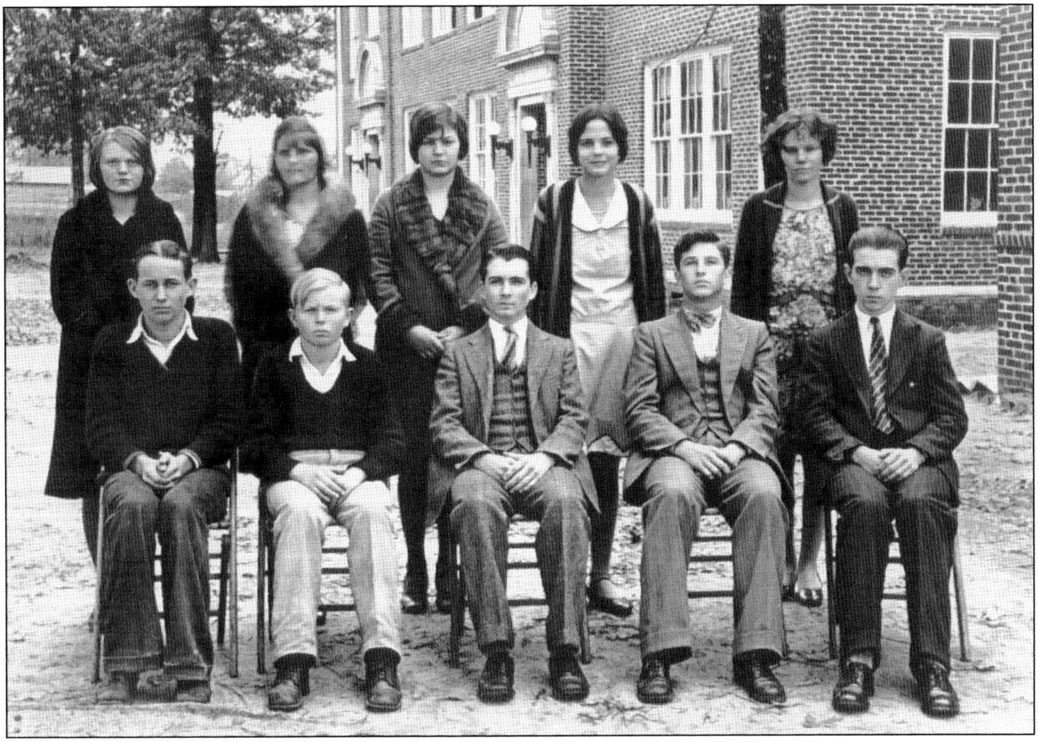

In 1929, Saline High School's choir includes, from left to right, (first row) Slayton Hennigan, Wayne Toms, Wilburn Rogers, Wilson Payton, and George Rogers; (second row) Mamie Fields, Ollie Dison, Pauline Payton, Myrtle Crawford, and Muriel Sullivan, The choir participated in programs throughout the parish, performing hymns and folk songs. (Courtesy of Bruce Evans.)

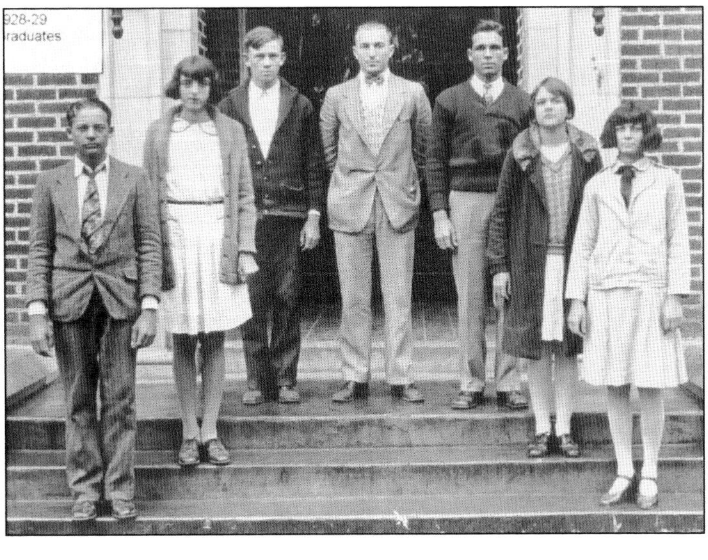

Saline High School's graduating class of 1928–1929 consisted of just seven students. They are, from left to right, Benton Fields, Lorraine Caskey, Aubrey Hood, Levi Thomas, W.C. Stewart, Christel Walters, and Verta Trussel. In 1910, only about 10 percent of Americans had a high school education. By 1935, the number had grown to 40 percent. Few rural Southerners went beyond the eighth grade until the 1940s. (Courtesy of Bruce Evans.)

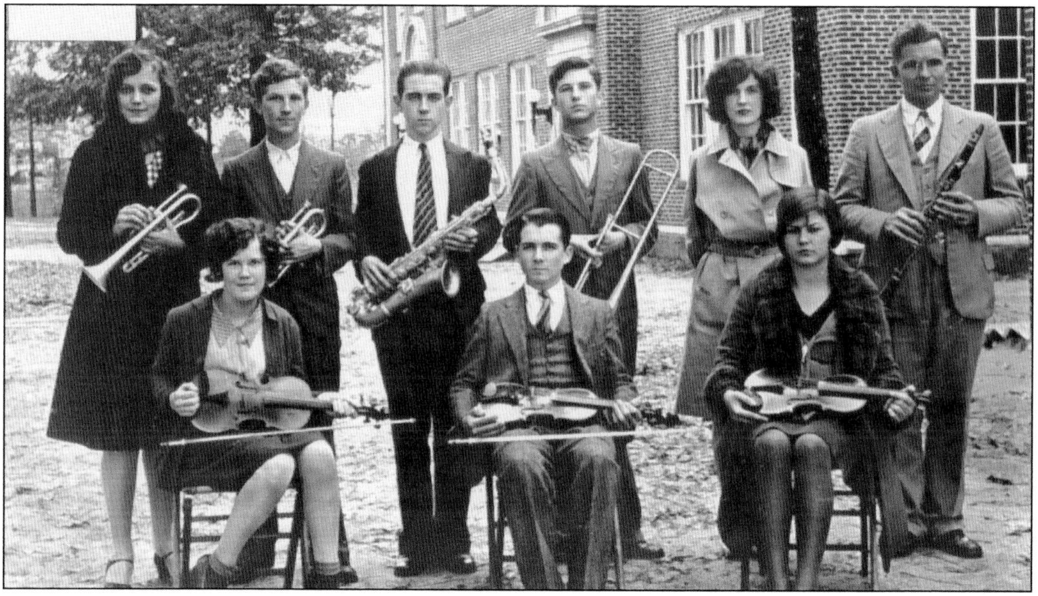

The 1929 Saline High School orchestra has gathered for a photograph. Shown are, from left to right, (seated) Ethel Singleton, Wilburn Rogers, and Pauline Payton; (standing) Lillian Krousel, Mason Payton, George Rogers, Wilson Payton, Irene Lucky, and principal G.E. Jones. Following World War I, professional and military orchestras declined, and instrument makers desperately sought a new market for sales. Schools increasingly added music to their curricula, and manufacturers began to build a new market base. (Courtesy of Bruce Evans.)

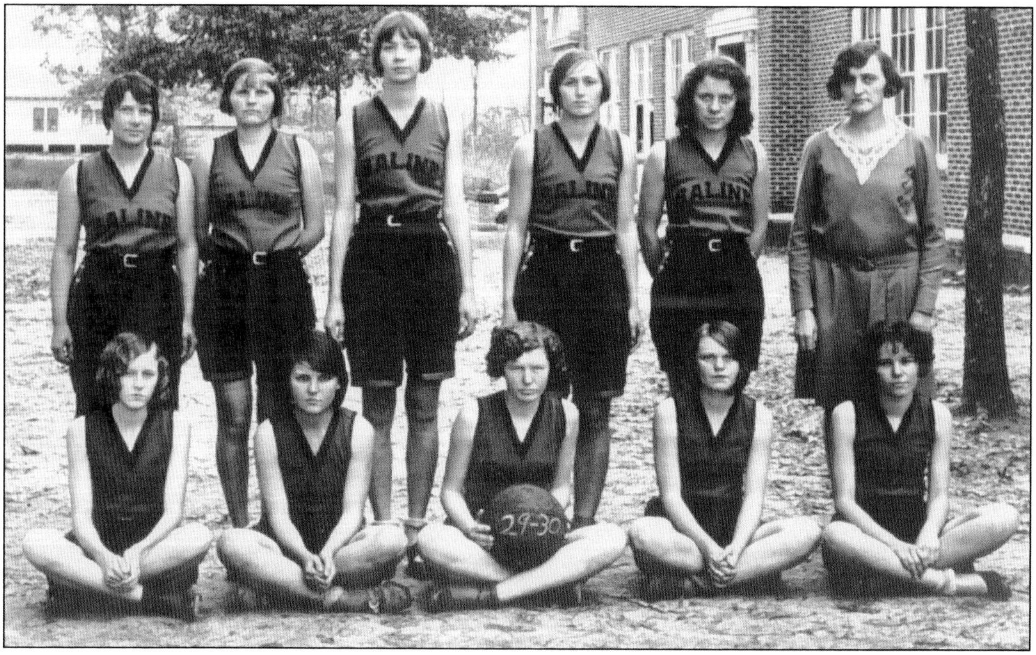

The 1929–1930 Saline High School girls' basketball team consists of, from left to right, (seated) Lenora Rivers, Wilmar Sample, Ola D. Watts, Mamie Fields, and Muriel Sullivan; (standing) Marie Madden, Ollie Dison, Irene Frey, Juanita Allison, Dorothy Walker, and coach Maggie Mae Hortman. (Courtesy of Bruce Evans.)

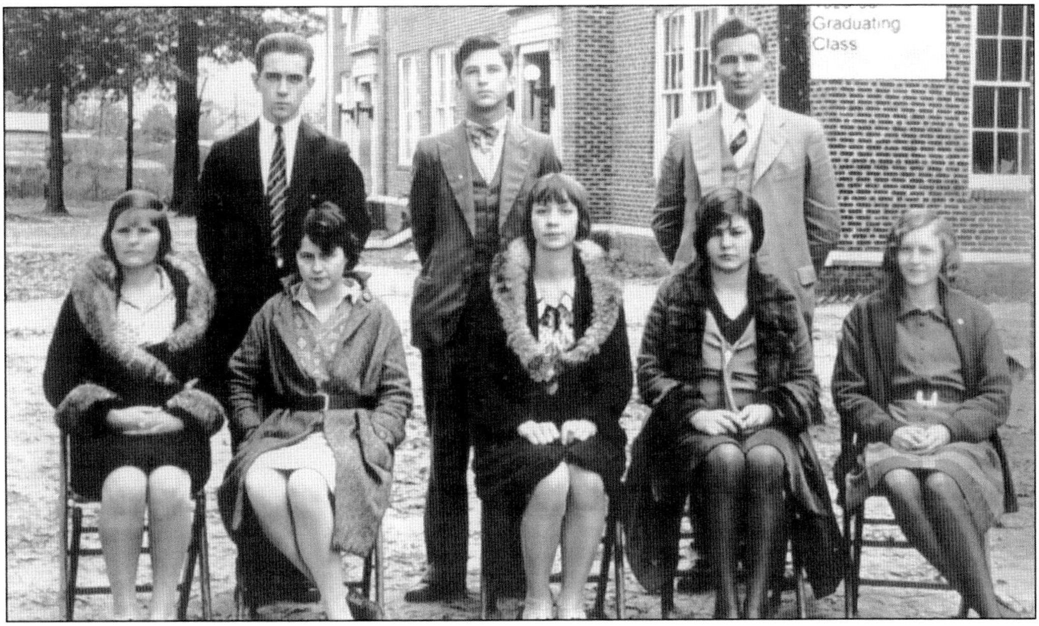

In 1930, principal G.E. Jones and the graduating class of Saline High School pose for a photograph. Pictured are, from left to right, (seated) Ollie Dison, Grace Windgate, Irene Frey, Pauline Payton, and Lenora Rivers; (standing) George Rogers, Wilson Payton, and Jones. Rogers went on to serve as principal at Saline High School from 1938 to 1966. (Courtesy of Bruce Evans.)

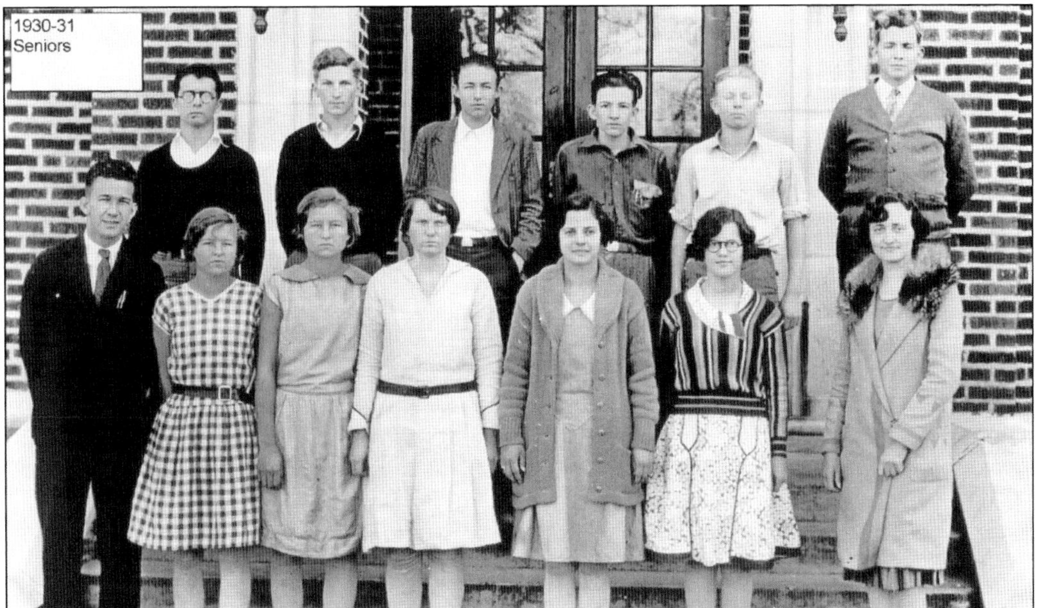

The graduating class of 1931 was slightly larger than that of the previous year. Posing here are the senior class and some of Saline's faculty. Shown are, from left to right, (first row) assistant principal George Strickler, Rugh Humphrey, Ruby Humphrey, Lucille Dison, Myrtle Crawford, Ethel Singleton, and teacher Maggie Mae Hortman; (second row) Wilburn Rogers, Mayson Payton, Vester Williams, Claude Montgomery, Wayne Toms, and principal G.E. Jones. (Courtesy of Bruce Evans.)

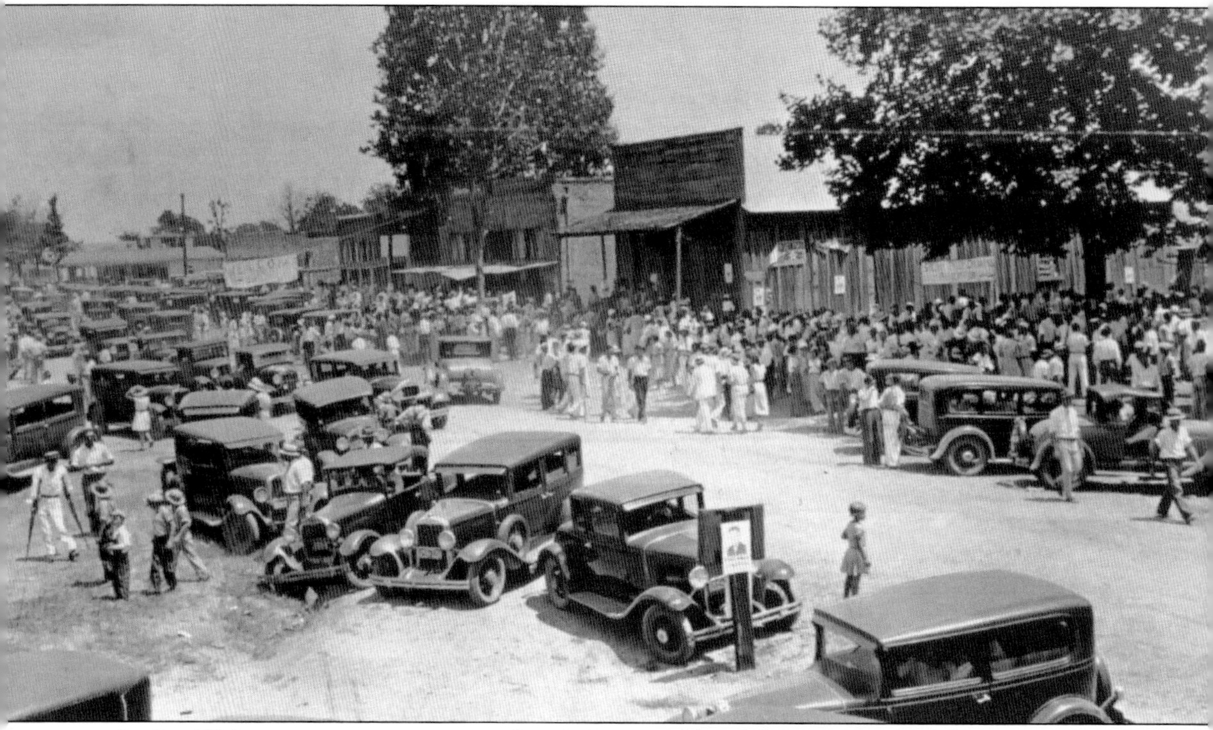

In the 1920s, cotton prices continued to decline, and local farmers searched for more profitable crops. They created the Saline Dairy & Truck Growers Association and diversified their yields, growing fruits and vegetables—most notably, watermelons. The annual Watermelon Festival celebrated the harvest. Saline became known for watermelon production, shipping the summertime staple worldwide. Customers included Pres. Franklin Roosevelt and King George V of the United Kingdom. (Courtesy of Bruce Evans.)

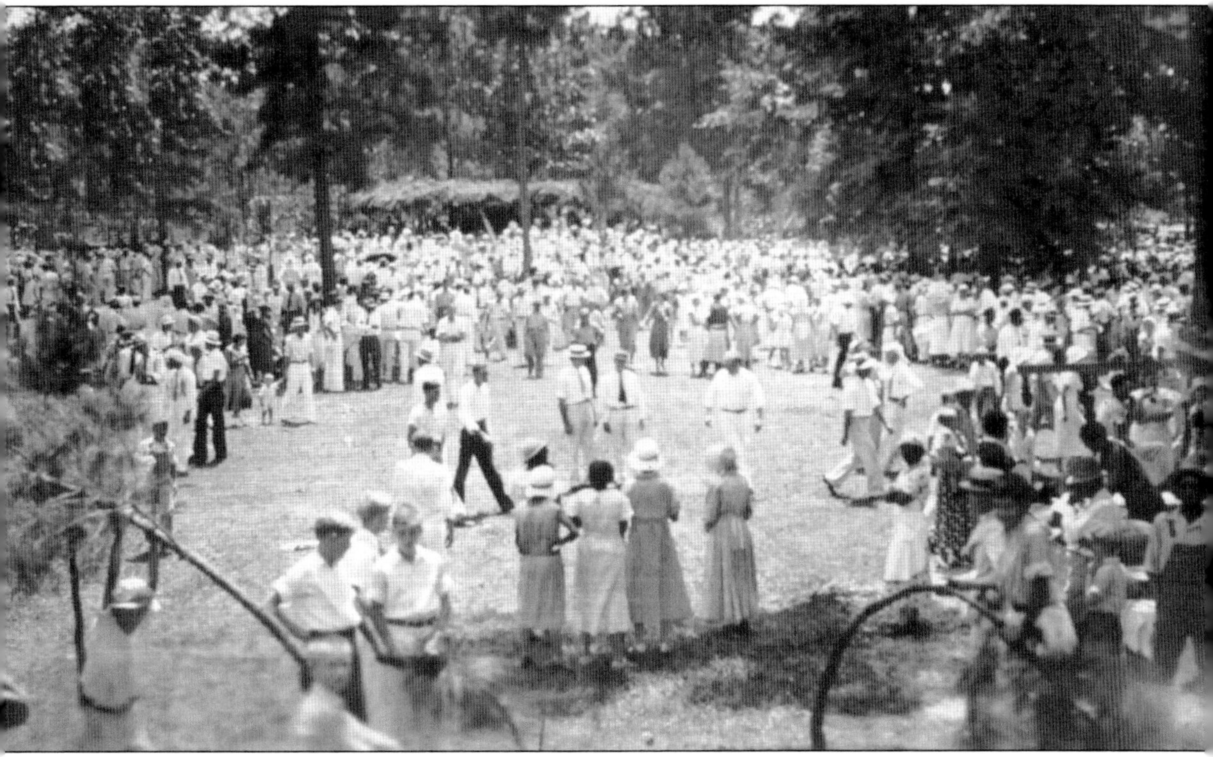

Originally held on Fridays, the annual Watermelon Festival drew large crowds from distant places. The *Bienville Democrat* boasted that the first Watermelon Festival attracted at least 5,000 people. Festivalgoers feasted on 1,000 ice-cold watermelons that local farmers hand-selected for the event. In 1932, the number of chilled watermelons rose to 1,500 and the number of festival attendees doubled. The 1933 festival also attracted approximately 10,000 people. (Courtesy of Bruce Evans.)

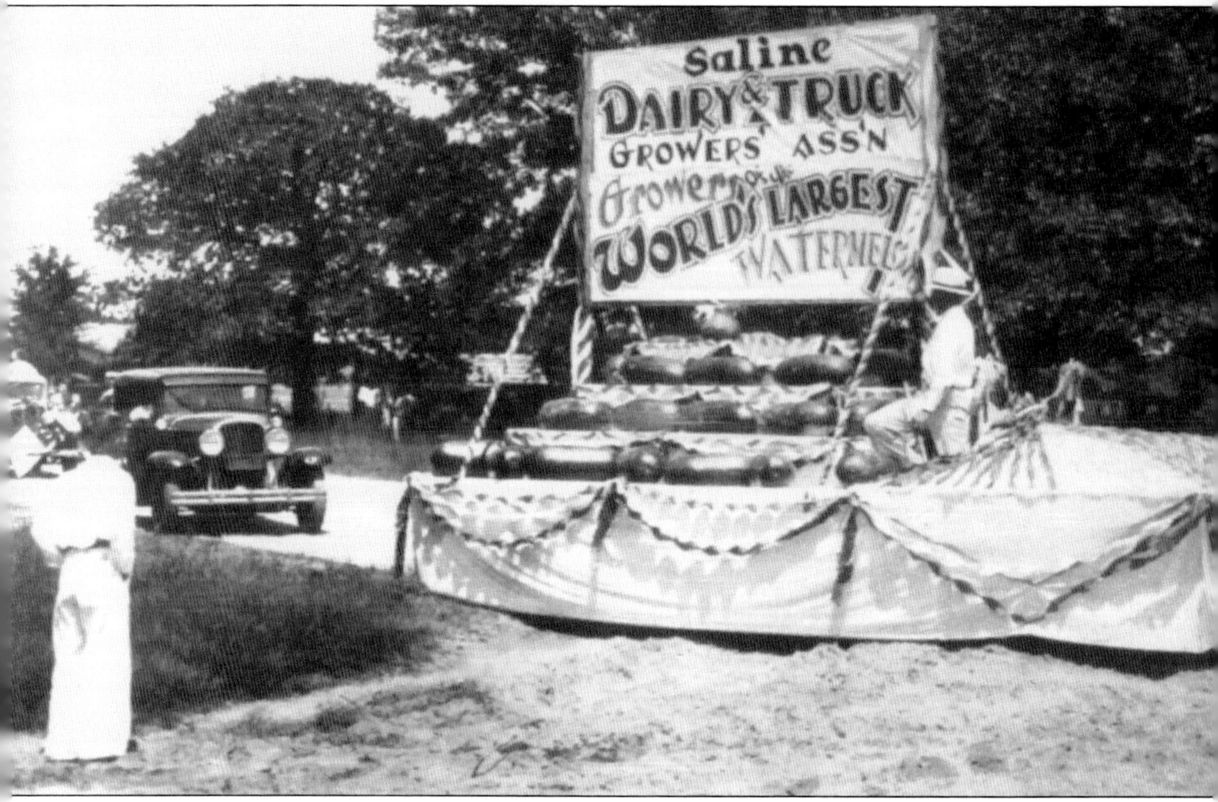

The Watermelon Festival parade began at the high school building and made its way through town to the festival grounds a half mile away. Following the parade, festivalgoers enjoyed two LN&W boxcar loads of iced watermelons. This float displays Saline's show melons, some of which weigh between 100 and 140 pounds. Based on tonnage, S.L. Rhodes of Saline was considered the champion melon-grower of Louisiana. (Courtesy of Bruce Evans.)

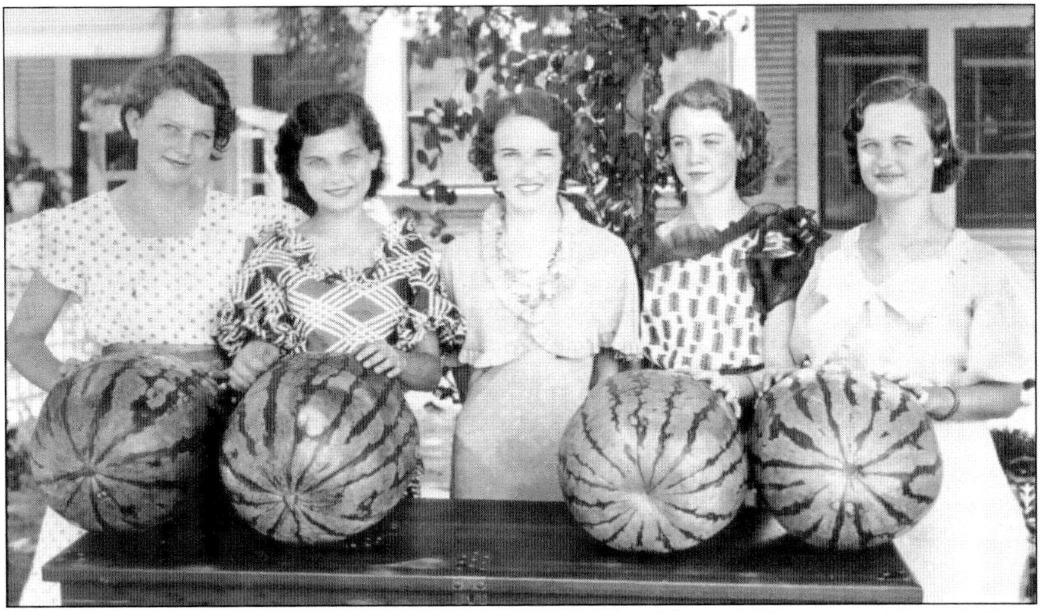

On July 20, 1933, Doris McCain reigned as queen of the third annual Watermelon Festival. Early beauty pageants were designed to build women's self-esteem and public-speaking abilities. The queen and her court were photographed with large watermelons from that year's harvest. Shown are, from left to right, Virginia Taylor, Camille Taylor, McCain, Mary Evelyn Frey, and Eleanor Stinson. (Courtesy of Bruce Evans.)

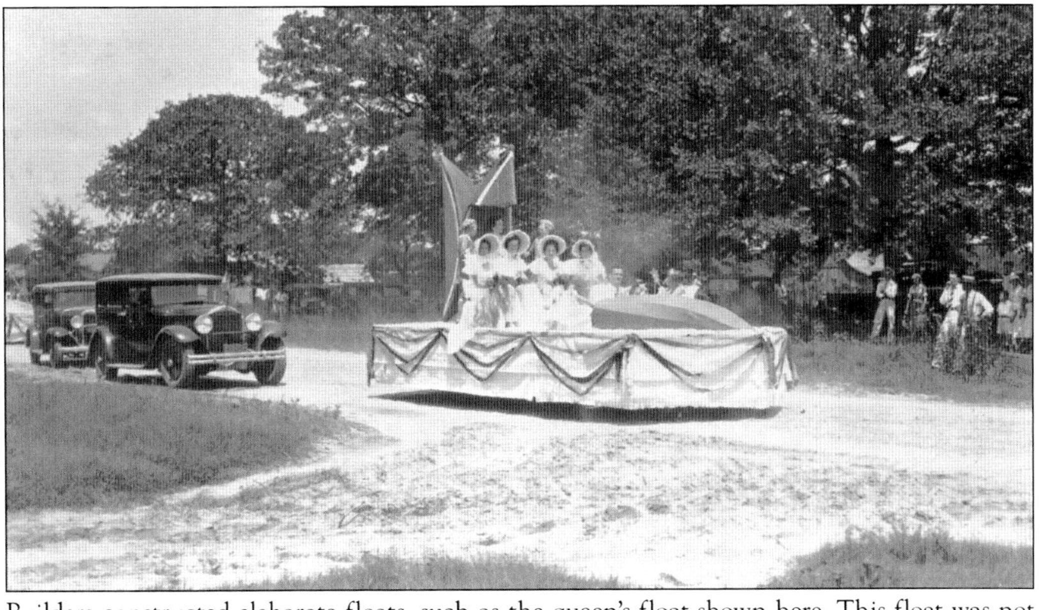

Builders constructed elaborate floats, such as the queen's float shown here. This float was not pulled by another vehicle, but was instead built upon a truck with no cab or bed. The driver is visible in front of the ladies on the float. The Watermelon Festival was discontinued after 1933, but was started again 50 years later, in 1983. (Courtesy of Bruce Evans.)

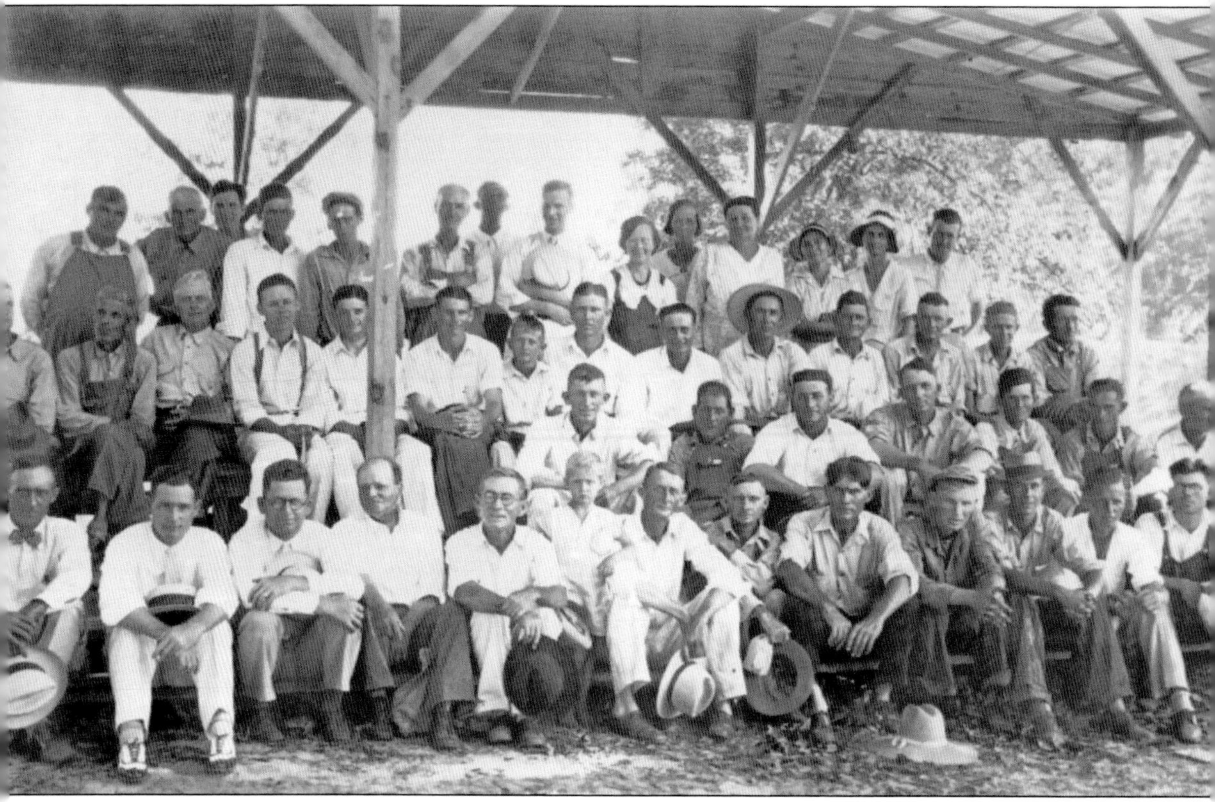

In 1928, approximately 40 local farmers created the Dairy & Truck Growers Association. They planted 85 acres of watermelons and 40 acres of cantaloupes, which yielded 21 train carloads of melons. In 1931, membership had grown to over 300, and 300 acres of watermelons had been planted. All 45 carloads of watermelons were shipped to foreign markets. This photograph, taken in 1933, shows only about one-tenth of the almost 400 members. (Courtesy of Bruce Evans.)

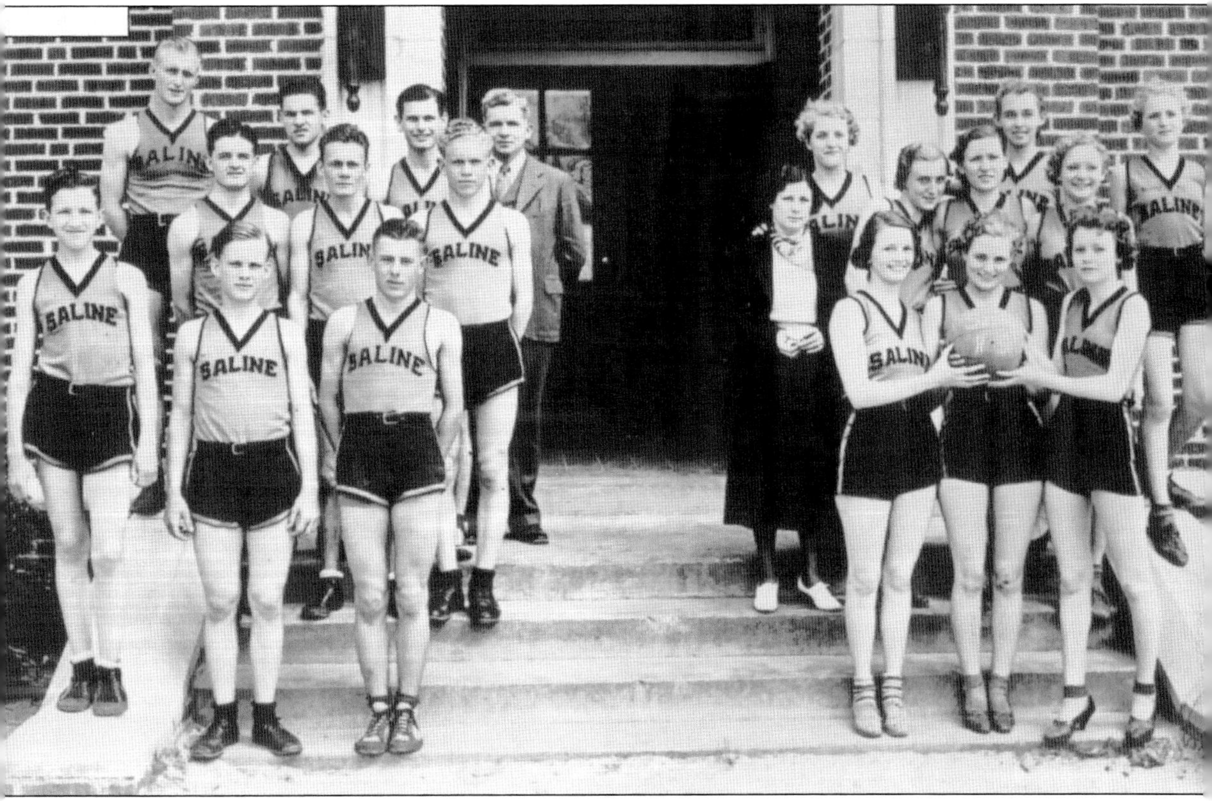

In 1934–1935, the Saline High School boys' and girls' basketball teams pose for a photograph. Pictured on the boys' side are, from left to right, (first row) T.T. Allison, Osborne Montgomery, and Lance Fair; (second row) Leland Readhimer, Lester Easley, and Leon Driggers; (third row) Jamie Montgomery, A.W. Rogers, David Riddle, and coach G.E. Jones. On the girls' side are, from left to right, (first row) Lena Caskey, Avis Crawford, and Madeline Caskey; (second row) coach Aline Marshall, Grace Watts, De Lane Watts, and Billie Smith; (third row) Katherine Norred, Syble Sullivan, and Bernice Allison. (Courtesy of Bruce Evans.)

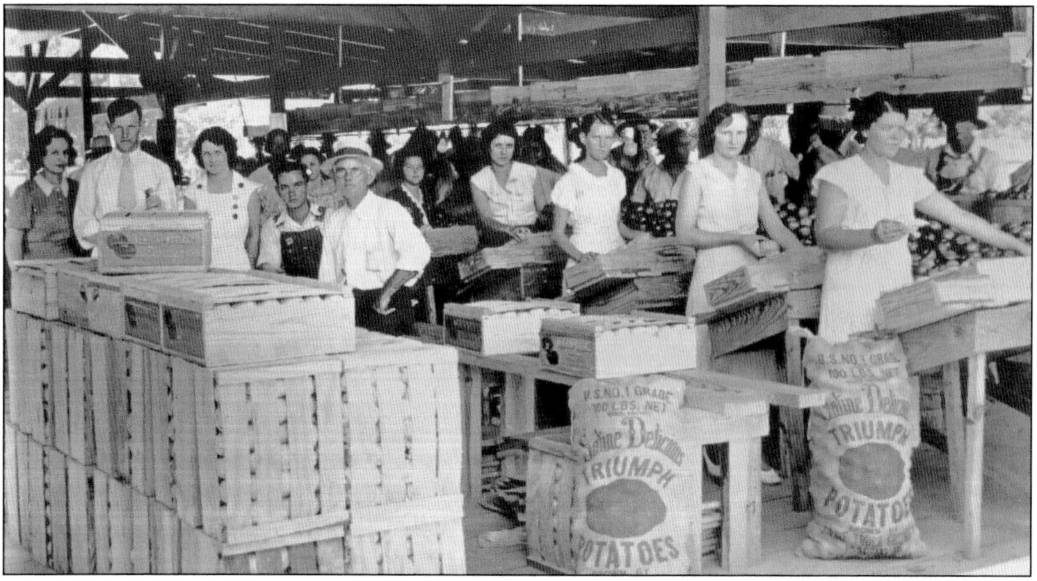

By June 1934, the Saline Truck Growers Association had shipped 28 boxcars of Irish potatoes and 5 boxcars of tomatoes. The potato and tomato shed employed about 35 people, who graded and packaged the vegetables. Shown in the foreground are, from left to right, (left row) De Lane Smith, Millard Toms, Estelle Thomas, A.D. Smith Jr., and A.D. Smith Sr.; (right row) Janice Fuller (in black, behind Smith Sr.), Carolyn Thomas, Louise Speir, Annie Lee Hennigan, and Eva D. Bishop. (Courtesy of Bruce Evans.)

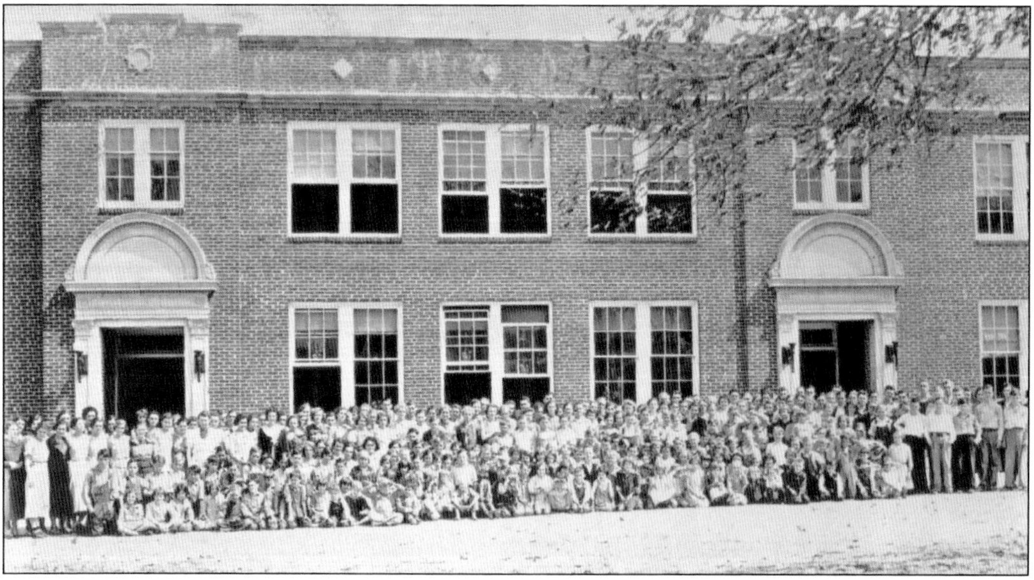

By 1935, the number of students and faculty at Saline High School had grown, as this photograph attests. In its first 30 years, Saline had grown from a small village of just a handful of families to a town with hundreds of citizens. The school had gone from a small, one-room building to a large, two-story structure. (Courtesy of Bruce Evans.)

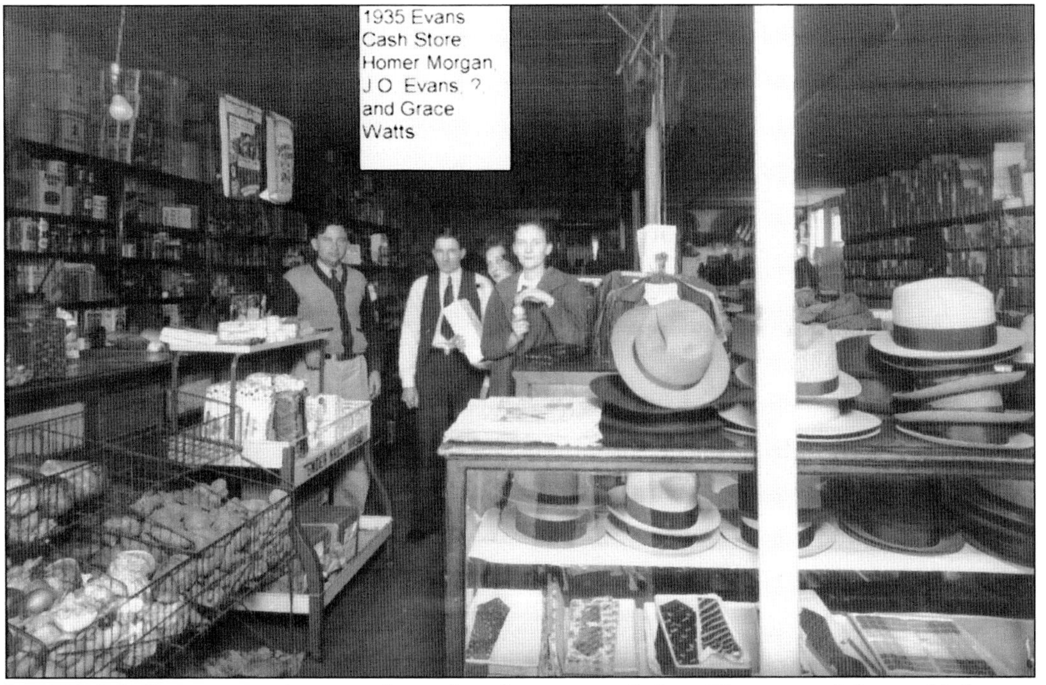

In 1930, J.O. Evans opened a general merchandise store in Saline. He operated the establishment from a little after daylight until 9:00 p.m. Since the store had no electricity, he used Aladdin kerosene lamps for lighting. By 1935, Louisiana Power and Light had installed electric lines in town, and the store acquired electric lighting. Evans operated his store in Saline for over 50 years. (Courtesy of Bruce Evans.)

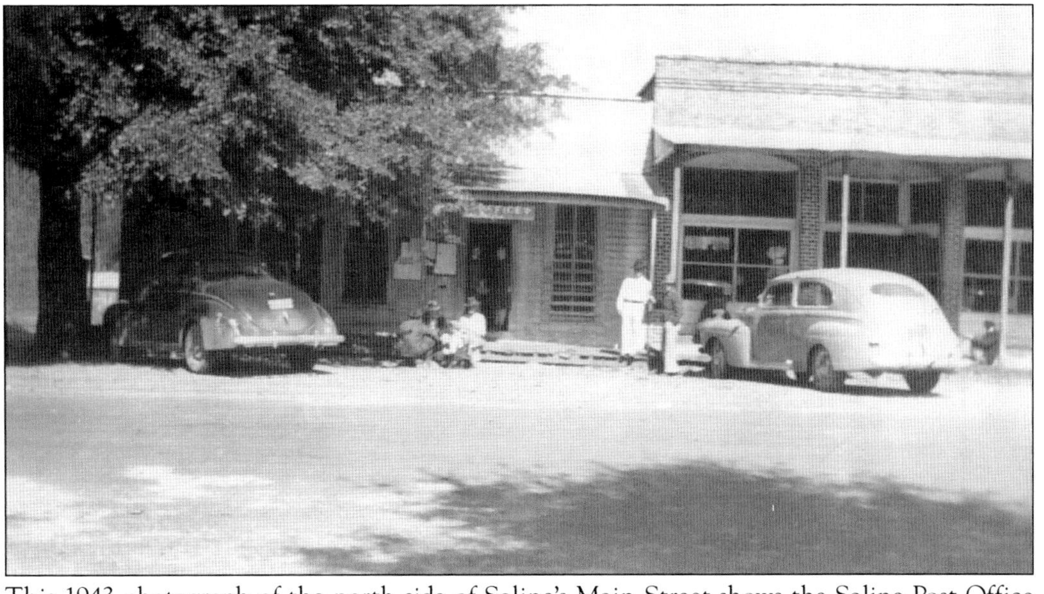

This 1943 photograph of the north side of Saline's Main Street shows the Saline Post Office and Many Williams' Grocery store. Beginning in the 1940s, Williams sold groceries and general merchandise in Saline. Years later, locals met up and played dominos in the post office building, and Opal Wafer's store sold groceries, including deli-style meats. (Courtesy of Cheryl Babers.)

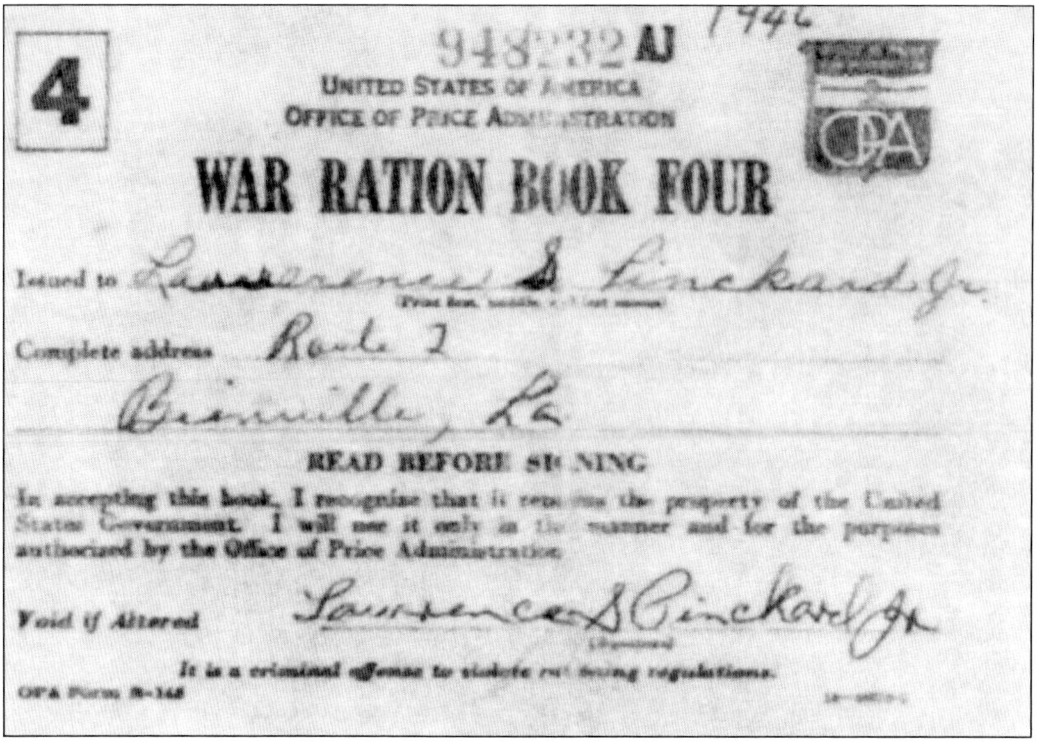

4

948232 AJ

UNITED STATES OF AMERICA
OFFICE OF PRICE ADMINISTRATION

WAR RATION BOOK FOUR

Issued to Lawrence S Pinckard Jr

Complete address Route 1

Bienville, La

Void if Altered Lawrence S Pinckard Jr

During World War II, material such as rubber and metal, and various grocery items, were in short supply. To ensure that goods were distributed evenly, the federal government created War Ration Boards to control the sale of scarce items. This war ration book belonged to Lawrence Pinckard Jr. Consumers could only purchase rationed items in limited quantities, if at all. (Courtesy of Saline High School.)

Sugar and coffee were the first items to be rationed, but the list of goods quickly spread to include tires, nylon stockings, meat, shoes, and gasoline. Ration stamps were not a replacement for money, but were used along with money. A common slogan during the war was "make do or do without." (Courtesy of Saline High School.)

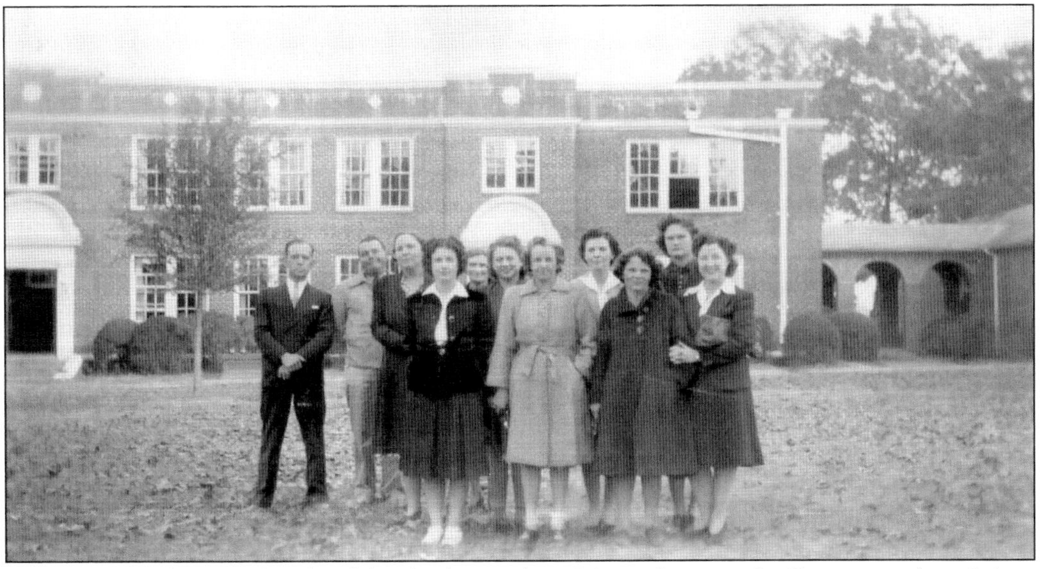

In 1943, the Saline High School faculty has gathered for a photograph. Shown are, from left to right, (back row) principal George Rogers, Van Burns, Hattie D. Corbitt, Cammille Hailey, Irene Mullis, Murlee Thomas, and Eloise Frey; (front row) Bessie Frey, DeLane Hickman, Gertrude Enloe, and Louise Lucky. The covered walkway that was removed during the school fire to keep the blaze from spreading is more easily seen in this photograph. (Courtesy of Cheryl Babers.)

The Future Farmers of America (FFA) is one of the largest youth organizations in the United States. The blue corduroy jacket is the most recognized symbol of the organization. FFA members have always been required to wear the jacket whenever participating in activities for the organization. These members of Saline High School's FFA built and erected signs welcoming locals and visitors to the town. (Courtesy of Saline High School.)

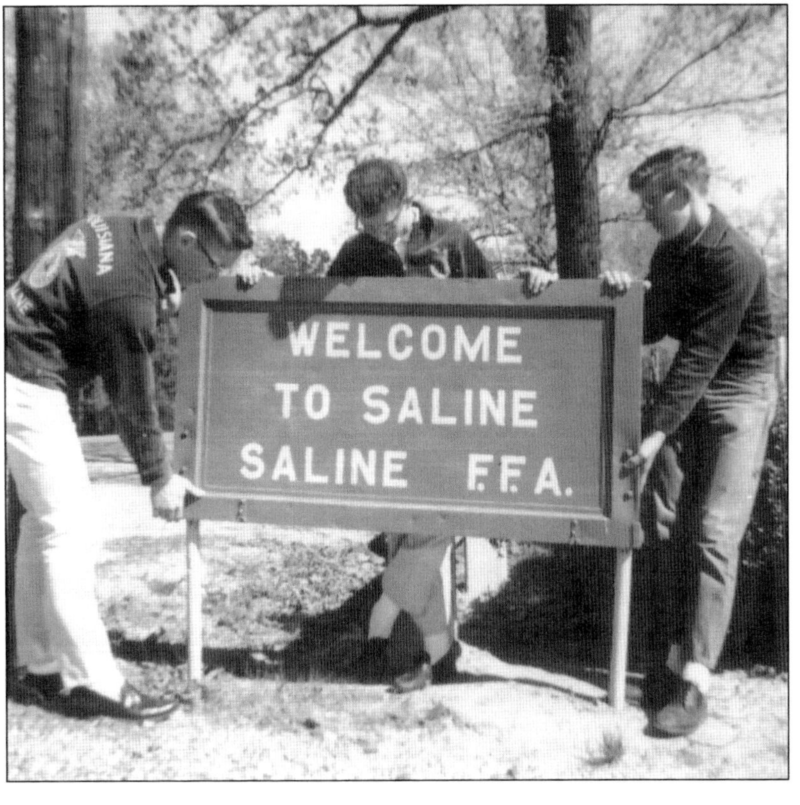

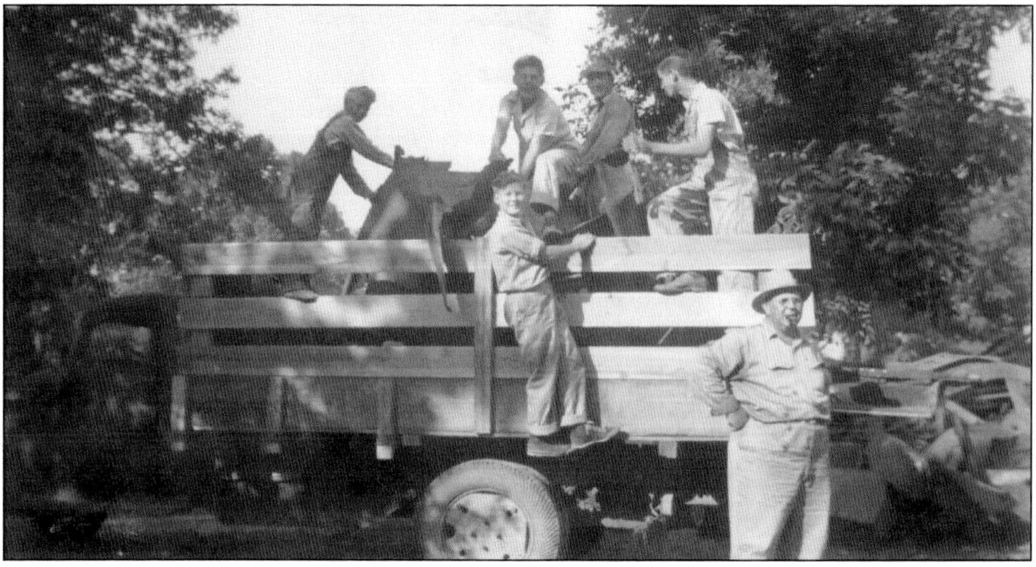

World War II was fought not only in foreign lands; it was also fought at home. Metal needed to build tanks, ships, airplanes, weapons, and other wartime necessities was in short supply. One tank required 18 tons of metal, and a Navy ship could require 900 tons. Americans were urged to recycle scrap metal, and the citizens of Saline were eager to do their part. (Courtesy of Saline High School.)

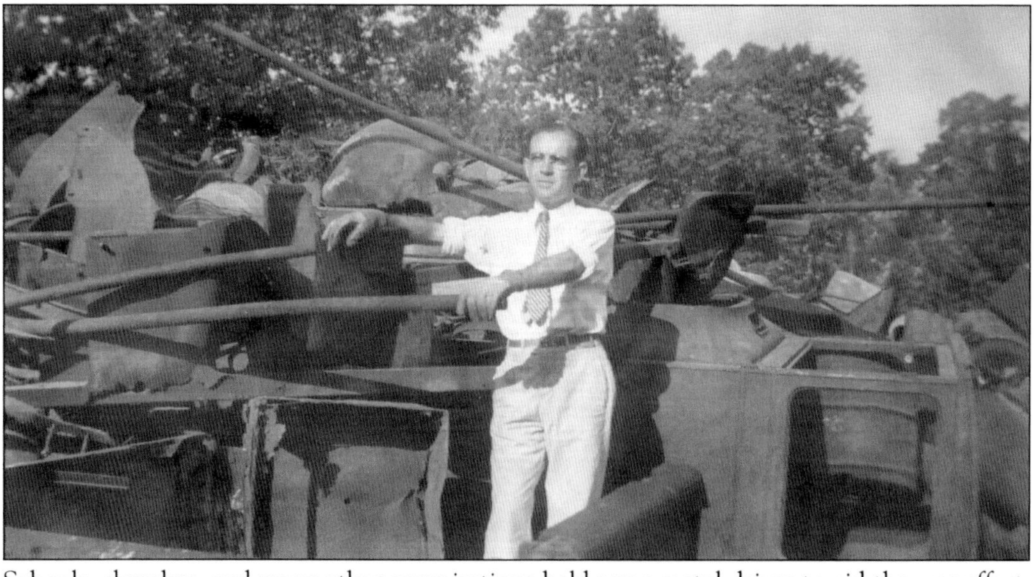

Schools, churches, and many other organizations held scrap-metal drives to aid the war effort. Here, Saline High School principal George Rogers stands amid the massive pile of scrap metal on the grounds of the school. In addition to providing the much-needed metal, the drives offered Americans at home a way to help win the war. (Courtesy of Saline High School.)

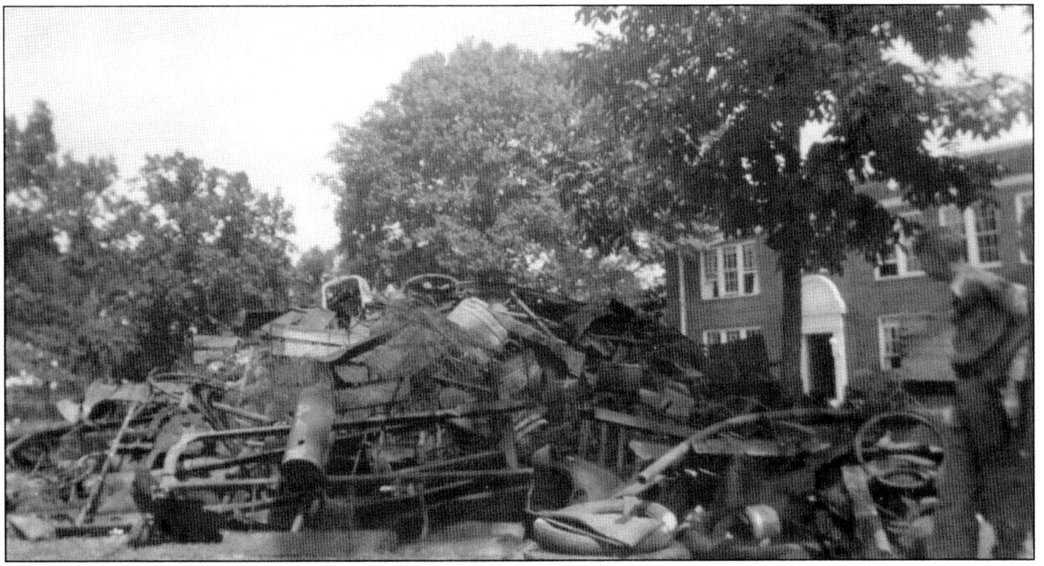

In one of their scrap-metal drives, Saline FFA members collected one ton of rubber, one ton of paper, and 125 tons of scrap metal. Rather than hiding the scrap metal out of sight, Saline High School proudly displayed its contribution to the war effort on the grounds in front of the main school building. (Courtesy of Saline High School.)

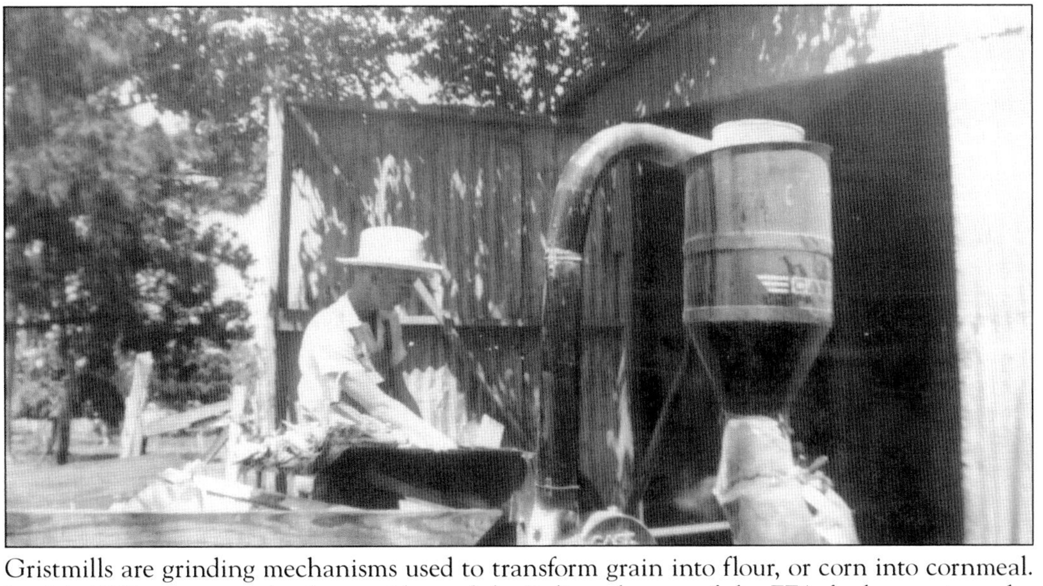

Gristmills are grinding mechanisms used to transform grain into flour, or corn into cornmeal. In this 1940s photograph, the president of the Saline chapter of the FFA feeds corn into the gristmill. Among other goals, the FFA focused on agricultural education, to improve students' careers after high school. (Courtesy of Saline High School.)

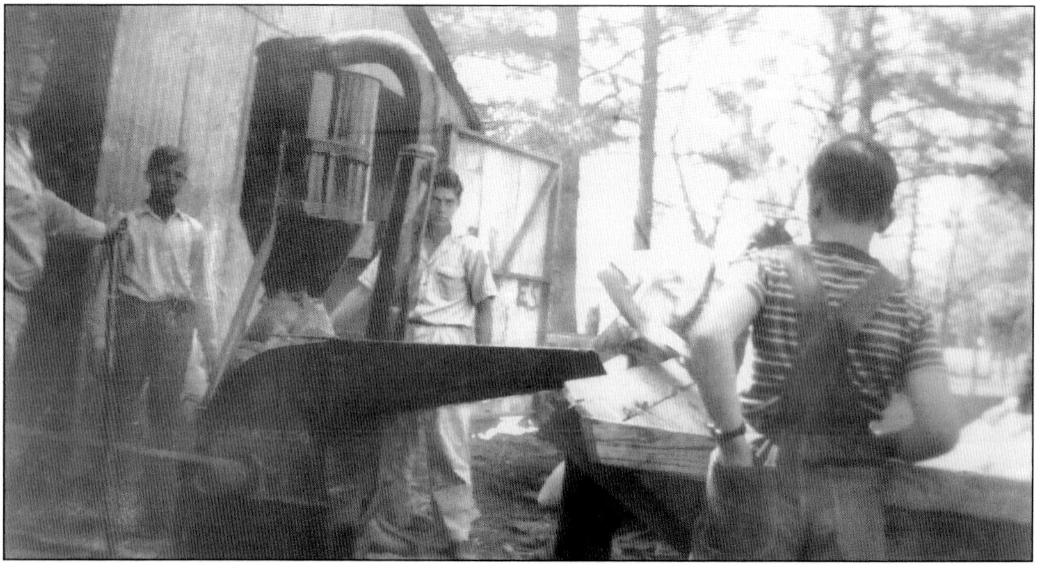

Saline High School FFA members used every part of the harvested corn. They loaded the corncobs and husks into a hammer mill. The mill then crushed or shredded the leftovers into a fine meal, which was then used to feed livestock. (Courtesy of Saline High School.)

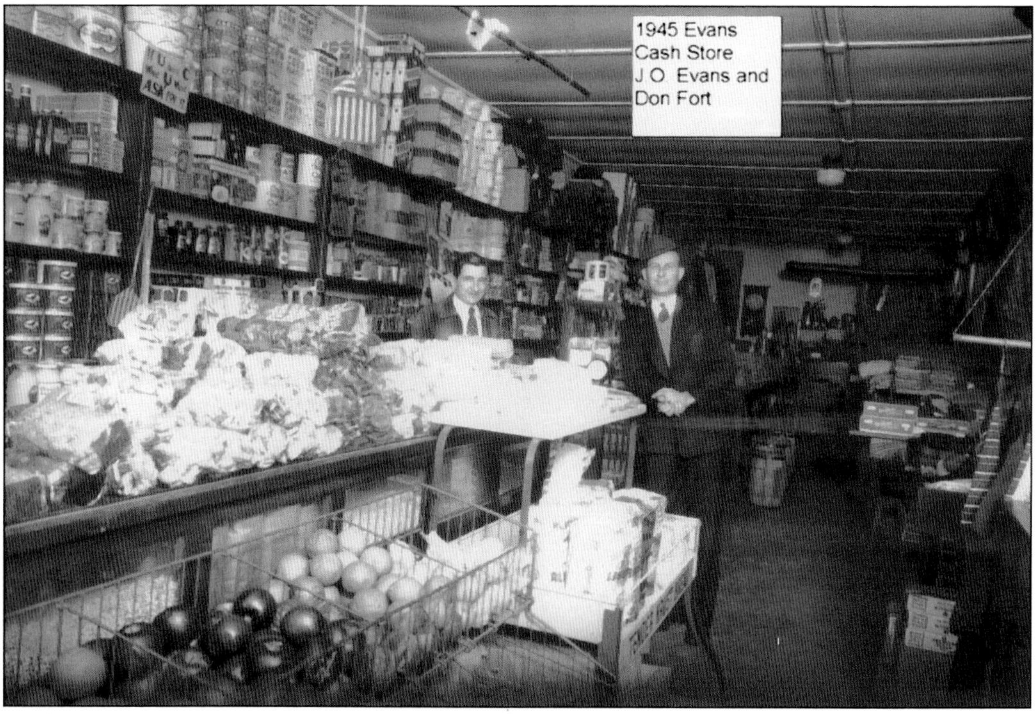

In the summer, J.O. Evans's store was extremely hot, but in the winter, woodstoves kept the store nice and warm. The first telephone in Saline was installed at his store, and he became the unofficial operator. Evans joked, "Sometimes I was up all night because that's when most women decide to have babies." Evans was mayor of Saline for 32 years. (Courtesy of Bruce Evans.)

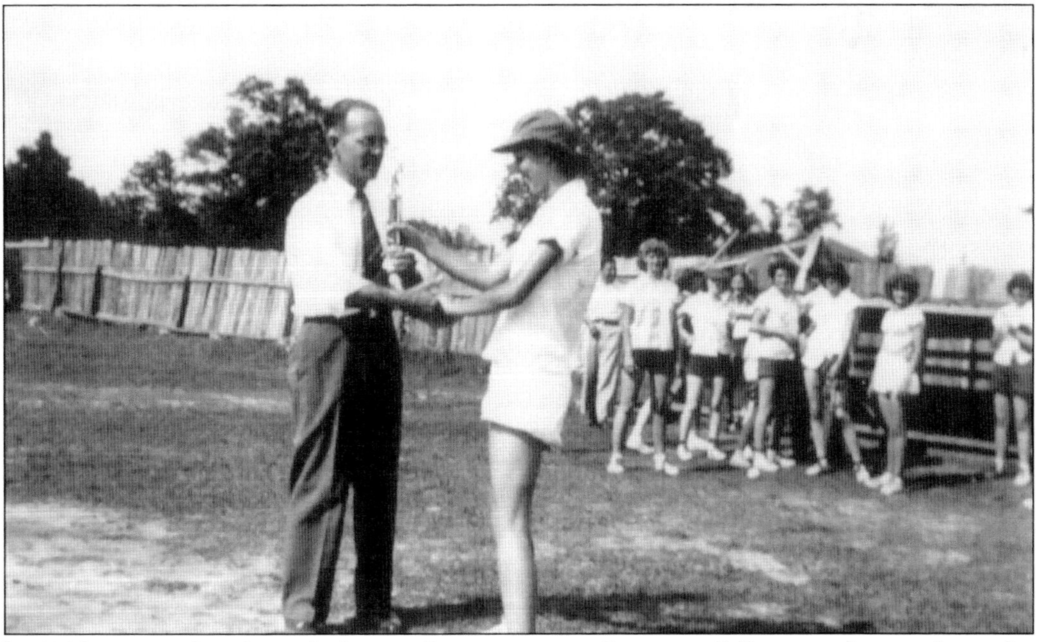

In 1948, principal and coach George Rogers presents Emogene Sullivan with a trophy at the Saline baseball field. The Saline High School girls' softball team won first place in the local softball tournament against other schools in the parish. The team continued its winning streak and competed in the North Louisiana District Championship. (Courtesy of Saline High School.)

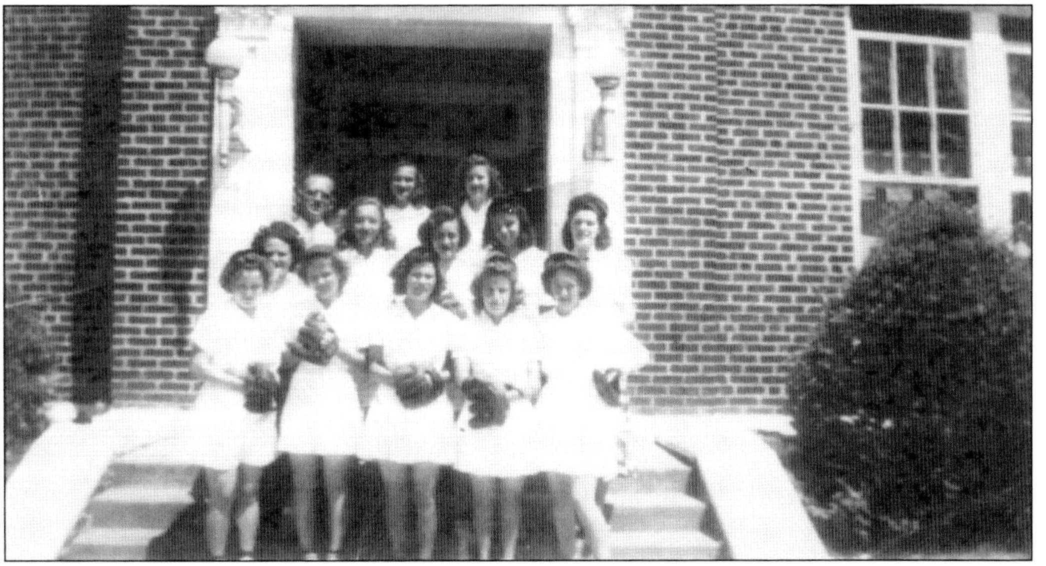

In 1947–1948, the Saline High School girls' softball team won the North Louisiana District Championship. The team consists of, from left to right, (back row) coach George Rogers, Patsy Moore, and Billie Joe Caldwell; (middle row) Doris Southern, Avanell Sullivan, Iris Jean Thrasher, Emogene Sullivan, and Betty Knotts; (front row) Mary Ellen Rogers, Glenda Toms, Viola Reynolds, Alice Harper, and Willa Dean Bryant. (Courtesy of Saline High School.)

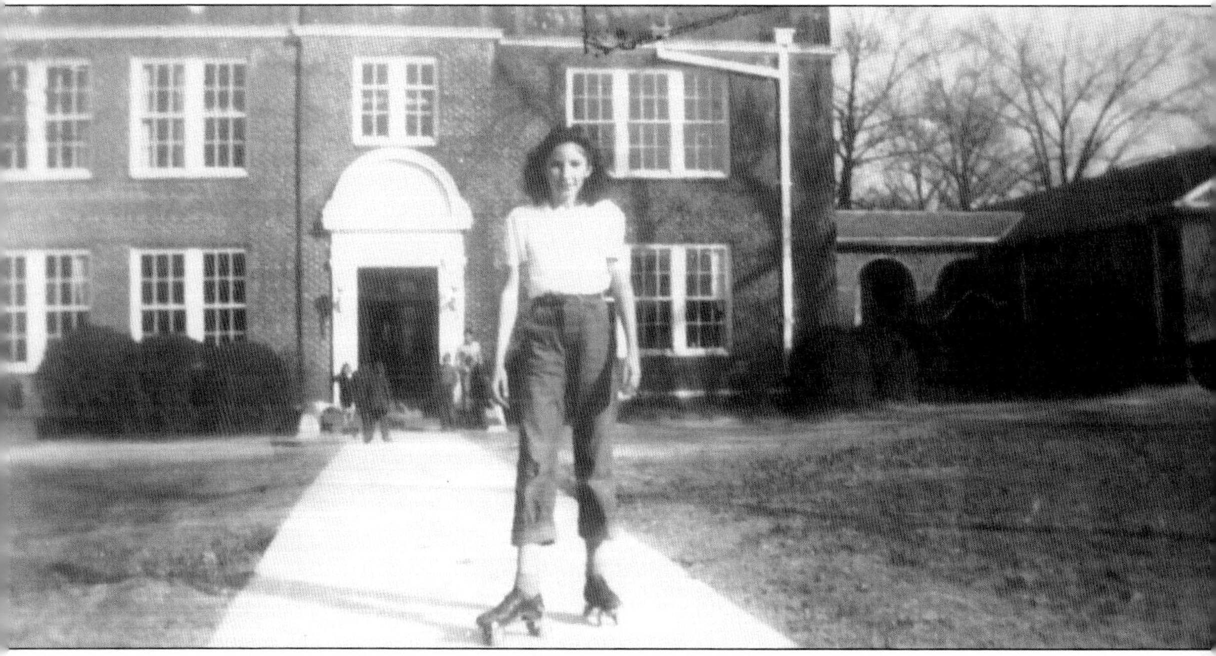

Seen here about 1951, Dot Peterson roller-skates on the sidewalk to Saline High School. In the 1950s, roller-skating became a popular pastime for the baby boom generation. Towns all across America, including Saline, built roller-skating rinks for the new fad. Birthday parties at local rinks became a rite of passage for children in the 1950s. (Courtesy of Saline High School.)

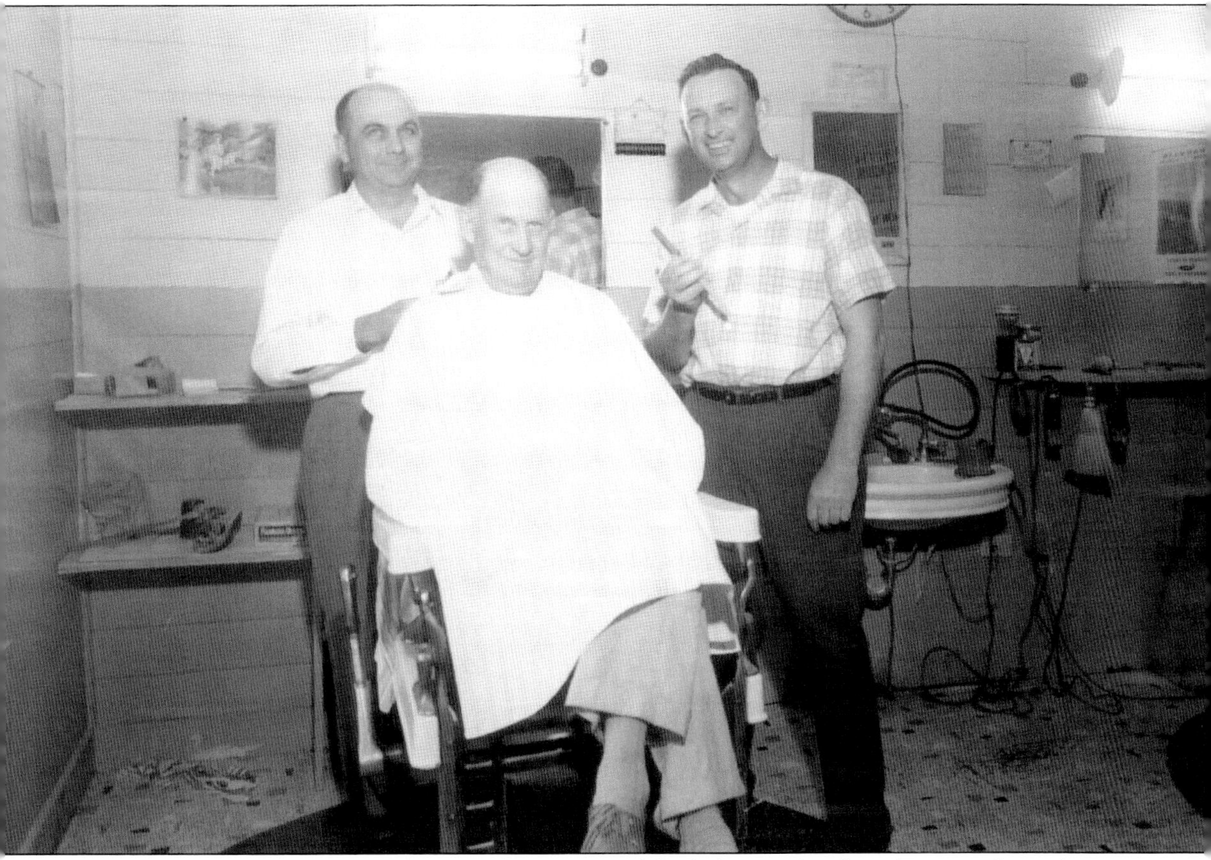

In 1962, Joe Harper (left) and Willard Cheatwood (right) pose for this photograph in their barbershop in Saline. In the 1950s, Harper, a skilled but unlicensed barber, cut hair at his home in the Carolina community. Customers recognized his talent and convinced him to enroll in barber school. Once licensed, he began cutting hair in Saline. Joe's Barber Shop served the community until his retirement in the 1980s. The man in the barber chair is unidentified. (Courtesy of Lavon Sullivan.)

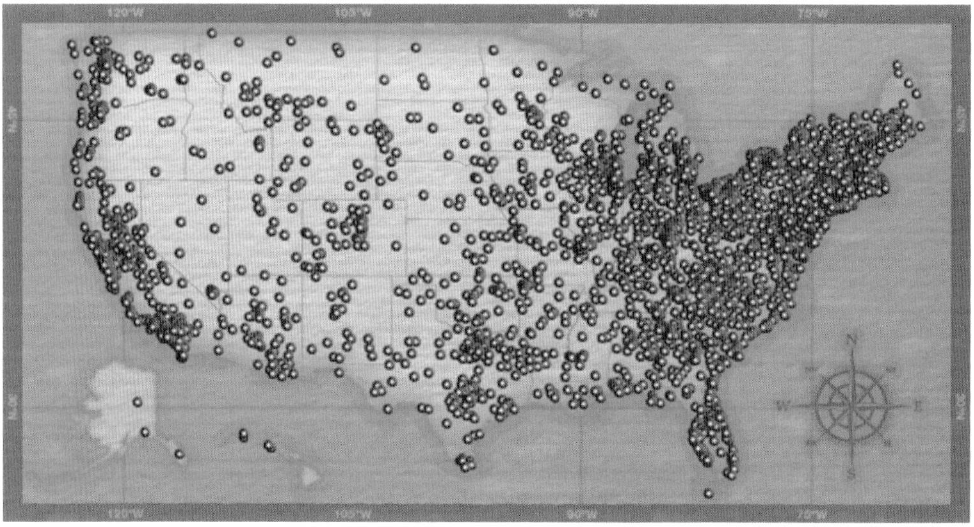